Charles E. Carlston is Norris Professor of New Testament Interpretation at Andover Newton Theological School.

The Parables
of the
Triple Tradition

CHARLES E. CARLSTON

The Parables
of the
Triple
Tradition

FORTRESS PRESS   Philadelphia

Library of Congress Catalog Card Number 74-26347

ISBN 0-8006-0402-4

4567L74   Printed in the United States of America   1-402

To my wife

CONTENTS

Part One:

THE MATTHEAN REDACTION

Part Two:

THE LUKAN REDACTION

Chapter 3.

Part Three:

THE MARKAN PARABLES

PREFACE

The following work is part of a larger study of the parables of the synoptic tradition. Its aim is to study the parables of Mark and the variant forms of them in Matthew and Luke, with special stress on the meaning of those parables not in themselves but as part of the *text*.

Those familiar with recent research in the Gospels will notice that this concentration on the text as a whole corresponds to the current shift away from an emphasis on the parables as part of the message of Jesus. That earlier emphasis, carried out with a high degree of skill and imagination above all in the works of Dodd and Jeremias, is important; without it, the historical development of primitive Christianity is distorted and its theological basis laid open to the charge of mythology.

But a single-minded concentration on the message of Jesus also carries with it two very great dangers. For one thing, it will create an almost irresistible temptation to rescue the authenticity of as much of the tradition as possible, to ascribe to Jesus at least the "kernel" of almost every parable. Jeremias' great study in particular seems to me to reflect this danger, and if his judgments about authenticity are right, many of those in this work are simply wrong. A second and even greater danger in an exclusive emphasis on the message of Jesus is that it leads almost inevitably to a neglect, if not an actual depreciation, of the contributions of the evangelists. In its worst form, it will come to understand later developments not as serious theological ventures but as simple "misunderstandings" of Jesus. Yet who today would deny that "Luke" wrote more of the New Testament than Paul did, and for equally serious theological purposes? Or that Matthew and Mark are to be properly understood not as mere compilers, or even as editors, but as important historical witnesses to changing situations in first-century Christianity and as theological witnesses to how the Christian tradition is to be appropriated and handed on?

If this is methodologically correct, one hardly needs to argue for the method adopted here of beginning with Matthew and Luke and working back through Mark to the pre-Markan tradition and to Jesus. Not only the "classical" solution to the synoptic problem—that Matthew and Luke used both Mark and another written source (Q) in addition to materials of their own—but *any* proposed solution to that problem requires some such method. (It is one of the most significant and striking failures of alternative solutions that their proponents have been able to produce so little redaction-critical work of this kind that will stand careful analysis.) In the long run, the best explanation of the varied texts of the three Gospels will commend itself as the best interpretation of the developments in primitive Christianity.

In a purely redaction-critical study, to be sure, one could stop once he had reached the Markan (or pre-Markan) stage, since then he would know what the three evangelists had done with the traditions that came to them. The matter of authenticity (does this material originate with Jesus rather than at some other point in the tradition?) would not have to be raised. Yet in this work I have tried to go beyond redaction-criticism in the pure sense and repeatedly asked the question about the authenticity of the materials of the tradition. The reason for this is twofold: For one thing, Mark's own contribution is sometimes understood differently as one makes different judgments about the form of the pre-Markan tradition (see the discussion below, for example, on the materials of Mk. 4). And again, both the pre-Markan tradition and the intention of Jesus have their own distinctive roles to play in understanding the theologies of the apostolic age. In other words, the question of authenticity must be raised somewhere, not for *redaktionsgeschichtlich* but for historical and theological purposes.

In addition to the general limitations imposed by thus restricting the analysis to the materials found in Mark (and ordinarily in the other Synoptic Gospels as well), two other limitations have been deliberately self-imposed. One is the elimination, for all practical purposes, of extensive discussion of the parables of the Gospel of Thomas, many of which have Synoptic parallels. This is due partly to the unsettled nature of the current discussion about Christian Gnosticism, a matter on which we shall happily be much better informed within the next five years or so as the Nag Hammadi materials become universally available for detailed study. It is also due in part, however, to the fact that many readings of the Gospel of Thomas and a considerable amount of time spent with the secondary literature (a small fraction of which is listed in the bibliography) have not yet convinced me that any of the parabolic material in Thomas is clearly independent of the Synoptic Gospels. I am not a specialist in Gnosticism and I am willing to be convinced by those who are; but I am not yet convinced, and I have occasionally tried to indicate in this study why I am not. In addition, there is still something to be said for dealing with the Gospels as both historical documents and part of Scripture. I can only hope that a serious commitment to the latter does not distort my judgment about the former.

The second, and in some ways more significant, limitation is the extremely small amount of attention paid to hermeneutical issues in general. This is not to be taken as an indication that I think either the philosophical or the literary questions being raised at the moment by existentialist interpreters on the one hand or literary critics on the other are not important. But for various reasons it does not seem appropriate to try to deal with them in a book that has become so large already, particularly since I have substantial reservations about the exegetical and theological methods widely in use in much very recent work.

Yet I have tried, quite unapologetically, to suggest for most forms of most of the parables studied here some things that might be useful in preaching, one venerable form of "hermeneutic." Some commentators, to be sure, insist that the exegete has no primary responsibility for sermonic practice. But if the transition from commentary to sermon were as simple as some suggest, the evidence of it would be far more widespread than it is. Naturally, this does not mean that the suggestions given here are thought to be somehow definitive; they are given in the hope of encouraging able practitioners of the art of preaching to go beyond them, no more.

The contributions, direct and indirect, of many people have gone into the making of this work, and I should like to express my appreciation to them:

To the faculty, students, and especially the library staffs at Dubuque Theological Seminary, the State University of Iowa, the Kirchliche Hochschule in Berlin, the École Biblique and the Ecumenical Institute in Jerusalem, Andover Newton Theological School, and the University of Tübingen for encouragement and assistance in ways too numerous to mention. To Prof. Everett Harrison of Fuller Theological Seminary, who first awakened my interest in the scholarly study of the New Testament; to Profs. Henry J. Cadbury, Amos N. Wilder, and Krister Stendahl of Harvard for advice and encouragement in graduate school and since; and perhaps above all to Prof. Ernst Käsemann of Tübingen, whose personal and professional kindnesses to me can never be repaid. To my colleagues, Profs. William C. Robinson, Jr. and William Holladay, for invaluable suggestions at various points in the preparation of the manuscript. All have contributed something to the general outlook and the specific content of this work, although its failures and shortcomings are of course entirely my own.

Finally, I would like to express my appreciation to my family, particularly to my wife, for patience and understanding over the years as the manuscript has been conceived, reconceived, written, revised, pondered, and finally prepared for publication.

Two technical matters may be noted briefly. The transliteration follows the system used in the *Catholic Biblical Quarterly*, except that iota-subscript is omitted and in the case of the titles of Talmudic tractates, the more familiar forms of Danby's Mishnah and the Soncino edition of the Babylonian Talmud have been regularly adopted. Perhaps the reader will eventually appreciate the attempt made here to distinguish between books (Matt., Mk., and Lk.) and authors (Matthew, Mark, and Luke). The distinction, whatever its demerits, will remind the reader that behind the present Gospels were real people, Christian people struggling for faith in a non-Christian world, trying not merely to learn the traditions about Jesus but to appropriate them and to pass them on as living words. We may learn much for our own situation if we carefully inquire after the intention of those who expressed their faith in our present Gospels and try simply to take "the text of each of the evangelists . . . seriously in its own right."[1]

1. Wolfgang Trilling, *Christusverkündigung in den synoptischen Evangelien* (Munich: Kösel-Verlag, 1969), 173.

ABBREVIATIONS

ARW	*Archiv für Religionswissenschaft*
ASNU	Acta Seminarii Neotestamentici Upsaliensis
ATANT	Abhandlungen zur Theologie des Alten und Neuen Testaments
BAG	Bauer-Arndt-Gingrich (English of Bauer's Lexicon)
BAH	Bibliothèque archéologique et historique
BETL	Bibliotheca Ephemeridum Theologicarum Lovaniensium
BibZeit	*Biblische Zeitschrift*
BZNW	Beihefte zur Zeitschrift für die Neutestamentliche Wissenschaft und die Kunde der älteren Kirche
CBQ	*Catholic Biblical Quarterly*
ETL	*Ephemerides Theologicae Lovanianses*
EvTheol	*Evangelische Theologie*
ExpT	*Expository Times*
FRLANT	Forschungen zur Religion und Literatur des Alten und Neuen Testamentes
HTR	*Harvard Theological Review*
ICC	*International Critical Commentary*
Interp	*Interpretation*
JBL	*Journal of Biblical Literature*
JBR	*Journal of Bible and Religion*
JTS	*Journal of Theological Studies*
M-M	Moulton and Milligan, Vocabulary of the Greek Testament
n.F.	neue Folge
NovTest	*Novum Testamentum*
NRT	*Nouvelle Revue Théologique*
n.s.	new series

NTD	Das Neue Testament Deutsch
NTS	New Testament Studies
RAC	Reallexikon für Antike und Christentum
RB	Revue Biblique
RHPR	Revue d'histoire et de philosophie religieuses
RSPT	Revue des sciences philosophiques et théologiques
RSR	Recherches de science religieuse
SBT	Studies in Biblical Theology
ScotJTh	Scottish Journal of Theology
SNTS	Studiorum Novi Testamenti Societas
StudTh	Studia Theologica
TDNT	Theological Dictionary of the New Testament
Theol. Stud. u. Krit.	Theologische Studien und Kritiken
ThLit	Theologische Literaturzeitung
ThZ	Theologische Zeitschrift
TThZ	Trierer theologische Zeitschrift
TU	Texte und Untersuchungen zur Geschichte der Altchristlichen Literatur
VT	Vetus Testamentum
VigChr	Vigiliae Christianae
WMANT	Wissenschaftliche Monographien zum Alten und Neuen Testament
ZDPV	Zeitschrift des Deutschen Palästina-Vereins
ZNW	Zeitschrift für die neutestamentliche Wissenschaft und die Kunde des Urchristentums
ZRG	Zeitschrift für Religions- und Geistesgeschichte
ZSystTh	Zeitschrift für Systematische Theologie
ZThK	Zeitschrift für Theologie und Kirche

PART
ONE

THE
MATTHEAN
REDACTION

Chapter One

MATTHEW'S INTERPRETATION
OF THE MARKAN THEORY
OF THE PARABLES

(13:10–17; cf. Mk. 4:10ff.; Lk. 8:9f.)

In the collection of parables of Mk. 4 some of Jesus' listeners are said to ask "about the parables" (4:10ff.). His reply includes, among other things, the statement that for some men all things occur in parables, "so that they may indeed see but not perceive, and may indeed hear but not understand; lest they should turn again, and be forgiven." This text is the basis of the so-called hardening theory, according to which God has hardened the hearts of some men lest they convert and be forgiven. The significance of the statement in the teaching of Jesus or in the theology of Mark is not of central concern here. But the Matthean modifications of the Markan text exhibit several important motifs in the theology of Matthew, some of them quite different from those reflected in his Markan source. Inserted at the same point as in Mk. (between the parable of the Sower and the explanation of it) and introducing in a similar fashion a collection of parables, these words concern not only the parable of the Sower or even the parables immediately adjacent to it but also the message of the parables in general. It may be helpful, consequently, to begin the examination of the Matthean parabolic material with his use of Mark's theory.

Mark describes Jesus' questioners as "those who were around him with the twelve." Both Matthew and Luke modify this extremely awkward phrase to a simpler one: "the disciples" (Matthew) and "his disciples" (Luke). The similarity between the Matthean and Lukan forms here is hardly due to Q, for which there is little tangible evidence elsewhere in the passage; it is rather the obvious way to simplify Mark's complex expression. This obvious change, however, points to an important motif in Matthew's conception of the disciples as a group. They are no longer blind, as in Mk. (4:13; 6:52; etc.). And the third person (". . . the eyes which . . .") of Q (and Lk.) has been modified to a second person (". . . your eyes, because . . ."), shifting the emphasis from joy over the fulfillment of the promises to joy and gladness over the ability to "see" metaphorically, i.e., to comprehend.[1] Thus the positive evaluation of the disciples' eyes and ears (Matt. 13:16f.) finds its exact counterpart at the end of the discourse: when the disciples are asked if they have understood everything, they answer bluntly, "Yes" (13:51).

Two different motifs are at work here. On the one hand, the disciples, though less obtuse than in Mk., are still the recipients of special instruction on such matters as the necessity of suffering (20:17) and the End (24:3). On the other, they are ideal representatives of what a disciple should be in any age, especially the writer's own age,[2] and fully suited for this responsibility in spite of whatever limitations they may possess.

A second change of some significance occurs in the wording of the question itself. Mk.'s general ". . . asked him about the parables" has become explicit: "Why do you speak to them in parables?" Matthew has tried, both here and in v. 13, to answer this question on the basis of the materials in his Markan source. In doing so, he has created two difficulties. For one thing, the question is never really answered; v. 13 in particular does not explain why parabolic speech is any more appropriate than any other form of address for a stiff-necked people. And, secondly, he has

---

1. See Jacques Dupont, "Le point de vue de Matthieu dans le chapitre des paraboles," in M. Didier et al., *L'Évangile selon Matthieu. Rédaction et Théologie* (Gembloux: J. Duculot, 1972), 221–259 (236f.).
2. Pierre Bonnard, *L'Évangile selon Saint Matthieu* (Neuchâtel: Delachaux & Niestlé, 1963), 193, Dupont, "Point de vue," 248. On discipleship in Matt., see Günther Bornkamm, Gerhard Barth, and Heinz-Joachim Held, *Tradition and Interpretation in Matthew* (Philadelphia: Westminster Press, 1963), 105–125.

removed the motivation for the explanation of the Sower which immediately follows: until the explanation is given—an explanation for which the disciples have not asked and for which "understanding" disciples would not ask—we have no indication (as we do in Mk.) that they do not understand (cf. Mk. 4:10, 13). In other words, the materials are not fully appropriate for the contrast the author really wishes to present, which is the ignorance (and concomitant judgment, 13:12) of "outsiders"[3] and the knowledge and blessedness of disciples.

Another significant modification occurs in the first part of Jesus' answer to the question. Mk. says that the disciples have been given the "mystery" (sing.) of the Kingdom. Matt. and Lk., probably on the basis of the oral tradition,[4] read instead "to know the mysteries" (Matt. 13:11; Lk. 8:10). Whatever the Markan singular may have meant, the plural must imply that the disciples understand Jesus' *teaching* or his message as a whole.[5] Particularly

3. Matthew, like Luke, eliminates the Markan *hoi eksō*. But the term *autois* is, in the light of v. 12f., highly pejorative. It would be only a minor excess to translate, "Why do you speak *against* them in parables?" Bonnard, *Matt.*, 193 stresses the *"nuance d'agressivité"* with which the disciples speak. Wilhelm Wilkens, "Die Redaktion des Gleichniskapitels Mk durch Matt," *ThZ* 20 (1964), 304–327 (308) notes that the *autois* reflects the sharp separation of the disciples from the crowds, a Matthean theme.

4. It is unlikely, though barely possible, that this text in this form comes from Q, since the agreements between Matt. and Lk. are minimal. On the other hand, the statement is brief and easily committed to memory, so its general familiarity may be assumed. There is no particular reason to assume the originality of the Matt./ Lk. form over against Mk. (vs. Friedrich Hauck, *Das Evangelium nach Markus* [2. neugearb. Aufl., Berlin: Evangelische Verlagsanstalt, 1959], 54) or to cite Qumranian parallels (!) to show that the plural is original and Mk.'s singular a *Pauline* modification of it (vs. Lucien Cerfaux, "La connaissance des secrets du Royaume d'après Matt. xiii.11 *et par.*," NTS 2 [1955/56], 241). Chap. 13 *"prend tout son sens si l'on y reconnaît une version remaniée du texte de Marc"* (Dupont, "Point de vue," 232).

5. Bornkamm-Barth-Held, *Tradition*, 19, n. 2; Julius Schniewind, *Das Evangelium nach Matthäus* (Göttingen: Vandenhoeck & Ruprecht, 1968), 166; Joachim Gnilka, "Das Verstockungsproblem nach Matthäus 13, 13–15," in Willehad Paul Eckert et al., *Antijudaismus im NT?* (München: Chr. Kaiser Verlag, 1967), 119–128 (121); J. C. Fenton, *St. Matthew* (London: Penguin, 1963), 216 ("the ways of God which he knows and only he can reveal to men so that they may know them"); W. D. Davies, *The Setting of the Sermon on the Mount* (Cambridge: Cambridge University Press, 1963), 214 (apocalyptic, "the eschatological purposes of God"); Wilkens, "Redaktion," 309 (*"das in der Himmelreichsbotschaft angezeigte Heil in seiner ganzen Fülle"*). Georg Strecker, *Der Weg der Gerechtigkeit* (Göttingen: Vandenhoeck & Ruprecht, 1962; 2. Aufl., 1966), 230 would limit the understanding here to the explanation of the parable of the Sower, which follows.

in Matt. understanding is characteristic of the true disciple; lack of understanding is a mark of unbelief, as the additions to Mk. in vv. 19, 23 (". . . and does not understand," ". . . and·understands it"), as well as Matthew's elimination of Mk. 4:33 (which might imply that the crowds are capable of partial understanding), clearly show.[6] What is given or withheld, therefore, is understanding of the content of Jesus' teaching. In spite of the question in 13:10, the parabolic *form* of that teaching is not really relevant.[7]

The saying, "For to him who has will more be given; and from him who has not, even what he has will be taken away" (Mk. 4:25) undergoes curious treatment at Matthew's hands (v. 12). This saying, which may originally have been secular, was apparently well-known in the early church, since it occurs both here and in Matt. 25:29 (=Lk. 19:26, Q). In its Markan form, which Matthew follows here, it is used to distinguish different degrees of discipleship. Since Matthew insists that believers do understand, however, he is not interested in this point. He consequently moves the saying (the only verse from Mk. 4:21–25 which he uses in this section) from its position following the explanation of the Sower (where differences among Christians are spelled out) and inserts it at this point to illustrate the sharp contrast between disciples and non-disciples. To do this, he constructs a balanced phrase (". . . but to them it has not been given") to complete the thought of v. 11, which he is interrupting, and provides the introductory "This is the reason I speak to them in parables" in v. 13. The effect of inserting v. 12 is to heighten the contrast between disciples and others;[8] its intention is to point out God's judgment,

---

6. Cf. Strecker, *Weg*, 72, n. 2. and see below, chap. 5.

7. In 21:45 the chief priests and Pharisees hear Jesus' *parables* and perceive that he has been speaking about them. What failure to understand they do reflect is related to the Matthean theme of ignorance/judgment, not parabolic speech; see Jack Dean Kingsbury, *The Parables of Jesus in Matthew 13: A Study in Redaction-Criticism* (Richmond: John Knox Press, 1969), 49f.

8. This contrast is further heightened by the Matthean addition "and he will have abundance," a phrase which Matthew also adds to the Q form of the saying in 25:29. It is fully in keeping with Matthew's practice elsewhere in the Gospel to understand "having" as implying a Christian reference as well: "To everyone who has . . ., but from anyone who has not . . ., etc."; so Gnilka, "Verstockungsproblem," 121f.

both within and beyond history,[9] perhaps initially toward the Pharisees[10] but primarily on any who irresponsibly claim "discipleship" but without understanding.[11] The curious inconsistency that those who have not been given something (v. 11b) should have it taken away (v. 12) does not trouble the author.[12]

By means of these modifications, then, the Markan "hardening theory" is softened almost into nonexistence. In the context of Mark's theology, Mk. 4:11f. can only mean that Jesus' ministry (including, perhaps, his parabolic teaching) is enigmatic to outsiders "in order that they may . . . not perceive . . . ; lest they should turn again. . . ." But this theory Matthew either does not fully understand or rejects or both. The natural interpretation of the change of conjunctions from hina to hoti (and consequently in the moods of the following verbs) is that Matthew intends to state as the result of Jesus' ministry what Mark sees as its purpose. The wording is now a description of unbelief, not an explanation of it, and the thought now concerns the hardness of men's hearts, not the fact that they have been hardened by God. Matthew moves further in this direction by eliminating Mark's Semitism, "indeed see but not perceive . . . , etc." and omitting the "lest . . ." clause completely; in Mk., people see without discerning—but in Matt. they do not even see![13] Even if the citation of Is. 6:9f. were original at this point, which it probably is not,[14] the verse could

---

9. The eschatological reference is clear in 25:29; see Bonnard, *Matt.*, 194. For the reference to Israel, see Joachim Gnilka, *Die Verstockung Israels: 6, 9–10 in der Theologie der Synoptiker* (Munich: Kösel-Verlag, 1961), 92 (incl. bibliog. in n. 12). But here, as in 21:43, the author's intention is to portray the transfer of the Kingdom of God as a present or trans-temporal reality to the church, not to describe eschatological judgment on Israel; see Gnilka, "Verstockungsproblem," 126 and esp. Wolfgang Trilling, *Das wahre Israel: Studien zur Theologie des Matthäus-Evangeliums* (3. umgearb. Aufl., Munich: Kösel-Verlag, 1964), 58–63.

10. Bonnard, *Matt.*, 192.

11. Dupont, "Point de vue," 234f. and *passim*.

12. See Alan Hugh McNeile, *The Gospel according to St. Matthew* (London: Macmillan & Co., Ltd., 1915), 190. M.-J. Lagrange, *L'Évangile selon Saint Matthieu* (8e ed., Paris: Librairie Lecoffre, J. Gabalda et Cie, 1948), 259 takes the saying *cum grano salis*, not literally, and cites as a rough parallel the Arab proverb, "*Aucun cavalier ne peut dépouiller un homme nu!*"

13. Dupont, "Point de vue," 236.

14. The originality of the passage at this point is denied by Sherman Johnson, "The Biblical Quotations in Matthew," *HTR* 36 (1943), 135–153 (137f.); Krister

not provide the key to Matthew's meaning. The use of the text in full, even with the "lest" clause, is not really in conflict with v. 13,[15] since it attests only the fulfillment of Scripture in the opponents' unbelief, not the rooting of that unbelief in the obscurity of Jesus' words.[16] And vv. 16f., as we have noted above, are inserted by Matthew into this context to render more explicit the contrast between the understanding disciples[17] and the uncomprehending outsiders.[18]

To sum up: The Markan "hardening theory" has been almost completely transformed in the Matthean revision. The question toward which the materials in vv. 11–17 are purportedly oriented, the purpose of Jesus' use of parabolic discourse, is never really answered. Instead, Matthew has created out of the materials of Mk. and Q a kind of double-edged beatitude in which the blessedness of the disciples (vv. 16f.) who do understand (vv. 23, 51), is contrasted with the judgment on non-disciples, presumably the Jews (v. 12) or anyone else who does not understand (v. 19).

Two things must be kept clearly in mind in the use of this double-edged beatitude today: "Understanding" in this sense can hardly be primarily cognitive, which would shift the initiative in faith from God to man and even from the whole man to his intellect alone; to "understand" is to know, to have faith, and to act

---

Stendahl, *The School of St. Matthew* (Uppsala: ASNU 20, 1954), 131; Strecker, *Weg*, 70, n. 3; Gnilka, *Verstockung*, 103ff. and "Verstockungsproblem," 127. It is accepted, however, by Adolf Jülicher, *Die Gleichnisreden Jesu* (Tübingen: J. C. B. Mohr [Paul Siebeck], I², 1899; II², 1910), I, 128, n. 1; Trilling, *WI³*, 78, n. 18; Hans-Theo Wrege, *Die Ueberlieferungsgeschichte der Bergpredigt* (Tübingen: J. C. B. Mohr [Paul Siebeck], 1968), 49, n. 43.

15. Vs. Strecker, *Weg*, 70, n. 3.

16. "The hardening of the Jews, in Matthew's view, is not 'Fate' but the consequence of the rejection of Jesus—and thus at the same time also a fulfilling of the reprobation-history *(Unheilslinie)* of the OT" (Wrege, *Bergpredigt*, 50).

17. Cf. also 17:13 and the very similar addition in 16:12. Note too the *removal* of the theme of non-understanding from Mk. 4:13; 6:52; "little faith" has replaced "little discernment" in Matt. See Gnilka, "Verstockungsproblem," 122f.

18. Note the catchword connection between seeing/hearing in the Q passage and in Mark's citation of Is. 6:9f. Note further that the order is hearing/seeing in the MT, the LXX, the Targum, and even in the citations of the Is. passage in Matt. 13:14f. and Acts 28:26f. The reverse order, seeing/hearing, in both vv. 13, 16 shows that Matthew in these passages is interpreting Mk., who initiates this order.

accordingly. Furthermore, Matthew's own view of the church as a *corpus mixtum* requires us to apply the dialectic of understanding/non-understanding to ourselves first, not to the church as over against the world. (And certainly not to Christians compared with Jews!) His point is quite different from Mark's, but it does not follow from this that Mark's is the only word we need to hear in "understanding" the parables.

Chapter Two

THE MARKAN PARABLES
IN MATTHEW

1. The Physician (9:12f.; cf. Mk. 2:15ff.; Lk. 5:31f.)

Matthew clearly takes over this brief saying from his Markan text and equally clearly uses it to express his own concerns. This can be seen in the small modifications introduced particularly in the narrative framework. (This framework, as elsewhere in both Matt. and Lk., has been modified more freely than the sayings-materials, not because the words of Jesus are too sacred to modify but because the author's interest is commonly in the "apotheg-matic" character of the tradition as a whole.)[1] Changes of some importance include the following:

Mark's description of the questioners, "the scribes of the Pharisees," has been modified to read simply, "the Pharisees" (v. 11). The unusual grammar and the difficulty of the concept were generally recognized, as is shown by the fact that both Matthew and Luke modify the wording, while the Markan textual tradition becomes quite uncertain.[2] In Matt., the change is probably also motivated by his generally favorable attitude toward "scribes," whom he elsewhere removes from unfavorable situations,[3] and by his understanding of "Pharisees" as a kind of negative ideal.[4]

---

1. See Charles E. Carlston and Dennis Norlin, "Once More—Statistics and Q," *HTR* 64(1971), 59–78.

2. See also Oxyrhynchus Papyrus 1224, vol. 2 verso, col. 2: "the scribes and Pharisees and priests." The secondary nature of this fragment and its dependence on Lk. are evident.

3. For the removal of scribes from pejorative contexts, see (besides our passage) Matt. 12:24; 17:14; 21:23, (45f.); 22:35, 41; 26:3, 47; 27:1. For *Christian* scribes, see Matt. 13:52; 23:34.

4. Pharisees are secondarily inserted into the context at 9:34; 12:24, 38. On the Pharisees in Matt., see Trilling, *WI*³, 198ff.; Strecker, *Weg*, 137–143; and

The question too has been slightly modified. The simple "Why does he eat . . . ?" might be taken to imply disrespect or even scorn. Matthew has felt this and substituted the less hostile "your teacher."[5] While such an expression is not historically improbable, its secondary nature in this context is evident, and it must be interpreted as an element in Matthew's Christology: even Jesus' opponents recognize him, willy-nilly, as a *teacher*.

The modification of the parable itself by the insertion of "I desire mercy and not sacrifice" (v. 13a) between the two parts of the parable poses more than one interesting problem. The citation, Hos. 6:6, is given only twice in the NT, both in Matt. alone (here and 12:7), and in both instances slightly closer to the Hebrew than the LXX. Since the author elsewhere regularly cites the OT in its LXX form, it is occasionally urged that the connection with this parable is pre-Matthean and possibly taken over directly from the homiletic tradition.[6] This argument, however, is precarious. The differences from the Hebrew are minor, while the other quotation (12:7) is buried in M material that looks like free composition; furthermore, in the present passage the quotation does not really fit the text. It is thus a pointer toward Matthew's insistence on a "better righteousness"[7] and it is compatible with the view that his Jesus has rabbinic traits.[8] Its function here is, among other things, to justify Jesus' conduct on the basis of Scripture itself, properly interpreted by an authoritative teacher.

The actual effect of this scriptural insertion on the *form* of the parable, however, is harder to judge. Jülicher[9] argues that it de-

---

esp. Reinhard Hummel, *Die Auseinandersetzung zwischen Kirche und Judentum in Matthäusevangelium* (Munich: Chr. Kaiser Verlag, 1963), 12–17.

5. This reading is preferable. Note that Jesus is called *didaskalos* by his opponents in 12:38. It is also important to note that following chaps. 5–7 (the Messiah of the Word) and chaps. 8–9 (the Messiah of the Deed), Matthew summarizes Jesus' work as "teaching . . . , preaching . . . , and healing" (9:35).

6. So, e.g., G. D. Kilpatrick, *The Origins of the Gospel According to St. Matthew* (Oxford: Oxford University Press, 1946), 90, 93.

7. On this concept, and Matt. 23 in particular, see Bornkamm-Barth-Held, *Tradition*, 24–32.

8. The citation is introduced by the rabbinic formula, "Go and learn"; cf. also 11:29, M.

9. *Gleichn.*, II, 177.

stroys the unity of the parable and turns it into an allegory in which the strong are identified with the just, the sick with sinners, Jesus with the Physician, etc. Bonnard,[10] on the other hand, argues for the literary unity of vv. 9–13 as a whole and sees the call of Matthew as an illustration of the "mercy" emphasized in v. 13. Both views are overstated. Allegory lies very near the surface in the Markan combination of two disparate statements, a secular saying about physicians and an explicitly christological comment on fellowship with sinners. That Jesus is the Physician is thus implied even in Mk., and Matthew has contributed little to the allegory. On the other hand, one ought not to argue that everything in vv. 9–13 is connected with the theme of "mercy," since the insertion of the Hosea passage is adequately accounted for by the context of eating with sinners; in everything else Matthew simply follows the Markan order, where "mercy" is not mentioned. That Jesus' whole ministry is seen as a ministry of mercy, at least by the time vv. 11ff. were composed as a unity,[11] is, again, something that cannot be established on the basis of v. 13 alone.

In its present context, then, the parable of the Physician justifies Jesus' conduct in eating with sinners,[12] and Matthew has added a biblical ground for this action. As a prophetic word addressed to the people of God, it is anti-Jewish, and so Matthew must have understood it. In a Christian context, however, it would be applicable as well in an anti-rigorist sense: Jesus' action and his authoritative interpretation of Scripture both condemn those with an excessive zeal for the purity of the church. Since Matthew seems to be fighting a two-front war against both antinomians[13]

---

10. *Matt.*, 128. Bonnard is partially correct, however, in that Matthew (like Luke) treats the two disparate sayings in Mk. 2:17 as a single parable.
11. Ibid., 131.
12. This is a broad term, with the specific meaning to be determined by the context; cf. Lk. 6:32 with Matt. 5:46; Matt. 11:19 (=Lk. 7:34, Q); Lk. 15:1; Gal. 2:15; Karl Heinrich Rengstorf, "*hamartōlos, ktl.*," *TDNT*, I, 317–335 (327–333). Among the Pharisees, it is used specifically for those who do not follow a strict interpretation of the Law. If Matthew means this, he has not noticed that Jesus is not included in the category by his opponents.
13. On the antinomians, see Bornkamm-Barth-Held, *Tradition*, 67–75, 159–164.

and rigorists[14] in the Christian church we may understand an additional anti-rigorist motif as part of his intention. Its application today is self-evident: any stress on the grace and generosity of God will find many opponents, especially among the religious.

2. The Sons of the Bridechamber (9:14f.; cf. Mk. 2:18ff.; Lk. 5:33ff.)

The contextual modifications of this parable are minor and primarily literary. The rather loose Markan connection at v. 18 has been tightened up by the use of the distinctively Matthean *tote*, which creates an impression of chronological continuity, and the setting in a context of fasting has disappeared. On form-critical grounds, of course, a concrete situation for controversy-discourses is ordinarily required; but the Markan text at this point is quite general, implying at best some unspecified fast.[1] If the legitimacy of any particular fast was ever behind this incident, it has long since disappeared from the text.

The participants in the discussion are also differently treated. In addition to changing "scribes of the Pharisees" to read simply "Pharisees," Matthew has revised the text so that the Pharisees ask the question about eating with sinners and the disciples of John ask about fasting. In this way he smoothes out the passage while avoiding the use of "the people" entirely. By doing so, however, he has associated the disciples of John with the Pharisees even more intimately than Mark, since they ask, "Why do we[2] and the Pharisees fast?"—an association that in Mk. is made only in the minds of the people, not by the participating groups, who can hardly be imagined as supporting one another, even against

14. The clearest evidence of anti-rigorism is the parables of the Tares (12:24–30, M).

1. The view that the text of Mk. used by both Matthew and Luke did not contain the phrase "and . . . were fasting" is unnecessary; vs. B. Harvie Branscomb, *The Gospel of Mark* (New York: Harper & Bros., 1937), 53.

2. ". . . Which they should know better than anyone" (Alfred Loisy, *Les Évangiles synoptiques* [Ceffonds: Chez l'auteur, 1907–08], I, 495). Hence it is hard to follow Lagrange's suggestion (*Matt.*, 182f.) that the Matthean form is both independent and primitive or his insistence that Mark really uses a Semitism in which (cf. Is. 58:3) the actual speaker is not necessarily included in the "we."

Jesus. For Matthew, however, they are aligned in fasting[3] against Jesus' disciples.

A very interesting Matthean variation occurs in Jesus' parabolic answer to the unfriendly question: fasting is interpreted as *mourning* (v. 15). Fasting is a common penitential practice, and the added fasts observed by the Pharisees are primarily of this type.[4] A contrast with the wedding as a symbol of joy[5] is certainly intended. Yet it would be too much to insist that the *primary* reference is to mourning, of which fasting is simply a sign[6]—the argument has to do with fasting, not mourning! Matthew's term would then strengthen the contrast between the joy of the wedding and the mourning (?) when it is ended, and it would make explicit what is at best implicit in Mk.: here Jesus predicts his own death. Whether in addition Matthew intends "mourning" ethically, characterized by reserve toward this aeon and expectation toward the aeon to come[7] is difficult to decide, although the reference in this passage seems a bit forced. But by eliminating Mark's "in that day" Matthew apparently reflects a "historicizing" of Jesus' past and accepts the time since the crucifixion as not so much a single "day" as an extended and continuing period in history.[8]

3. The Patched Garment and the Old Wineskins (9:16f.; cf. Mk. 2:21f.; Lk. 5:36–39)

Matthew, in his interpretation of these two brief parables, rests fairly completely on Mk.; the parables follow the discussion about fasting, they are treated as a pair, and the wording seems to

3. *polla* (v. 14, supported by C D W Θ λ Φ ℛ syᵖ bo) looks very much like a gloss, probably influenced by the somewhat similar Lukan reading *pykna*.
4. See mTaʾanith (Danby, 194–201).
5. Cf. I Macc. 9:41, where Jonathan and Simon kill many of the sons of Jambri and "the wedding was turned into mourning."
6. Vs. Vincent Taylor, *The Gospel According to St. Mark* (London: Macmillan & Co., Ltd., 1957), 211. Note too that the Markan wording becomes almost totally inexplicable on the hypothesis of Matthean priority.
7. So Strecker, *Weg*, 189. On Matt. 5:4, see Rudolf Bultmann, "*penthos, ktl.*," *TDNT*, VI, 43.
8. Strecker, *Weg*, 189 suggests that Matthew thus indicates the continuing practice of fasting as over against Mk., which might be understood to imply fasting only at the time of the bridegroom's departure. But there is little evidence that Matthew read Mk. this way; see further below, chap. 6, sec. 2.

be entirely dependent on Mk.[1] A primary reference to fasting thus lies close at hand.

The extent to which fasting is only symptomatic of something else, however, is more problematic. The addition to v. 17, "and so both [i.e., new wine and new skins] are preserved," indicates that for Matthew, as for Mark, the emphasis lies on the preservation of the new, not the old.[2] If this is hardly central in the Patched Garment—of what value is a patch?—the general notion of incompatibility between the old and the new has in this second parable moved imperceptibly into a defense of the new.

But what is the "new" thing which must not be put into old wineskins? Like Mark, Matthew believes that Christianity is in some sense incompatible with the Judaism of his own day and of course superior to it. But whether he draws from this any conclusion about specific Christian practices as opposed to their Jewish counterparts we cannot say. Perhaps the most judicious course is "not to press this double parable too hard."[3] The homiletic tradition of Matthew's day, like that of our own, doubtless found many applications, some of them mutually exclusive. But for our purposes its greatest importance may lie in its value as a warning against excessive enthusiasm for the generalization that everything in the Gospel tradition was handed down for a theological purpose, since a theological purpose which we cannot recover is not, in the last analysis, much different from the old "historicist" view that the author simply handed on the words because they were part of the tradition. The falsity of this "historicist" view is amply demonstrated by the tiny changes, none of which an "objective" redactor would have bothered to make. But beyond this we can hardly go.

---

1. Only two agreements between Lk. and Matt. against Mk. are important: the use of *epiballei* for *epiraptei* (which is apparently suggested by the noun *epiblēma* and the use of *ekcheitai* (Lk: *ekchythēsetai*, a thought that could have arisen independently or might have crept into the Matthean text from Lk., just as the reading of D it has come in by assimilation to Mk. On other minor details, see Jülicher, *Gleichn.*, II, 189f.
2. Schniewind, *Matt.*, 121. Yet note that Matthew "seems to fight shy of the suggestion in Mk. that Judaism is abolished by the Kingdom" (Fenton, *Matt.*, 140).
3. Bonnard, *Matt.*, 134.

4. The Beelzebul Parables (12:22–30, 43ff.; cf. Mk. 3:22–27; Lk. 11:14–26)

This section, in both Mk. and Q, is highly composite, including in its Matthean form two parables (the Strong Man and the Return of the Unclean Spirit Seeking Rest) and a number of sayings. We may justifiably discuss it as a single section because that is apparently what it was in Q, and in calling it a collection of parables we use Mark's own terminology (3:23).

Several of the most interesting and most important aspects of Matthean interpretation have to do with the order of the sayings and their context. It is obvious that this section is a doublet of Matt. 9:27–34, in which Jesus heals two blind men who confess him as Son of David and then heals a dumb demoniac. At the second healing the crowds marvel, suggesting that Jesus must indeed be the Son of David,[1] but the Pharisees say, "He casts out demons by the prince of demons." Whatever non-Markan materials, if any, lie behind these two similar passages, they are surely redactional in detail: *daimonidsomenos* occurs in both; the demoniac is *brought*[2] to Jesus; and the distinctive christological title, Son of David,[3] is common to both.

Matthean redaction in 12:22ff. even extends to small words. He has omitted the Markan introduction to the Beelzebul charge (3:19b–21), no doubt because the suggestion that Jesus' friends thought him mad was offensive, though the *eksestē* of Mk. must reappear in the "amazement" (*eksistanto*) of the people, since the Q rendering, as the Lukan text here and the Matthean doublet in 9:33 show, was probably *ethaumasan*. Similarly, the charge that he (Jesus) is possessed by Beelzebul and drives out demons by demonic means, a charge introduced by a scornful refusal to

---

1. The wording of the question seems to imply that the crowds, unlike the Pharisees, recognize Jesus' true nature. On *mēti* here, see Ernst Haenchen, *Der Weg Jesu. Eine Erklärung des Markus-Evangeliums und der kanonischen Parallelen* (Berlin: Verlag Alfred Töpelmann, 1966), 151, n. 17; Blass-Debrunner-Funk, sec. 427, 2. Lagrange, *Matt.*, 241 sees it as a hesitant affirmation.

2. *prosēnechthē:* Matt. 14; Mk. 3; Luke-Acts 7.

3. On the importance of this title in Matt., see Hummel, *Auseinandersetzung*, 116–122.

address Jesus directly, is modified and heightened. The accusation
of being possessed disappears (v. 24; so also Lk.), but Matthew
adds, "It is *only* by Beelzebul. . . ." And he repeats the "this man"
of the people's confession in reformulating the charge that "this
man" casts out demons by Beelzebul. He has removed the typically
Markan note that the conversation takes place at the house,
although he obviously knows it (12:46; 13:1), and thus has left
the conversation without a setting. In all of this we may justly
speak of Matthean redaction of Mk.

In the identity of the accusers, however, Matthew is obviously
working with a double tradition, Mk. and Q. In Mk. 3:22 "some
scribes who come down from Jerusalem" make the Beelzebul
charge; in Matt. (as in the doublet, 9:34), it is the Pharisees.
Q, like Lk., probably read not "Pharisees" but "some of them,"
since, although Luke has some preference for anonymity, the
trend in the tradition is generally from anonymity to specificity,[4]
while for Matthew the Pharisees are the typical theological opponents of Jesus. Furthermore, the expression "your sons" a few
verses later in Q (Matt. 12:27 = Lk. 11:19) can only refer to Jews
in general, not to Pharisees in particular, since "sons of the Pharisees" is an impossible concept.[5] (It is most improbable that this
phrase should be understood of "followers," somewhat on the analogy of "sons of the bridechamber" [Mk. 2:19] or that it was created by the tradition as a counter to the Christian "Son of God").[6]
In any case, it is fully consistent with Matthew's outlook that the
charge should be made by Pharisees and that here, as in 9:34, the
Pharisaic accusation should be motivated less by the exorcism
itself than by the people's confessional response.[7]

In response to the charge, which Jesus "knows" without having

---

4. See Rudolf Bultmann, *The History of the Synoptic Tradition* (Oxford: Basil
Blackwell, 1963), 14, 309f., who however overstates the case.
5. Ibid., 52.
6. Josef Schmid, *Das Evangelium nach Lukas* (4. Aufl., Regensburg: Verlag
Friedrich Pustet, 1960), 204 accepts the former explanation; Jülicher, *Gleichn.*,
II, 230 hesitates between the two because he accepts Pharisees as the original
reference and does not ask what Mk. meant.
7. Lagrange, *Mk.*, 64 rightly notes that Mark would not have set aside a source
like Matt., where the Christian confession is clear and useful.

heard (v. 25=Lk. 11:17, Q), Jesus in all three Gospels makes a
rather long speech. It is composite—the presuppositions behind
v. 27 and v. 28, for example, are incompatible—and in Matt. includes some material which may legitimately be omitted from a
study of the parables. But many individual items fit easily into
the larger pattern of Matthew's overall concern.

The first response to the charge, vv. 25f., rests largely on Q,
though it contains Markan elements (cf. 12:26a with Mk. 3:23b),
and consists of a counter-question based on a simple parable:
Every kingdom divided against itself is laid waste; so if Satan is
divided against himself, how will his kingdom stand?[8] In Mk. the
general principle that strength lies in unity is applied to a kingdom
and a "house," which is at most a household, since in v. 27 the
house as a building is prominent. Matthew inserts between these
two items, however, a "city," which makes a natural progression:
kingdom, city, house.[9] As in Q, the disaster implied in the question
is still future.[10] The force of this first argument is to show that
Jesus' opponents condemn him illogically: either he casts out
demons by the power of God, in which case the Kingdom has
come upon them (v. 28), or he casts them out by the power of a
divided and thus "wasted" Satan. *Tertium non datur.*

The second argument rests on the presupposition that Jewish
exorcists[11] are also effective. Since obviously they cannot be in
league with Beelzebul their activity shows the absurdity of the
charge that Jesus is; they are[12] therefore (v. 27b) evidence against

8. Q's form is a question, Mk.'s a statement. Since development is ordinarily from
a question to a statement (Bultmann, *HST,* 93) we may cautiously assume that Q
here is more primitive than Mk.; vs. Taylor, *Mk.,* 240. In v. 29 Mk.'s statement
has also become a question, but here, on balance, it seems best to explain the
question form in Matt. as a redactional parallel to the earlier question and to
identify Q with Luke's version.

9. If house were interpreted, as in Semitic thought, as a political line ("house of
David," etc.), this progression would be obscured. The Matthean emphasis seems
to mean "from the largest to the smallest political/social unit."

10. In Mk. Satan's kingdom "has an end," which seems to imply that this end
has already begun.

11. By introducing the Pharisees (12:24) into his source, Matthew has made
"your sons" in v. 27 sound like a charge against *Pharisaic* exorcists. But doubtless
he, like Q and Luke, understood the saying in a more general sense.

12. On the grammar, see McNeile, *Matt.,* 176; Jülicher, *Gleichn.,* II, 230.

Jesus' opponents. In v. 28 (also from Q) a different (and inconsistent) aspect of the same argument is used: since the case for a
Satanic explanation has collapsed, the true explanation must be
that Jesus casts out demons by the Spirit of God, an indication that
the Kingdom of God[13] is at work, not at a future time, but now.[14]

To these arguments another is now added, the parable of the
Strong Man, which seems to have come from both Mk. and Q and
in Matt. differs from the Markan form only in two very minor
details: the parable is connected with all that precedes by the simple "or" ('ἤ), which has the effect of making it a variant argument
for what has just preceded; and the statement (Mk., v. 27) becomes a question (Matt., v. 29). In neither case can we be quite
sure what the Q reading was. In the absence of any noticeable
modification, we may assume that the Matthean interpretation
was much like Mark's. The Q saying, "He who is not with me is
against me, etc." follows, in this context obviously anti-Pharisaic.[15]

Two verses on blasphemy against the Holy Spirit then follow,
representing an amalgamation of Mk. (3:28) and Q (Lk. 12:10)
into one long and balanced saying. In its Matthean form it could
imply either a chronological distinction between rejecting Jesus
and rejecting the apostolic preaching or a material distinction between degrees of unbelief.[16] In favor of the latter—understood as
a warning to the hearers of Matthew's own day—is Matthew's
elimination of Mark's redundant comment in 3:30 and his general
inclination to view the rejection of the Jews as final. In any case,
Matthew has added to the saying the phrase, "either in *this age*
or in *the age to come*," a contrast which, with a slight variation in
wording,[17] is taken from Mk. 10:30 with a significant Matthean

---

13. The contrast between Satan and God requires that Matthew simply follow
Q in reading "Kingdom of God" instead of using his more usual expression,
"Kingdom of Heaven."

14. Schniewind, *Matt.*, 159.

15. The (reverse) Markan form of the saying, "He that is not against us is for us,"
9:40, is less polemic and refers to irregular exorcists.

16. On this see Strecker, *Weg*, 190, n. 3. Quite probably Mark intended to distinguish two kinds of sins, Q two periods of history. Matthew assumes the two
periods of history but generalizes the saying in a parenetic sense.

17. *ho aiōn ho erchomenos* instead of *ho aiōn ho mellōn*.

modification. Mark's promise that "There is no one who has left house or brothers . . . who will not receive in this time houses and brothers, . . . and in the age to come eternal life" has been modified to read simply "And every one who has left houses or brothers . . . will receive a hundredfold and inherit eternal life (19:29)." Matthew's elimination of the phrase and the thought represented by "in this time" has the effect of restricting the reward to the world to come, one example of his "spiritualizing" and "apocalypticizing" tendencies.[18] Yet we must not assume that because he is loath to speak of a reward in this time he is equally reluctant to assert a proleptic judgment within history, at least on unbelieving Jews. His specific mention of *both* this age and the next where his sources apparently do not contain such a contrast must imply some such anticipation of the Judgment even in this world, although ordinarily judgment *on the Christian church* is for Matthew an eschatological event of the End time.

After the parable of the Tree and Its Fruit and an interesting but obscure comment on what might be called a judgment of words (vv. 36f.), Matthew adds a Q section on seeking a sign (vv. 38–42), which he apparently understands as part of the same dialogue ("Then . . . ," v. 38), and closes with the parable of the Return of the Evil Spirit Seeking Rest (vv. 43ff.).[19] If we read these as a single speech in the Matthean order, the parable of the Return of the Evil Spirit Seeking Rest is addressed to "some of the scribes and Pharisees" (v. 38), one of the very few instances of a gratuitous Matthean addition of scribal condemnation to his sources, although the addition in v. 45b ("So shall it be with this wicked generation, too") shows that the condemnation is intended for the whole people, not for individuals within it.[20]

18. See Strecker, *Weg*, 151, n. 1.
19. The description is almost a caricature of 11:28ff.! (See Schniewind, *Matt.*, 163.)
20. *poneros* is Matthean (Matt. 24; Mk. 2; Q 8; Lk. 11); added by the evangelist here and at 13:19, 38, 49; 22:10 (Kilpatrick, *Origins*, 21). But the phrase "evil generation" occurs only in the Matthean doublet (12:39; 16:4) of a Q saying (=Lk. 11:29), while all 8 occurrences of "this generation" outside our present passage rest on either Mk. (so 16:4; 17:17; 24:34) or Q (so 11:16; 12:38, 41, 42; 23:36). On balance, therefore, it seems best to assign Matt. 12:45b to Q, not Matthew; vs. Loisy, *ES*, I, 716.

The effect of v. 45b in Matt. (as in Q, if it originated there) is to make the Return of the Evil Spirit Seeking Rest unmistakably a parable. But of what? Clearly, of a judgment on the Jews. But the identification of the two periods of demonic habitation is difficult. One possibility is that the latter stage is the ministry of Jesus, the former the ministry of John or even the period characterized by the presence of Jewish exorcists.[21] But since John is not described as an exorcist in any contemporary source and so sharp a distinction between two chronological periods as this parable demands is nowhere implied in the descriptions of Jewish exorcisms, it is better to find here a reference to the time of Jesus' ministry and the days of the apostolic church.[22] In association with v. 45c the parable thus reflects an understanding of history in which the Jewish rejection of Jesus has occurred twice—once in his ministry, once in the response to the apostolic preaching—and is presumed to be final.[23] In its Matthean context it provides a connecting link between the long Beelzebul discourse and the following apothegm on Jesus' true relatives (vv. 46–50), ending the discourse without dismissing the crowd. The man to whom the "will of my Father in heaven" (v. 50, Matthean terminology) is commended as the key to a true relationship to Jesus is thus an example of those in Matthew's own day who must learn that the Father's will is connected with the Strong Man who plunders Satan's house and casts out demons by the Spirit of God in the power of the inbreaking Kingdom.

5. The Sower (13:1–9, 18–23; cf. Mk. 4:1–9, 13–20; Lk. 8:4–8, 11–15)

In Matt. 13, as in Mk. 4, several parables are given successively. Until v. 35 this chapter may be considered a modification of Mk.[1]

21. See Bonnard, *Matt.*, 185. Older commentators speak of pre-Christian periods of Jewish history; cf. Loisy, *ES*, I, 716.
22. Strecker, *Weg*, 105f.
23. Vs. McNeile, *Matt.*, 184, who understands the phrase simply as a stern warning, no doubt because he attributes it to Jesus.

1. The items suggested by Ernst Lohmeyer, *Das Evangelium des Matthäus*, hrsg. v. W. Schmauch (3. Aufl., Göttingen: Vandenhoeck & Ruprecht, 1962), 190–212

Matthew then diverges from Mk. to add the explanation of the Tares (vv. 36-43), three parables from his special tradition (the Hid Treasure, v. 44; the Pearl, vv. 45f.; the Net, vv. 47-50)', and a concluding parabolic statement about the scribe trained for the Kingdom of heaven (v. 51f.).

Broadly speaking, the modfications of the Markan material have the net effect of minimizing still further the Markan hardening theory; they also illustrate in minor ways different details of Matthew's own theology and situation.

The most striking changes are to be found in vv. 10-15, in which Matthew has revised the materials of the Markan hardening theory, and in v. 34, which interprets Jesus' use of parables as the fulfillment of Ps. 78:2, a non-Markan note. In vv. 16f. Jesus sharply distinguishes the eyes and ears of the disciples, which are blessed because of what they see and hear, from the closed eyes and heavy ears of those whose hearts have been hardened but who hear only parables. The theory that even the disciples do not understand (Mk. 4:13) is gone. Gone too is the inconsistency between Mk. 4:33b, which he does not cite, and Mk. 4:34, according to which the parables demand explanation and are incomprehensible otherwise. Insofar as a parable is obscure it is spoken "to them" (13:10), not to the disciples, since the latter have "understood all these things" (v. 51).[2] Explanations are given—three of the four explained parables in the Gospel tradition are in this chapter of Matt.[3]—but they are not really necessary, since a true disciple understands. Just as the unbeliever is one who "hears the word of the kingdom *and does not understand it*" so the seed sown on good soil is "he who hears the word *and understands it*" (vv. 19, 23). This emphasis, which is paralleled elsewhere in the

---

to establish the primacy of the Matthean form of the Sower over against Mk. are by no means persuasive. Wilkens's admirable study ("Redaktion") establishes Matthew's dependence on Mk. beyond reasonable doubt, in spite of Xavier Léon-Dufour's insistence (*Études d'Évangile* [Paris: Éditions du Seuil, 1965], 287) that the hypothesis of such absolute dependence is "*ruineuse.*"

2. Since the crowds do not understand, Jesus "tells" many things to them (13:30), but he does not, as in Mk. 4:1f., "teach" them.

3. The Sower (vv. 18-23), the Tares (vv. 36-43), and the Net (vv. 49f.); the Things That Defile (15:1-20) is retained at its later Markan place.

Gospel,[4] refers not to general understanding, still less to general intelligence, but to the Christian message in its full import. It is thus not accidental that in the explanation of the Sower (vv. 18–23) the second and third groups are never said to understand; understanding is soteriological (and perhaps also ethical),[5] not primarily intellectual.

Other changes are more minor. The context has been clarified, though perhaps not really changed, over against Mk. In v. 1, Jesus leaves the house;[6] in v. 36 he goes back into it to explain the Tares and tell the three small parables of the Kingdom (vv. 44–50); in v. 53 he finishes the parables and leaves the region. (Just where the disciples "came" from in v. 10[7] is not clear, although the difficulty is no greater than in the Markan text on which he depends.) Matthew also revises Mark's wording (v. 1) to avoid the possible misunderstanding that Jesus actually sat in the water (although he does so by making him sit down *twice*, vv. 1, 2), omits the solemn "listen" at the opening of the parable (Mk. 4:3),[8] varies the words used for "choke" (vv. 7, 22), modifies "the word" (abs.) to "the word of the Kingdom" (v. 19),[9] omits the Semitizing *egeneto* (v. 4) and adds a redundant *kai poiei* (v. 23), and modifies Mark's *ho satanas* (v. 15) to *ho poneros* (v. 19). Of these details only the last calls for comment.

The Matthean change is characteristic: *poneros* is a Matthean word.[10] Luke also changes the word *satanas* (v. 12), although *ho diabolos*, which he substitutes, is not particularly characteristic

---

4. Cf. above, chap. 1, n. 17. On understanding as a characteristic of the disciples, see 15:10; 16:12 (both from Mk.); 13:51; 17:13; and note the elimination of *non*-understanding from Mk. 4:13; 6:51f.; 8:17f.; 9:10, 32. Quite possibly this motif explains Matthew's preference for the form *ho echon ota* vs. Mk.'s *hos echei ota akouein akoueto*. (Both external and internal textual criteria show that the shorter form is primitive in all three Matthean passages.)

5. See Strecker, *Weg*, 229.

6. The dependence of Matt. on Mk. is evident in the fact that the "house" of v. 1 has not previously been mentioned in Matt.

7. *proserchomai* is Matthean: Matt. 52; Mk. 5; Lk. 10; Jn. 1.

8. But is it not implied in "Hear the parable . . ." (v. 18)?

9. This absolute use of "the Kingdom" is non-rabbinic: Lohmeyer/Schmauch, *Matt.*, 27, n. 2 (in dependence on Dalman).

10. Above, chap. 2, sec. 4, n. 20.

of his language.[11] Since both Matthew and Luke feel it necessary
to change Mark's term, Matthew into his own vocabulary, Luke
into the common terminology of his own generation, it is possible
to argue that *ho satana(s)* represents an earlier stratum of Gospel
tradition than *ho diabolos* and even to draw tentative conclusions
about the authenticity of the explanation from this fact.[12] But such
a conclusion is unwarranted. It is true that Mark never uses *ho
diabolos*. And it is also true that this term is common in the later
books of the NT as well as in Matt. 13:39; 25:41. But both *ho
satana(s)* and *ho diabolos* are pre-Christian[13] and *ho diabolos* does
occur in the Q account of the temptation, which is at least as early
as Mark. Furthermore, TNaph. 8:4, 6, on which the Markan
account of the temptation may well rest, uses *ho diabolos*. The
argument that *satana(s)* is more primitive than *diabolos* is thus
unpersuasive.

Three other changes are of some significance. In the parable
proper Matthew consistently thinks of the "seed" as a plural, not,
like Mark, as a collective singular. This parenetic concern is no
doubt the reason that he also changes Mark's singular *to petrōdes*
to the plural, *ta petrōdē* (v. 5). (Since Mark *also* uses the plural
in the explanation, it is probable that the plurals in the parable
represent the influence of the explanation, where interest in the
application has taken precedence over the story of the sowing
itself.) A similar shift to a parenetic interest is reflected in Matthew's omission of Mark's "The Sower sows the Word" (v. 14).
These traits show that Matthew continues a process begun long
before Mk., and in his Gospel the connection between parable and
explanation, and thus the parenetic purpose of the whole, is clear.

11. It occurs in Acts 10:38; 13:10; in Lk., nowhere except here and in the
temptation narrative (4:2f., 5, 13), where it clearly comes from Q.
12. Joachim Jeremias, *The Parables of Jesus* (rev. ed., New York: Charles
Scribner's Sons, 1963), 81.
13. *Satanas* is the Gr. form of the Heb. *śāṭān* (Aram. *sāṭānā'*), of which however
diabolos is the ordinary LXX translation. In the confused textual tradition of the
Test XII. Patr. both terms seem to be about equally frequent: *Satanas*, Dan
3:6; 5:6; 6:1; Gad 4:7; Asher 6:4(β). *Diabolos*, Sim. 4:8(a); Naph. 3:1(β-g);
8:4, 6; Gad 5:2(β-b); Asher 3:2(β). (Citations taken from Charles's edition
304, 320). See esp., for the Qumran material, W. Foerster, "satanas," *TDNT*, VII,
151–163. *Ho satanas* seems to appear for the first time in Sir. 21:27 (30).

In v. 8 Matthew has described the harvest in descending order, 100-60-30 (so too the explanation, v. 23), a reversal of Mark's ascending order, 30-60-100 (vv. 8, 20). The effect of this seems to be to move the center of interest from an *ever greater* or *certain* harvest to a *varied* harvest; in a sense, it places three successful categories over against three unsuccessful ones. In the context of Matthew's theology as a whole, it is plausible to assume that differences in degree of fruitfulness among various types of Christians (soils) is a central concern. The reverse order might also reflect an idealizing of the earlier more successful days of the church.

But Matthew specifically calls this "the parable of the sower" (v. 18). Does that mean that he understands it primarily christologically? Bonnard[14] argues that it does and holds that Matthew intends a contrast between the "Christ" of the Pharisees, whose might is irresistible (see especially the Psalms of Solomon), and the Christ of the believer, who is finally victorious only after many rejections. But the sower never appears in the parable after the opening line (v. 3), and Matthew has even taken the reference out in the explanation (v. 19) where it occurs in his source (Mk. 4:14)—a most peculiar way of showing christological concern! His generalized "when any man hears the word..." (v. 19) is a revision of Mk. that points with exceptional clarity away from the sower to a discussion of the various ways in which the Word may be heard. And his central concern is, as in the section immediately following the explanation (vv. 24–30, the Tares), the various possible responses to the one Word or, to stay with his own figure, the variety of both failure and harvest that the Word brings forth from encountering different types of soil. To be fruitful—not merely to have heard the Word[15]—is the perennial demand which Matthew understands to have been laid upon the Christian.

---

14. *Matt.*, 192; so also Theophylact: *tis oun estin ho speirōn; autos ho Christos* (cited, Henry Barclay Swete, *The Gospel According to St. Mark* [London: Macmillan and Co., Ltd., 1898], 74.)
15. "'Understanding' and 'bearing fruit' are inseparable"; Dupont, "Point de vue," 238.

6. The Mustard Seed (13:31f.; cf. Mk. 4:30ff.; Lk. 13:18f.)

In Matt. the Mustard Seed is part of a paired parable; the other member, the Leaven, follows immediately. Although in Matt. the two doubtless have the same intention, they may not have the same origin: the Mustard Seed is a conflation of Mk. and Q, while apparently[1] the Leaven was never in Mk. or his source.

Several minor changes in the Markan and Q forms of the Mustard Seed bear upon the Matthean interpretation. For one thing, the parable itself is introduced by a question in Mk. (and probably in Q), but a statement in Matt. It is generally agreed that the question form is more primitive.[2] But a question might well have seemed to Matthew too solemn a way to begin what is really only part of a longer discourse, the third and fourth in a series of parables. His statement form blunts the rhetorical edge and moves in a parenetic direction.

The most curious Matthean modification of Mk., however, is not this purely literary one. It is rather that by conflating Mk. and Q he has made the text into something different from either, so that "when . . . [the Mustard Seed] has grown it is the greatest of shrubs [Mk.] and becomes a tree [Q]." More significantly, in Mk. the parable consists of present tenses: this is what happens whenever a mustard seed is sown. In Q the parable is of a single past event, told in aorists: a man took the seed, etc. But in Matt. the tenses are mixed and the resulting parable is neither a timeless possibility nor a past event; the seed grows, and the Markan general possibility (the birds *can* come) becomes instead a general rule (the birds *do* come).

Here surely the presence of allegory is at work, a presence confirmed by both the location and the language of the parable. It

1. Vs. Jülicher, *Gleichn.*, II, 580. Jacques Dupont, in "Les paraboles du sénevé et du levain," *NRT* 89 (1967), 897–913 (899–902) argues with great plausibility for the priority of the Markan wording of the Mustard Seed in most respects, though he holds that the *narrative* form (Lk.; cf. the Leaven) is more primitive.
2. Sherman Johnson, *The Gospel According to St. Mark* (London: Adam and Charles Black, 1960), 95. Swete, *Mk.*, 82 sees the original question as an attempt by Jesus, a wise teacher, "to take his audience into his counsels, and to seek their help." But the emphasis is either polemic or (as rabbinic parallels show) rhetorical. (Schmid, *Mk.*, 103; rhetorical.)

immediately follows the Matthean allegory of the Tares and is followed within a few verses (vv. 47–50) by the allegory of the Net. It maintains the Markan contrast, not central in Q, between the small beginning and the great ending, and includes (like Q) a clear reference to the LXX of Dan. 4:9, 12, 20f., which suggests to practically all commentators a reference to Gentiles in the church. But what precisely is this allegory of the Kingdom supposed to teach? We may rule out the view that Matthew emphasizes the sudden bursting forth of the Kingdom, its surprising power,[3] which his grammar does not imply. And we may also set aside as unduly speculative that interpretation which says that Matthew retained Mark's "the smallest of all seeds" because this (faulty) horticulture would point toward the paradoxical nature of the Kingdom.[4] There is no evidence that Matthew even saw the difficulty, much less deliberately emphasized it.[5]

What does seem to be intended is a portrayal of growth; in Matthew's view the Kingdom is like a tiny seed which becomes the greatest of shrubs. There is little reason to understand Matthew's intention as primarily parenetic, as if he meant no more than that in the realm of religion small acts can have great consequences,[6] the parenetic implications of which would be hard to draw. Rather it must somehow relate either to the church as such —an ancient view, still common especially among Roman Catholics[7]—or to the Kingdom insofar as it had "grown" or become a reality by the adherence of believers to Jesus. While it does not

3. Bonnard, Matt., 201.
4. It is not the smallest for the botanist—but it is for the ordinary peasant; see Lohmeyer/Schmauch, Matt., 217. That it reflects the "least"= "the disciples" (ibid.) is very unlikely.
5. According to the later regulations in mKilaim (Danby, 30f.) Jews were permitted to sow mustard seed only in fields, not in gardens. It is possible that Matthew's "field" is nearer to first-century Palestinian custom than Luke's "garden"; so Johnson, Mk., 95.
6. Rudolf Bultmann, Theology of the New Testament (ET, 2 vols., New York: Charles Scribner's Sons, 1951, 1955), I, 8.
7. See, e.g., Otto Kuss, "Zum Sinngehalt des Doppelgleichnisses vom Senfkorn und Sauerteig," Biblica 40 (1959), 641–653) (=Auslegung und Verkündigung, 85–97). Wilkens, "Redaktion," 319 sees the parable as contrasting not the Church as a corpus mixtum with the final Kingdom but the disciples with "hardened" Israel; although the Church might be only a minority enduring temptation, "against all appearances God creates His Kingdom."

particularly emphasize the weakness of the beginning of the process, as a *theologia crucis* would have done, it does contrast a measure of incompleteness with a great (and presumably complete) consummation. For Matthew, of course, the time of this beginning is now long past. Equally certainly, society or even the earthly growth of the church is not his primary concern; if it had been, he would not have said so much about the end product of the process of growth, so little about all the intermediate stages. What he does emphasize is what the small seed becomes. A tree great enough to support nesting birds must have seemed to him a fitting parallel to the church "*en pleine expansion*"[8] of his own day, a haven for "all nations" (28:19). But this was itself at best a foreshadowing of a consummation, perhaps not far away, when the Kingdom should fully portray what was implicit even in its tiny beginnings.

7. The Things That Defile (15:1–20; cf. Mk. 7:1–23)

Actually the parable in this section is the single statement in v. 11 (=Mk. 7:15): "It is not what enters the mouth that defiles the man but what comes out of the mouth. . . ." Its metaphorical nature is stressed by both evangelists in their insistence that it is a parable, i.e., that it contains a meaning beyond the superficial one. And it is interpreted both specifically, in vv. 17–20, and generally, by the context in which it is placed, vv. 1–20.

Generally speaking, Matthew's revision of his Markan source has four tendencies. He blurs the sharpness of the Markan insistence that foods are unrelated to purity. He represents Jesus, even more sharply than Mark, as opposing the scribal tradition but not Mosaic law. He eliminates Mark's rather awkward explanations of Jewish customs. And he makes the whole section smoother and somewhat more logical in expression and development. The significance of these changes can best be illustrated by examining the details.

8. Dupont, "Sénevé," 903.

The most striking and important modification is Matthew's
insertion of vv. 12ff., which are made up largely of Matthean
material (although v. 13 may rest on earlier tradition and v. 14 is
clearly a reworking of the Q parable in Lk. 6:39). In spite of the
fact that these three verses contain one and possibly two metaphorical statements, the request for an explanation of "the parable" (v. 15) refers back to the statement in v. 11, not to anything
in vv. 12ff., clear evidence of Matthew's dependence on Mk.
Essentially, then, vv. 12ff. are an elaboration of the scene,[1] which
point out that the Pharisees are offended by the parable. Since the
questioners were originally described as Pharisees and scribes
(v. 1), this limitation to the Pharisees is unusual. Yet it is quite
in keeping with Matthew's special understanding of the Pharisees,[2]
whom he considers symbolic of the people as a whole, a kind of
negative ideal of Judaism. (The neutral attitude toward the people, taken over from Mk., is purely formal and does not really
suggest a separation of Pharisees from the people in Matthew's
intention.) This passage, like much else in the Gospel, suggests
that any hope of healing the breach between Jews and Christians
has long since disappeared.

Jesus responds to the information that the Pharisees are offended
by using two brief figurative statements. The first insists that the
Pharisees (or, less probably, the doctrines they represent) are a
plant not planted by God; hence they will be rooted up, i.e.,
judged. This figurative promise of judgment is then linked with
the second, the Q parable about the Blind Leading the Blind, with
the admonition "let them alone." While the interpretation of these
words is disputed, they can hardly be primarily words of consolation: "Be not disturbed at their disapproval,"[3] since by Mat-

1. The artificiality of their connection here is shown among other things by the
fact that the disciples must *come* to him (a Matthean word), although the text,
unlike Mk. 7:17, has not yet indicated that anyone has left.
2. Mk. uses the Semitizing expression "walk according to . . .," Matt. (the equally
Semitic) "transgress." The effect of this is to equate tradition and written Law.
The Markan wording more precisely reflects the spirit and rationale of Pharisaic
teaching (Lagrange, *Matt.*, 301).
3. So McNeile, *Matt.*, 227f., paraphrases the saying.

thew's time any Christian would have rejoiced in Pharisaic disapproval, not been disturbed by it. The words must therefore imply primarily a rejection of the Pharisees; their disapproval is to be expected and should consequently be ignored. The Q parable of the Blind Leading the Blind need not be discussed here, although it should perhaps be pointed out that in this period many favorable statements about "guides" exist; only blind guides (as here) are to be rejected.[4]

Within the text of vv. 10f., 15–20 there are also modifications of the Markan material that point to special Matthean emphases. The most important of these involve the blunting of Mark's absolute rejection of any connection between foods and cleanliness. Matthew does keep the brief parabolic statement itself (v. 11), since otherwise he would be forced to omit the entire discussion. But he softens it in various ways. For one thing, he twice omits Mark's (incorrect) notion (vv. 2, 5) that unwashed hands are "defiled." Again, Mark's blunt "there is *nothing* outside a man which . . . can defile him" becomes "Not what goes into the mouth defiles a man, but what comes out of the mouth . . ."—which in Matthew can be read as a simple contrast between internal defilement and (an imaginary) defilement by eating *with unwashed hands*, exactly the contrast he intends in v. 20. In v. 17 he omits both the statement that whatever goes into a man *cannot defile him* and Mark's editorial explanation (v. 19b) of the significance of this: "Thus he declared all foods clean." Finally, Matthew's smoothing out of the language and balancing of the various phrases at one point creates a difficulty of its own: by adding the "mouth" in v. 11, he is forced in v. 18 to modify Mark's "what comes out of a man" to "what comes out of the mouth proceeds from the heart"; then, having made the connection between the mouth and the heart, he can continue approximately along Markan lines.[5]

---

4. For parallels, see Rudolf Bultmann, *The Gospel of John: A Commentary* (ET, Oxford: Basil Blackwell, 1971), 574, n. 2.

5. This is necessary, among other things, because few of the vices mentioned have anything to do with the mouth.

It would be a mistake, however, to see these modifications as unimportant literary changes; they amount to a change in substance as well. In Mk. the question of eating with unwashed hands serves only to introduce the controversy-discourse; after v. 5 this question is not mentioned again. Instead it is combined with other traditional usages (v. 4) and biblical passages (vv. 6f., 10) as well as the Corban controversy (vv. 9–13) to move to the larger question of the whole nature of defilement. By v. 23 even the broad question of clean and unclean foods has been settled and passed over. Matthew shares Mark's rejection of the Pharisees, and he also shares his insistence on internal defilement. But what he does not do is allow any of this or even the flat rejection of hand-washing (v. 20) to involve him in a rejection of the distinction between clean and unclean foods. This circumspection can hardly be due to any sensitivities about *Jewish* feelings, especially if, as seems probable, the Pharisees for Matthew in some respects represent all unbelieving Jews. The basis of his judgment must, consequently, be related to his position within the Christian church—and his dealing with the problem must indicate an inner-Christian controversy in the church of his own day. Since he does not, like Mark, simply reject the distinction between clean and unclean, and since he does not, on the other hand, insist on it, either here or elsewhere, the natural conclusion is that he is willing to leave the matter open, finding authority in the practice and teaching of Jesus only for the rejection of obligatory hand-washing.[6]

It is possible that one minor linguistic phenomenon points toward a plausible explanation of this attitude. Matthew's version of this whole incident is somewhat closer than Mark's to the typical *Streitgespräch* (controversy-discourse) pattern in that the bib-

---

6. Davies, *Setting*, 104 sees v. 20 as evidence that Matthew intends to restrict the dispute to oral tradition, in which alone hand-washing was enjoined. It is surely correct that Matthew does not reject the (written) distinction between clean and unclean. But it is less certain that he accepted every written provision of the law as binding on Christians in a simple biblicist fashion. Strecker, *Weg*, 30f. sees in v. 20 only a *reemphasis* on Mk.'s rejection of the cult, but this hardly squares with the persistent Matthean softening of Mk.'s broad generalizations.

lical quotation (Is. 29:13) is at the end, rather than the beginning, of the dispute (vv. 8f.). Since the biblical quotations in these verses in both Matt. and Mk. rest on the LXX,[7] we cannot explain Matthew's language as showing the influence of Palestinian Aramaic.[8] We are left, then, with a mixed Jewish-Christian and Gentile-Christian milieu in which the language of both groups was Greek. Matthew knows, better than Mark, the customs discussed in such controversies, and he is more familiar with the *Streitgespräch* form. But his native tongue is not Semitic, and in the controversies he can reject the Jews without necessarily rejecting certain practices in their Jewish-Christian form. If such be the explanation of the rearranging and modification of the Markan text in its handling of the biblical passages it is unnecessary to go further afield and argue for a Palestinian or even primitive influence on the Matthean account at this point.

Familiarity with the *Streitgespräch* form, rather than primitive tradition, is probably also the explanation of two other minor Matthean differences. A question ("Why...?") is answered with another question ("Why...?"), and the two "transgress" clauses[9] are exactly antithetical; both the counter-question and the use of balanced parallel clauses are well-known devices in this type of controversy (and in the related inner-Christian *Schulgesprächen*). This particular passage, then, becomes one in which any requirement of hand-washing is specifically rejected but the possibility that food laws might be kept (or broken) within the Christian community is left open. This would mean that Jewish practices are rejected but that Christian practices might differ, something that is impossible on the basis of the unequivocal statements in Matthew's Markan source.

The introductions to the citation from Isaiah in both Gospels also show similarities and minor differences. Both evangelists agree that the Pharisees and scribes make void the word (law?)[10]

---

7. Stendahl, *School*, 54–58.
8. Vs. McNeile, *Matt.*, 223.
9. *Parabainō* occurs only here in the NT in this sense.
10. The very interesting reading *ton nomon tou theou* (ℵ* C 084 Φ *pc*; Epiph) is clearly harder than *ton logon tou theou* (B ℵ corr D Θ 700 pc it sa bo; Ir),

of God through their tradition (Mk. 7:12; Matt. 15:6), and both agree that their hypocrisy was prophesied in Is. 29:13. But Mark, who has somewhat awkwardly spoken of the "commandment of God" twice in vv. 8f., contrasts (vv. 10f.) "For Moses said . . ." with "But you say. . . ." Matthew, who has rearranged both the language and the order of this section to avoid just such duplications, has mentioned the commandment of God only once (v. 3), so his contrast reads "For God commanded . . ." (v. 4) and "But you say . . ." (v. 5). It is quite possible that Matthew's substitution of "God" for "Moses" is theologically as well as literarily motivated: What Moses said is God's word, not to be set aside by "your tradition" (v. 3). Note, however, that he does not, like Mark (7:8), set the word of God against *all* human tradition.

The Corban controversy itself is not of direct concern here; both evangelists see in Jewish practice, as they understand it, a violation of the Fifth Commandment and an illustration of the hypocrisy (Mk. 7:6; Matt. 15:7) of Jesus' opponents. The commonly noted difference that Mark explains what Corban means and Matthew does not may simply mean that Matthew's readers were more familiar with Jewish custom and terminology than Mark's,[11] although this does not necessarily make them Jews or Jewish-Christians.

A much more important question is what the evangelists say about Jesus' hearers. In Matt. the emphasis differs greatly from that in Mk.: the Jews as a whole are never mentioned directly; although the Pharisees and scribes are, as in the Markan source, given as the opponents of Jesus (v. 1), it is the Pharisees alone who are offended (v. 12) and who are rejected as competent guides (vv. 13f.), not merely on the key issue of hand-washing (v. 20) but presumably on other matters as well (v. 14); the dis-

---

which is identical with Mk.; but it is much less well-attested and probably (like, *tēn entolēn t. th.* ℛ L W Δ **0106** λ 565 *pm* lat; Or Cyr) secondary.

11. So, e.g., McNeile, *Matt.*, 221; Bonnard, *Matt.*, 225. This familiarity would also explain why Matthew modifies Mk.'s "father or mother" (Mk. 7:12) to "his father" (Matt. 15:6), since on Jewish terms "father" may be used for "parents." The omission of *ē tēn mētera* in 15:6 (B **א** D *pc* a e sy^c sa; Or) was apparently not understood by later scribes.

tinction between the people and their leaders is taken over from Mk. but in a purely formal way (cf. Mk. 7:14, 17 with Matt. 15:10, 15); and the esoteric note implied by Jesus' leaving the people and entering the house (Mk. 7:17) is omitted.

Who is it, then, against whom the Corban controversy is directed—Jews, Pharisees, or some Christian party within the Markan and Matthean churches? If we reserve for the moment the question of Markan intentions, it is evident that Matthew singles out for condemnation a single group, the Pharisees, whom he treats as beyond hope; that he utilizes a comparatively neutral view of the people (v. 10) which he does not really hold (v. 16);[12] and that he goes out of his way to make it clear that Jesus' teaching on this matter is given not only generally to all the disciples but specifically to Peter (v. 15), a reference that must come out of a Christian context, like the other Petrine passages in Matt.,[13] since the Jews cannot have had any interest in what Jesus said to Peter. It is not only plausible but highly probable that we have here dominical instruction to Peter on the kind of question which he is so shortly to be given authority to decide, viz., which commandments are binding and which are not (16:19). The special prominence of Peter eliminates any purely Jewish reference— whether to the Jews of Jesus' day or Matthew's—and shows that here, as so often elsewhere, the argument passes quickly and subtly from the past to the present, and almost certainly reflects Matthew's primary parenetic concern.

This same concern is indicated by a comparison of the vice lists in the two Gospels. Matthew's list is closer to the decalogue and also (in spite of what one commonly reads about his "spiritualizing" of the Law) much more externalized than Mark's. If Jülicher is right that grammatically Mark's "evil thoughts" are the general category of which all the other vices are really examples,[14] the

12. See below, chap. 6, sec. 10, n. 7.
13. Matt. 14:28–31; 15:15; 16:17ff.; 17:24-27; 18:21; etc. It is begging the question to describe these as "natural in a Gospel for Jewish Christians" (McNeile, *Matt.*, 131). And in any case the lists of apostles show that Peter's prominence is pre-Matthean.
14. *Gleichn.*, II, 61.

externalization of sin in Matthew's list is immediately obvious, since he revises the word order to make this vice only the first of a long list (cf. Mk. 7:21f. with Matt. 15:19). But even without this valid grammatical observation, the details establish the same point.[15] Mark uses six plurals, which imply various evil acts, then six singulars, which refer to specific vices. Several of these are omitted by Matthew, whose list (after the "wicked thoughts" which he has taken over from Mk.) consists of the sixth through ninth commandments of the decalogue (in biblical order), followed by "acts of slander," (*blasphēmiai*), which is apparently put at the end to correspond to Matthew's own emphasis on the mouth. The content, the order, and the fact that he uses plurals throughout (acts, not vices) show a dependence on the Jewish parenetic tradition and, at least *vis-à-vis* Mk., an externalizing of sin, although he has retained at least formally Mark's insistence that all of these things come from the heart.

In this brief section, then, Matthew's Jesus clearly rejects the Pharisaic (and scribal) custom of hand-washing, as well as the Pharisees and the people whom they represent. He insists that concrete unethical acts defile a person, since they spring from the heart, but what goes into the mouth does not. All of this—and much more—could be said by the Hellenistic, even the antinomian, tradition in Matthew's own church. But Jesus does not, as in Mk., settle the question of clean and unclean foods unequivocally. On this matter he explains to Peter and to all the disciples, whose understanding is growing but not yet complete, that what comes from the heart is more important than what goes into the mouth. No food law is given, not even a negative one like Mark's. Presumably this is a matter not worth dividing the church over. If guidance is needed, v. 15 suggests, Peter and the disciples (which means, in Matthew's terms, their successors) can provide it. In short, Mark's account is ecclesiasticized.

---

15. For a statistical analysis of the terms and their occurrence in the NT, see Taylor, *Mk.*, 346f.

8. Children and Dogs (15:21–28; cf. Mk. 7:24–30)

The brief parabolic saying, "It is not good to take the children's bread and give it to the [little] dogs" (Mk. 7:27b = Matt. 15:26) is embedded in a larger miracle-story.[1] It is apparent that the section is an apothegm,[2] since the saying and the woman's reply are actually the center of interest, although one can see traces of the miracle-form in the fact that the woman cries out, that her cry is for mercy, that the daughter is "sorely" oppressed by the demon, that the daughter is healed "from that very hour," etc. The basic source is Mk., although Matthew has evidently enlarged the Markan form by adding material of his own and sayings from his tradition,[3] including one or two archaizing touches,[4] and he has rewritten the whole in the service of his own theology. That Luke, with a strong Gentile bias, omits the incident entirely requires no explanation.

The location of the healing is vaguely described in both Gospels. Mk.'s "the regions (*ta oria*) around Tyre"[5] are in Matthew "the regions around Tyre and Sidon" (*ta merē Tyrou kai Sidōnos*), a traditional Gentile area (cf. Matt. 11:21 = Lk. 10:13, Q) on the north-northwest borders of Palestine. More important than the precise geography is the Matthean note that the woman *comes* from there to Jesus (v. 22), which could mean that Matthew is trying to be consistent with 10:5 and thinks of the encounter as taking place on non-Jewish territory.[6] Similarly, he eliminates the "house" of Mk. 7:24 (as well as the note that Jesus went there for

---

1. Josef Schmid, *Das Evangelium nach Markus* (5. durchges. Aufl., Regensburg: Verlag Friedrich Pustet, 1963), 142, notes that form-critically the pericope is a *Streitgespräch*, but with a difference: here *Jesus* is conquered! This shows that neither Mk. nor his tradition understood the pericope primarily as a controversy-discourse.

2. Bultmann, *HST*, 38.

3. See B. H. Streeter, *The Four Gospels* (London: Macmillan & Co., Ltd., 1924, repr., 1956), 260; T. W. Manson, *The Sayings of Jesus* (London: SCM Press, 1949), 200f.; Taylor, *Mk.*, 347.

4. Mk.'s Syrophoenician woman is described in biblical terms as a Canaanite (cf. Gen. 12:6 LXX), and Tyre becomes the biblical "Tyre and Sidon" (cf. Is. 23:1f.; Jer. 25:22; 27:3; 47:4; 1 Macc. 5:15; Jud. 2:28 reads "Sidon and Tyre"), although Sidon is a long way north of Tyre.

5. On the textual problem in Mk., see below, chap. 6, sec. 11, n. 6.

6. Loisy, *ES*, I, 971; McNeile, *Matt.*, 230; S. Légasse, "L'épisode de la Cananéenne d'après Mt. 15, 21–28," *Bulletin de Littérature Ecclésiastique* 73 (1972),

purposes of secrecy), not because he recognizes the theological significance of "house" in Mk., but because keeping it would imply that Jesus entered a Gentile house. His elimination of the note that Jesus was "unable to escape recognition" is probably theologically motivated.[7]

Several important changes also take place in the body of the narrative. The woman's request that Jesus heal her daughter (Mk. 7:26) is greatly elaborated (and stylized) as "have mercy upon me, Lord, Son of David" (v. 22), repeated in briefer form a few verses later (v. 25, following Mk.). This cry, practically identical in form with the twice-repeated cry of the two blind men in 20:30f., includes the characteristically Matthean "Son of David," here combined with *Kyrios*; and we may be sure that Matthew intended both terms to be taken in their full christological significance. It is most improbable that the description is historical, that she merely recognized Jesus as the eschatological Savior[8] or that Jesus recognized humility in her self-effacing terms,[9] still less that she here rejects the thought of Jesus as a mere individual thaumaturge and accepts him as the agent in God's plan for his elect people.[10] Just as Jesus' enemies often speak, willy-nilly, the full Christian truth, so here the woman, "great in faith" (v. 28, Matt. only) is a paradigm of the believer in Matthew's own day, who also acknowledges Jesus' Lordship and his Davidic sonship.

To this remarkable address, however, Jesus remains silent (v. 23a). This equally remarkable response can hardly be squared with what our knowledge of Jesus would lead us to expect. Literarily, however, it springs from the fact that he must instruct the disciples (vv. 23f., peculiar to Matt.) before dealing directly with her problem. The insertion of the disciples into the dialogue at this point is probably motivated in several ways. For one thing,

---

21–40 (24). In v. 29, "Jesus does not come out . . . because he never went in [to the territory]"; ibid. Cf. also Matt. 19:1 with Mk. 10:1.

7. "It may be that he does not wish to say that there were things Jesus could not do" Taylor, *Mk.*, 349.

8. Lohmeyer/Schmauch, *Matt.*, 252f.

9. Bonnard, *Matt.*, 231.

10. Ibid., 232.

the disciples' failure to have her dismissed[11] highlights her persistence, which in turn reflects the heroic nature of her faith.
Matthew also allows Jesus to speak directly and unequivocally to
the *disciples* about his mission (v. 24), so that his correction of
their mistaken views on this important matter would be known to
all in Matthew's time. The saying itself, "I have been sent [rever-
ential passive] only to the lost sheep of the house of Israel" (= "all
Israel") is a traditional saying, much like 10:5f. in content, which
probably arose during the controversy over the Gentile mission
long before Matthew's day.[12] Matthew's familiarity with such sayings in his tradition, coupled with the universal acceptance of the
Gentile mission long before his time, doubtless explains his own
theory[13] that Jesus and his disciples deliberately restricted their
mission to Jews and went to Gentiles ("all nations," 28:19) only
after the resurrection.[14]

This incident, then, is portrayed by Matthew as one of the
exceptional cases which "announce the participation of the pagan
multitudes, by faith, in salvation after Jesus' death and resurrection."[15] It is not unequivocally clear, however, just what the basis
of her acceptance by Jesus is. It is, in some sense, obviously her

11. The suggestion of Lagrange (*Matt.*, 309), the Jerusalem Bible (40f.), Fenton
(*Matt.*, 255), and Légasse ("Cananéenne," 28) that *apolyson* means "send her
away (healed)" or "(give her what she asks and) let her go" is unnatural and
runs counter to both the context and Matt. 19:14; 20:31 (both from Mk.).
12. So Taylor, *Mk.*, 347; Bultmann, *HST*, 163. Vs. Lohmeyer/Schmauch, *Matt.*,
254, where the saying is understood as indicating a *prophetic* calling only, Jesus'
Messianic consciousness is here taken for granted. It is, as its Semitic nature
shows (Légasse, "Cananéenne," 29f.), probably somewhat earlier than most of
the other "I have come . . ." sayings (Bultmann, *HST*, 153, 155, 163), though
not necessarily authentic. The attempt by Joachim Jeremias, *Jesus' Promise to the
Nations* (Naperville, Ill.: Alec R. Allenson, Inc., 1958), 26ff. to establish its
authenticity on the grounds that it could only shock the church, familiar with a
Gentile mission since pre-Pauline days, and that Mark and Luke omit it but Matthew keeps it because it has the authority of Jesus himself behind it assumes
that a) it was known outside the Matthean tradition, and b) Matthew had some
way of distinguishing genuine sayings of Jesus in the Jesus-tradition.
13. Strecker, *Weg*, 109. Lagrange, *Matt.*, 307f. misunderstands this theory as a
simple fidelity to historical fact.
14. If Matthew has any theological reason for omitting Mk. 7:27a ("let the
children first be fed"), it could be for fear that it be understood as basing the
Gentile mission on the completion of a mission to the Jews, rather than on the
command of the Risen Lord. Légasse, "Cananéenne," 34 suggests that it might
have seemed to him to mitigate slightly the full privileges of Israel.
15. Bonnard, *Matt.*, 231.

great faith (v. 28). It can hardly be denied, however, that her faith is not very precisely spelled out. It is reflected in her persistence, her double cry for mercy, and may be remotely Pauline, at least in the sense that she admits to having no claim on Jesus.[16] Yet in what she actually says she merely recognizes the prior rights of Israel, and it would be going beyond the evidence to see this recognition, even for Matthew, as a sign of her *humility*.[17] The best commentary on the text is the healing of the centurion's son (8:5–13, Q), which shows many parallels to our passage, and in which the greatness of the centurion's faith is specifically praised as exceeding that of anyone in Israel (8:10).[18] "As you have believed," Jesus promises, "it shall be done to you" (8:13). Both healings-at-a-distance show that while Gentiles have no direct claim on Jesus during his lifetime, even then access to the Kingdom was not to be denied them if they truly believed. They thus confirm the view that the whole of Matthew's Gospel is written from the standpoint of the Great Commission and teaches that Jesus comes not to those who are merely called as part of the earthly people of God, but to those who are chosen, to men and women of faith. The "Canaanite" woman is granted a great faith— of which the text offers little specific evidence—in order that Matthew may use her as a paradigm of an important Christian virtue. It is particularly important to note that her "faith" is not simply a sturdy optimism in the face of harshly adverse circum-

---

16. This is clear however we translate the difficult phrase *nai; kyrie; kai ktl.*, which is surely the correct reading in both Mk. 7:28 and Matt. 15:27. Probably Matthew has inserted *gar* in v. 27 (assuming that the omission of the word in B e sy^sy,p sa is secondary and that—vs. *R* A L N λ *pm*—it did *not* originally occur in Mk. 7:28), thereby softening the controversial nature of the woman's response ("Yes, indeed, Lord—why, even the dogs . . . ," etc.); so Légasse, "Cananéenne," 37. If this is correct, it squares fully with Matthew's tendency to minimize the woman's wit and stress her *faith*.
17. So Bonnard, *Matt.*, 230ff. The point is rather that Matthew assents to the Gentile mission, "but only on condition that Israel's religious primacy be recognized." (Roy A. Harrisville, "The Woman of Canaan," *Interp* 20 [1966], 274–287 [274]).
18. On internal grounds we may hesitantly accept this as the correct reading rather than *oude en tō Israēl* (א C *R* Θ Φ pl [lat sy^s,p]), which, though rather well-attested, seems to have come into the Matthean text from Luke rather than Q. Theologically, it is most unlikely that Matthew would speak so favorably as Q apparently did of the state of faith in Israel.

stances; it is rather the unwavering assurance that Jesus is fully capable of meeting her needs. Matthew would never have imagined that optimism as such is of any theological significance.

9. The Wicked Husbandmen (21:33–46; cf. Mk. 12:1–12.; Lk. 20:9–18)

The context of this parable in Matt. is clearly taken from Mk., although it is somewhat modified. Told in the Temple (21:23; cf. Mk. 11:27), it is a polemic and largely negative piece of *Heilsgeschichte*, with minor changes from the Markan source which tend to sharpen this negative polemic and, in some ways, to add (not substitute) parenetic concerns as well.

In keeping with Matthew's favorable estimate of scribes, the parable is told in the presence of the chief priests and elders of the people (21:23) or against the chief priests and the *Pharisees* (21:45) (not, as in Mk. 11:27, against the chief priests, scribes, and elders). The people, so far as they appear at all, are good, holding Jesus (21:46), like John (21:26), to be a prophet.[1]

The rather loose Markan context—the questions about authority (11:27–33), the Wicked Husbandmen (12:1–12), and the question about paying taxes to Caesar (12:13–17)—is tightened up,[2] and new material is inserted, as follows:

1. Question about Jesus' authority (21:23–27, Mk.)
2. The Two Sons (21:28–32, M)
3. The Wicked Husbandmen (21:33–46, Mk.)
4. The Marriage Feast (22:1–10, Q)
5. The Wedding Garment (22:11–13, 14, M)
6. Question about taxes (22:15–22, Mk.)

Items 1, 3, and 6 are Markan, but the others are new in this context. Broadly speaking, one can perceive a shift from the exclusive preoccupation with Jesus' opponents in Mk.[3] to a parenetic interest

---

1. His Markan source contains this view with respect to John (11:32), not Jesus (12:12; but cf. 8:28).
2. "Hear *another* parable" (21:33); "and *again* Jesus spoke to them in parables, saying . . ." (22:1); "*then* the Pharisees went . . ." (22:15).
3. The polemic against Judaism which runs from Matt. 21:23 through chap. 23 (so, rightly, Trilling, *WI*[3], 85; Richard J. Dillon, "Towards a Tradition-history

in Matt. as well, a concern that is evident (if at all) only contextually in the Two Sons, but reasonably clear in the details of
the Wicked Husbandmen (see below) and the Marriage Feast,
unquestionable in the Wedding Garment, and highly probable in
the question about taxes. In this series, then, the Wicked Husbandmen is both a heightened form of the anti-Jewish polemic in the
Two Sons (certainly the judgment is more severe) and a part of
Christian parenesis as well.

Several items in the language move in the direction of both allegory and parenesis. The owner of the vineyard is somewhat more
broadly conceived in Matt. than in Mk.: he has become an
oikodespotēs,[4] a prosperous landowner, though not necessarily an
absentee landlord[5] of great wealth. Both Matt. and Mk. reflect
LXX language in the description of the vineyard,[6] the details of
which suggest God's care and love. Matt.'s *kairos tōn karpōn* (pl.!;
cf. *kairos*, Mk./Lk.) implies a certain stress on the harvest as the
decisive time and introduces into the parable an additional emphasis on *fruit*, as in v. 43. That Matt. understands fruit allegorically is made clear in v. 34: the servants are to get "his fruit,"
not (as in Mk./Lk.) "some of the fruit," which is hardly agricul-
turally exact[7] but parenetically important (see below on v. 43).

The allegorical understanding of events has also affected Matt.'s
description of the servants. With most commentators, we may
understand the two groups of servants as representing the prophets, perhaps "former" and "latter" prophets,[8] a distinction which

---

of the Parables of the True Israel [Mt 21:33–22:14]," *Biblica* 47 [1966], 1–42
[6]) is a key part of the author's intention; parenesis is no mere substitute for it.
4. 13:27; 13:52 (of a Christian scribe); 20:1, 11 (M); 24:43 (=Lk. 12:39, Q);
Mk. 14:14 par.; Lk. 13:25 and 14:21 (Lk. only).
5. Vs. Charles Harold Dodd, *The Parables of the Kingdom* (London: James
Nisbet & Co., Ltd., 1935), 124ff., whose interpretation of the parable almost
requires the landowner to be so busy elsewhere that he hardly has time for the
situation in this one vineyard.
6. *phragmon, lēnon* (Matt.; Mk.: *hypolēnion*; LXX: *prolēnion*).
7. Schmid, *Matt.*, 305; Hans-Josef Klauck, "Das Gleichnis vom Mord im Weinberg (Mk 12, 1–12; Mt 21, 33–46; Lk 20, 9–19)," *Bibel und Leben* 11 (1970),
118–145 (122f.).
8. So Bonnard, *Matt.*, 316; M.-J. Lagrange, *Évangile selon Saint Luc* (Paris:
J. Gabalda, 1921; 7e éd., 1948), 307f.; Loisy, *ES*, II, 308; Fenton, *Matt.*, 342;
Schmid, *Matt.*, 305; similarly, Swete, *Mk.*, 251.

finds some support in the correspondence between v. 35 and the traditions regarding the fate of God's spokesmen in different periods.[9] There can be no gradual worsening of the treatment accorded the servants (as in Lk.) because neither history nor his Markan source suggests any such worsening; at most Matthew suggests such a motif by pointing out that the second group was even more numerous than the first (v. 36).

The third messenger from the landowner is the son, not specifically described as "unique" or "beloved" as in Mk., perhaps to soften the tragic error made by the fictional father—surely Matthew had no objection to the use of the term "beloved" for Jesus.[10] But the treatment accorded the son is, as in Mk., unconscionable: after agreeing among themselves, the tenants kill the son and throw him out of the vineyard (Mk.), or—to square the chronology allegorically with the tradition that Jesus died "outside the gate" (Heb. 13:12; cf. Jn. 19:17)—the other way around (Matt. 21:39).

In vv. 40f. important differences between Matt. and Mk. are evident. The rhetorical question, "What will the owner do?" (Mk., Lk.) becomes a genuine question: "When...[11] the owner... comes, what will he do to those tenants?" to which his hearers—presumably still the chief priests and the elders (v. 23)—answer solemnly: "He will put those miserable men to a miserable death."[12] It is hardly correct to say that they thus "unwittingly" condemn themselves,[13] for Matthew feels no compunction about

9. Matt. 23:29–36 (=Lk. 11:47–51, Q); cf. 2 Chron. 24:20ff.; 36:15f.; Mart. Is. 5:1, 11 and *passim*; Acts 7:52; Heb. 11:32–40; see also 1 Kgs. 22:26ff.; Jer. 7:25f.; 25:4; 37:14f.; Zech. 1:4ff.; Matt. 5:12 (=Lk. 6:23, Q); 23:37 (=Lk. 13:34, Q).

10. 3:17; 17:5. That the Matthean form is more primitive at this point, however, is, in the absence of supporting evidence, unlikely. (Vs. Léon-Dufour, *Études*, 322f.). Franz Mussner, "Die bösen Winzer nach Matthäus 21, 33–46," in Willehad Paul Eckert et al., *Antijudaismus*, 129–134 (130) rightly sees the omission as a slight shift in emphasis from the christological to the ecclesiological.

11. The thought that the owner *will come* (Mk., Lk.) is here subordinated completely to the notion that *whenever* he comes, it will be in judgment.

12. *Kakous kakōs apolesai autous*. A long list of parallels to this formal judicial pronouncement—Greek and Roman in provenance but known in Palestine (cf. Jos. *Antiq.* vii. 291)—is given in Lohmeyer/Schmauch, *Matt.*, 313, n. 1.

13. Jülicher, *Gleichn.*, II, 397; Lohmeyer/Schmauch, *Matt.*, 314; Klauck,

putting a Christian judgment on the lips of Jesus' opponents, as
the preceding parable (cf. v. 31a) makes clear.[14] But who is here
condemned, and who are the "other tenants" to whom the vineyard (in v. 43, allegorically, "the kingdom of God"!) will be given?
The question here is whether Matthew thinks of the judgment on
the wicked tenants as past or future or both.

Bornkamm[15] argues that, while for Mark the judgment lies in
the historical past, for Matthew the judgment is thought of as
eschatological and future. It is of course true that Matthew (unlike
Luke) generally thinks of judgment at the end of history not
within it, but this is especially true of *parenetic* sections. If the double reference to Jews and Christians suggested above is correct,
the parable may in the first instance allow for a judgment within
history on Judaism, with a future judgment for all mankind at the
Last Day. Bornkamm, to be sure, believes that the final break with
Judaism has not yet taken place and that consequently Matthew
cannot have seen, as Mark did,[16] the final rejection of the Jews as
implied in the householder's action. But this argument is not persuasive. For one thing, it practically requires that Matthew understood the parable to intend a sharp distinction between the Jewish
people as represented by their leaders,[17] perhaps the Temple leaders,[18] and the Jews as a whole. In general, however, it is hardly
the early Christian belief that the people had only to change their
leaders to become once again God's people,[19] and much in early

"Weinberg," 125. Swete, *Mk.*, 254 more correctly notes that "it is difficult to
suppose that Matt. xxi.41 can have been uttered by the audience." This fixed *topos*
rests on the convictions of the redactor, not the psychology of Jesus' opponents.
14. The parallel between v. 31a and v. 41 does not, unfortunately, settle the textual
question of which of the Two Sons responded first. (On this, see Josef Schmid,
"Das textgeschichtliche Problem der Parabel von den zwei Söhnen," *Vom Wort
des Lebens. Festschrift für M. Meinertz* [Münster: Aschendorff, 1951], 68–84).
But it does at least show clearly that Matthew cannot have created the reading
in D it sy[s]; in context, the son who says "I go" and does not go represents Jesus'
opponents, who reject the will of God.
15. Bornkamm-Barth-Held, *Tradition*, 43.
16. Note that even for Mark the master of the vineyard *will come*, etc., so that
the historical judgment anticipates the eschatological judgment.
17. Cf. Jülicher, *Gleichn.*, II, 398, 405; Erich Klostermann, *Das Markusevangelium*
(5. Aufl., Tübingen: J. C. B. Mohr [Paul Siebeck], 1971), 120.
18. Lohmeyer/Schmauch, *Matt.*, 315.
19. So, rightly, Bonnard, *Matt.*, 317.

Christian tradition specifically rejects this sharp distinction between people and leaders.[20] In addition it is very difficult to square
this view with Matthew's use of "nation" in v. 43, a distinctive and
unequivocal expression,[21] especially since Mk.'s "others" (allois)
would have been a clear way to refer to some but not all of the
people.

More probably, then, Matthew understands the rejection of the
Jews as past and final, the result of their rejection of Jesus.[22]
Bornkamm is quite right, however, in asserting that Matthew, by
inserting the theme of "fruits" into the story where he did not
have it in his source (vv. 41, 43, both as qualifications of the new
tenants), has made parenetic use of an originally anti-Jewish allegory.[23] A strikingly similar process occurs at the end of the (largely
parallel) story of the Great Feast, which immediately follows: an
anti-Jewish piece of Heilsgeschichte (22:1–10)[24] is enlarged to
include a warning of the high ethical standards to be demanded
of Christians at the Judgment (22:11–14, the Wedding Garment).
The "fruits," unexplained in the text, are doubtless "fruits of repentance" (3:8) or "fruits of righteousness" (Jas. 3:18), i.e., good
works,[25] and the broad expression used[26] shows that Matthew in-

---

20. Schmid, Matt., 306, citing such passages as Matt. 23:38 (=Lk. 13:35,
Q); Acts 2:23; 1 Thes. 2:15; etc.
21. Matthew uses the singular elsewhere only at 24:7, "Nation against nation."
But to argue that the transfer of the Kingdom from Jews to Gentiles would therefore require either the plural or laos and that the original reference was deliberately imprecise (so Léon-Dufour, Études, 342) is unpersuasive for Jesus and
impossible for Matthew.
22. Possibly, because of the centrality of the fruit-motif, of their ethical shortcomings as well. (So Trilling, Christusverkündigung, 175, citing 23:23 and 5:20
as additional evidence).
23. I find unconvincing Dillon's attempt ("Trad.-Hist.," 15–22) to deny v. 43 to
the final redactor and to ascribe it to an ethical orientation in his (written!)
special tradition. (Similarly, Léon-Dufour, Études, 341f., who finds Matthew's
catechetical perspective a return to the "sens ecclésial" [!] of the original parable.) The evidence that the verse is Matthew's own work is given fully in
Trilling, WI³, 58–63.
24. Note the Matthean insertion at v. 7, which implies a judgment on the Jews
within history.
25. Jülicher, Gleichn., II, 338; for the theme in Matt., see 7:17ff. Fenton, Matt.,
342 suggests "all that is due to God from man"; Trilling, Christusverkündigung,
174: "das Tun der Liebe."
26. "Fruits in their seasons" (both plurals!) is a reminiscence of Ps.1:3 (LXX),
where both terms are singular.

tends a general principle: in all ages, the Kingdom of God is only for fruit-bearers. The new "nation," then, is not the Gentiles as such (for which the plural would be more fitting), but the new people of God, the Christian Church, insofar as it "bears fruit."

In this context, the use of v. 42 by Matthew does not go much beyond his Markan source. The introductory phrase "Jesus said to them. . . , etc." is not stressed[27] and seems to mark not a new beginning but a return from the thought of v. 41c, Christian fruits, to the judgment expressed in the first part of the verse (v. 41): the rejected Stone in turn rejects his opponents and in a marvelous way gives their vineyard to others. With the warning that Christians must produce fruit (v. 43), the parable ends.[28] It is noteworthy that the emphasis Matthew feels he must add for the proper understanding of the parable is the very one commonly neglected or reinterpreted today.

10. The Fig Tree as the Herald of Summer (24:32f.; cf. Mk. 13:28f.; Lk. 21:29ff.)

In the midst of Jesus' final eschatological discourse[1] comes this small parable, which Matthew has kept completely in its Markan context, almost without changes of wording. Two modifications, however, are of some significance. In v. 33 (=Mk. 13:29), Jesus is now recorded as saying, "When you see all[2] these things you know [or: know, imperative] that he is near, at the very gates." In Mk., as

---

27. "Therefore I tell you . . . ," (v. 43) is, on the contrary, solemn and central. It introduces Matthew's primary concerns; cf. 6:25; 12:31; 18:18.

28. V. 44 is, in spite of its good attestation, a secondary addition from Lk. into the Matthean text, since no plausible reason can be given for its omission in D 33 b it ff¹ ff² r¹ sy⁸; Iren Or Eus. See the discussion, with bibliography, in Trilling, WI³, 57, n. 15 and Klauck, "Weinberg," 129ff.; per contra, Léon-Dufour, Études, 339f.; Strecker, Weg, 110f. Its meaning, if it were original, could only be: Every Christian who fails to bring forth fruit stands in danger of being crushed by the Stone, Jesus the Eschatological Judge.

1. It is possible that Matt. 25:13, which does not really fit the parable of the Ten Virgins (all slept, not merely the foolish), was formulated on the basis of the parenesis in Mk. 13, esp. Mk. 13:35; see Erich Klostermann, Das Matthäusevangelium (4. Aufl., Tübingen: J. C. B. Mohr [Paul Siebeck], 1971), 197.

2. The Matthean "all" is not very appropriate; strictly interpreted it would include the coming of the Son of Man (vv. 30f.) among the premonitory signs of the Parousia; cf. Jacques Dupont, "La parabole du Figuier qui bourgeonne (Marc xiii, 28–29 et par.)," RB 75 (1968), 526–548 (533).

in Matt., this saying comes immediately after the cosmic signs which
attend the coming of the Son of Man and immediately precede the
great final tribulation. But Mk. reads "When you see these things
taking place . . ." which seems to suggest a *process.*[3] Matthew is
probably thinking of a distinct but indefinite future moment; certainly the sense of immediacy and continuity are less.[4]

This emphasis is confirmed by the details of the context. Both
evangelists cite the saying in the context of the ending of the
apocalyptic discourse. But the briefer Markan form has been elaborated[5] in Matt. by the addition of a substantial amount of Q material (24:37–51) plus the three great parables of chapter 25.[6] In
general his treatment has moved from the promise of the Parousia,
so important for Mark, to a much greater stress on preparedness
for judgment. All evangelists are aware of the Christian life as
lived in the hope of the final consummation, but Matthew more
clearly than either Mark or Luke relates the judgment implied in
that consummation to the ethical demands laid upon the profess-
ing church.

11. The Savorless Salt (5:13; cf. Mk. 9:50; Lk. 14:34f.)

It has been convenient thus far to concentrate on those parables
which Matthew has clearly taken over and modified from Mk.,
since here his editorial work is most easily observed and evaluated.
In addition to these parables, however, Matthew has also made
use of parabolic material from Q, much of which does not occur
in Mk. and can only be reconstructed and evaluated by a careful
comparison of Matt. and Lk. The non-Markan material has no
proper place in the present work, which concentrates on the Triple
Tradition, but the Q material which is *also* in Mark may profitably
be discussed briefly.

There are (if we exclude the very fragmentary parallel in Mk.

3. Jülicher, *Gleichn.*, II, 6.
4. Strecker, *Weg*, 240f.
5. And, to some extent, allegorized: ". . . on what day *your Lord* is coming."
6. Matthew adds this material because "having transcribed the eschatological
discourse from Mark almost word for word, he cannot bear to close with so frail
a simile": M. D. Goulder, "Characteristics of the Parables in the Several Gospels,"
JTS n.s. 19 (1968), 51–69 (67).

13:34 to the Parable of the Pounds) five Matthean parables that occur in both Q and Mk.: the Beelzebul parables, the Lamp and the Bushel, the Manifestation of What Is Hidden, the Mustard Seed, and the Savorless Salt. Since the Beelzebul parables and the Mustard Seed in Matthew are a mixture of Markan and Q materials, they have already been discussed. The other three parables, which take their *form* entirely from Q although they also occur in Mk., can only be summarized very briefly here.

The first such parable is the Savorless Salt, which is built on the simple saying, "If salt has lost its savor, with what shall it be salted [or: seasoned]?" The position of the saying following the Beatitudes (5:3–12) is probably, for reasons which cannot be detailed here, due to Matthew rather than Q, and it continues the personalizing of the Beatitudes, evident in the shift from the third-person to the second-person plural at v. 11.[1] The introductory phrase, "You are [not: you ought to be!] the salt of the earth" (v. 13) is surely created, like the equally Matthean expression in v. 14, "You are the light of the world," to emphasize discipleship as a whole, rather than any single quality.

But what specifically does Matthew intend? The parallels show that salt is beneficial, almost essential to, human existence,[2] from which we may deduce, especially within the context of Matthew's theology as a whole, that the parable intends to portray discipleship as involving practical obligations within daily life. Salinity, whatever it is, can be lost—otherwise the parable has no point—and its loss will result in disdain on the part of others. The context, vv. 13–16, and especially Matthew's own v. 16, suggest that the paradoxical "salt without salinity" parable is intended to urge

---

1. Oscar Cullmann, "Das Gleichnis vom Salz. Zur frühesten Kommentierung eines Herrenworts durch die Evangelisten," *Vorträge und Aufsätze. 1925–62* (Tübingen: J. C. B. Mohr [Paul Siebeck], 1966), 192–201 minimizes this change (see p. 196) and points out that the salinity can be *lost*. But Matthew's wording seems to imply "paradox" rather than "loss"; further, any connection with "persecution" (5:12) and a *theologia crucis* (p. 189) in this text seems forced.

2. Pliny, Nat. Hist. xxxi.102 cites the maxim, "Nothing is of greater benefit to the whole body than salt and sun," and asserts that "Without salt a really civilized life is impossible" (ibid., 88); similarly, Sir. 39:26: "Basic to all the needs of man's life are water and fire and iron and salt. . . ." Further parallels are given in Friedrich Hauck, *"halas," TDNT*, I, 228f.

good works, actions which will shine before men and impel them toward the praise of God. Both a pure individualism—each of you individually[3]—and a limitation to the apostles or some other group of disciples[4] are foreign to Matthew's universalistic and missionary emphases. On the contrary, all disciples bear a total witness, not only in the preaching of the gospel but also in commending it concretely by their actions. To break this ineluctable connection between word and deed is to place the church in a fundamentally impossible and even dangerous position[5] and to refuse the world what the church alone offers it.

12. The Lamp and the Bushel (5:15; cf. Mk. 4:21; Lk. 8:16; 11:33)

This short parable is the third of a series of four brief sayings: 14a, 14b, 15, and 16. All have similar points, and all are to be interpreted together with the Salt (v. 13) which immediately precedes, since all stand between the Beatitudes (vv. 3–12) and the general interpretation of the Law (vv. 17–20) and with them provide the introduction to the specifics of the rest of the Sermon on the Mount. The parable of the Lamp and the Bushel is Q material, possibly Aramaic in origin,[1] which in this context can only mean: just as salt is for seasoning (v. 13), so a lamp is for providing light. But the exact significance of the light is elusive. We may eliminate allegorical references to customs like lighting a lamp to symbolize the presence of God or the Law (or, later, the human soul).[2] And we must not too quickly conclude from the use of the concept

3. So, rightly, Bonnard, *Matt.*, 58.
4. For this and other similar references in Methodius and Chrysostom, see Jülicher, *Gleichn.*, II, 74; cf. also Rudolf Schnackenburg, " 'Ihr seid das Salz der Erde, das Licht der Welt,' " *Mélanges Kardinal Eugène Tisserant* (I, Rome: Biblioteca Apostolica Vaticana, 1964), 365–387. (Reprinted in Schnackenburg's *Schriften zum Neuen Testament* [Munich: Kösel-Verlag, 1971], 177–200. Pages are cited from this work.) See esp. pp. 184ff.
5. J. B. Souček, "Salz der Erde und Licht der Welt," *ThZeit* 19 (1963), 169–179 (174f.) points out that the Salt is primarily *negative*, the light primarily *positive* in Matthew's interpretation.
1. Note the impersonal plurals in *kaiousin* and *titheasin*, as well as the paratactic *kai*.
2. Ex. 40:4, 25; 2 Sam. 22:29; Ps. 119:105; Prov. 6:23; 20:27. On this, see Bonnard, *Matt.*, 60.

of the Light of the World in Judaism[3] or in early Christianity[4] that a specific reference to the revelation of God in Christ is intended.[5] Rather here, as in vv. 13, 16, the primary reference is to good works.[6] Any refusal to do them is like lighting a lamp and hiding it under a bushel.

Those who do good works, however—and good works as a generic category, not any specific thing, is intended—will be a Light for men who, seeing the disciples' good works, will glorify God. Directly or indirectly (almost certainly the latter) this text runs counter to the esoteric attitude of the Essenes,[7] who have no intention of being a light to the world but only of maintaining their own purity.

This brief parable in its Matthean form, then, charts a clear course between sectarian withdrawal from the world, on the one hand, and simple conformity to it, on the other. Without service in the world the church becomes a self-serving institution, Christians an irrelevant group of high-minded people—Christians without Christianity, salt without salinity, light that illumines nothing. The world, correspondingly, does without the one thing above all else that the church could bring to it—the life-preserving, light-giving presence of God among his own.

13. The Manifestation of What Is Hidden (10:26; cf. Mk. 4:22, Lk. 8:17; 12:2f.)

This brief and complex parable is in Matt., as in Q, on which he depends, part of a collection of sayings of various provenance. It is commonly agreed that few if any of these sayings arose in the

---

3. Is. 42:6; 49:6; Wisd. 17:20; 18:4. Schniewind, *Matt.*, 51 notes that the concept is used of God, of the Law, of the People of Israel, and of outstanding individual teachers in later Judaism.

4. Jn. 8:12; 9:5; 12:46; cf. Phil. 2:15; 2 Cor. 4:6; Eph. 5:8.

5. So Bonnard, *Matt.*, 60.

6. Note Justin's citation of this passage: "Let your good works shine before men ..." (*Apol.* I.16.)

7. See Herbert Braun's brief remarks in his "Qumran-Billerbeck," *Qumran und das NT* (2 vols., Tübingen: J. C. B. Mohr [Paul Siebeck], 1966), I, 14, with the bibliog. cited there, and, on esoterism in Qumran and the NT, his *Spätjüdisch-häretischer und frühchristlicher Radikalismus* (2 vols., Tübingen: J. C. B. Mohr [Paul Siebeck], 1957), II, 18–23.

context of a mission charge; they are more probably eschatological[1] words of consolation, either created or expanded in a situation of persecution in the apostolic age and applied particularly to the twelve, here thought of as the first and model preachers. To them, and to all who suffer, comes a warning (v. 28) and a promise (v. 31).

To this general theme of bearing witness under persecution Matthew has added a reference to the twelve (cf. 10:5; 11:1) and modified a *promise* of proclamation to an *imperative* of proclamation—both fully consistent with his programmatic conclusion to the whole Gospel (28:16–20). But he has also, apparently, introduced into the text the theme of semi-esoteric teaching, private communications by Jesus to the twelve which they are (not to pass on secretly but) to proclaim publicly. Since he does not understand Christianity as an esoteric sect, and since he removes, as we have seen,[2] various Markan tendencies that might point in that direction, how are we to account for his language in this verse?

One possibility is that he knew of growing esoteric tendencies in the church, perhaps not unlike those we can see in second-century Gnosticism, and opposed them by showing that Jesus himself insisted on the public proclamation of even his most private utterances. The most serious difficulty with this view, however, is that no satisfactory case has ever been made for any contact between Matthew's church and early Gnosticism. The second possibility is that Matthew did not mean to stress "in the dark" and "whispered," which came in some form from Q, and has reworded the saying this way to harmonize its language with the christological form he has given to the whole section, from the express parallel between master and disciples in vv. 24f. to the substitu-

---

1. Ernst Käsemann, "Die Anfänge christlicher Theologie," *ZThK* 57 (1960), 162–185 (176f.) (=*NT Questions of Today*, 82–107 [98f.]) has noted that Matthew, unlike Mark and Luke, often preserves the eschatological context created by apocalyptic prophets for gnomic sayings; see, e.g., 7:2; 23:12; and esp. 25:29. See further below, chap. 4, sec. 11.
2. Above, chap. 1.

tion of "I" for "the Son of Man" in v. 32. The emphasis now is solely on the element of public witness, attestation of everything, without exception or limitation, that the church has learned from its Lord (cf. 28:18ff). He needs no esoteric tradition for the support of his faith.

PART
TWO

THE
LUKAN
REDACTION

Chapter Three

LUKE'S INTERPRETATION
OF THE MARKAN THEORY
OF THE PARABLES
(8:9f.; cf. Mk. 4:10ff.; Matt. 13:10–17)

Luke, like Matthew, uses the materials in Mk. 4:10ff. without fully accepting the "hardening theory" in the specific form in which Mark teaches it, although his statement is so brief that it can hardly be understood except by reading Mk.

In this section, as commonly in Lk., the language is greatly abbreviated and smoothed out. Mark's awkward description of Jesus' questioners, "Those who were around him with the twelve," becomes "his disciples," a natural modification for Luke, who often has Jesus speak to the disciples, but only rarely *alone*.[1] Ordinarily the situation implied is much like that in 20:45, "and while all the people were listening he said to the disciples . . . ," which greatly minimizes the contrast between the disciples and the crowd. The crowd seems to be considered "potential disciples,"[2] not (as in Matt.) a paradigm of non-understanding or (as in Mk.) the object of divine reprobation.

The ambiguity in the Markan text about the exact nature of the question asked Jesus is also removed in Lk.: the disciples ask "what this parable might mean." This modification, unlike the one in Matt. 13:10, has at least the virtue of being answered (in vv. 11–15). Between the question and its answer, however, is v. 10,

---

1. In 9:18 Luke is dependent on Mk.; in 10:23 no emphasis is placed on the fact that they are alone. It is thus by no means insignificant that Luke omits from Mk. 4:10 the phrase, "and when they were alone"; vs. Tim Schramm, *Der Markus-Stoff bei Lukas* (Cambridge: Cambridge University Press, 1971), 114.
2. 3:7 with 7:29f.; 7:29 with 18:43; 13:17; 20:19; 21:38; 23:27, 35.

which is not really relevant at this point and has obviously been included because of its position in Luke's Markan source.

Although Mk. 4:11 has been taken over (Lk. 8:10), it has not remained unchanged. It has been connected very closely to the question about the meaning of the single parable (vv. 9, 11) and is thus of restricted application as a general statement about Jesus' ministry (or the Kingdom of God) as a whole.[3] The express Markan contrast between the disciples and "those outside" has been greatly weakened by the use of the rather neutral term "the rest," a common Lukan expression[4] which does not imply the "rest" of the Jews, unbelieving Jews,[5] but simply "others." And what has been given to the disciples is, as in Matt., not the mystery of the Kingdom, but a knowledge of the mysteries of the Kingdom.[6] Finally, Mark's "everything is in parables" has become simpler and less precise: "But for others they are in parables" (8:10—the only occurrence in Luke of *parabolē* in the plural). The force of these changes is to blunt the distinction between those who believe and those who do not.

To put it differently: Luke apparently grants that outsiders find the Christian message something of a riddle, but not that *all things* are obscure. Certainly a parable as such is not enigmatic.[7] The last part of the Markan statement (v. 12) is abbreviated so drastically that its Lukan interpretation is extremely elusive.[8] He retains the Markan *hina* (plus the subjunctive), which taken in isolation

---

3. Friedrich Hauck, *Das Evangelium des Lukas (Synoptiker II)* (Leipzig: A. Deichertsche Verlagsbuchhandlung, 1934), 108.

4. 18:9, 11; 24:10; Acts 5:13; 17:9; 27:44; 28:9; cf. Lk. 11:2 *v.l.*; 24:9.

5. Gnilka, *Verstockung*, 123f. thinks this is the meaning in Acts 5:13; it could also mean simply "unbelievers," however.

6. The use of the plural seems to require a broad (but non-esoteric) interpretation of what is given. The "nature of the Kingdom of God" (Hauck, *Lk.*, 108; Hans Conzelmann, *The Theology of St. Luke* [London: Faber & Faber, 1960], 103f.; William C. Robinson, Jr., "On Preaching the Word of God," *Studies in Luke–Acts*, ed. Leander E. Keck and J. Louis Martyn [Nashville: Abingdon Press, 1966], 135) is perhaps too specific, unless we understand "nature" in an ethical as well as theological sense.

7. Gnilka, *Verstockung*, 127.

8. Luke's tendency to shorten the biblical quotations in his sources may also be observed in his use of Is. 5:1f. (20:9) and Ps. 118[117]:22 in 20:17; cf. Mk. 12:1, 10 par.

could mean that he also retains the hardening theory. Since he omits the phrase, "lest they should turn again . . . ," however, it is better to look for an explanation that will not bind him to that theory, for which there is so little support elsewhere in the Lukan writings. One way of doing this is to suggest that Luke uses *hina* only to introduce the scriptural quotation, i.e., as the equivalent of *hina plērōthē*, "that the Scripture might be fulfilled." While this is probably not the meaning in Mk., since it does not fit Mark's theology, there is no particular objection to this interpretation in the theology of Luke.

In short, while it is too much to say that Luke explicitly rejects the Markan theory in toto—since he could easily have omitted Mk. 4:11f.—he nevertheless renders it innocuous in various ways. Perhaps he is enabled to keep it because of his broadly "predestinationist" views, so that he intends to say only that faith understands more than unfaith. But he makes no sharp distinction between the believing disciples and the unbelieving crowds, and he either does not fully understand or does not share (or both) Mark's view that the *purpose* of Jesus' person and ministry is to harden men's hearts. Later, when he cites the Isaiah passage in full (Acts 28:26f.), he does so primarily to illustrate Israel's blindness and to justify the Gentile mission: what was potential during the ministry of Jesus has become actual in the preaching of the church. Yet even Israel's blindness is not total: some believe, and some do not (Acts 28:24). Luke has individualized and ethicized Mark's theory, but of the theory itself only a mere husk remains.

Chapter Four

THE MARKAN PARABLES IN LUKE

1. The Physician (5:31f.; cf. Mk. 2:15ff.; Matt. 9:12f.)

In this brief parable, which clearly rests on Mk. in both its wording and its context, Luke has made several small but significant changes. He has tried, for example, to smooth out Mark's awkward phrase, "the scribes of the Pharisees" (2:16) in the reading, "the Pharisees and their scribes" (5:30).[1] Quite possibly his understanding of the actual relationships between scribes and Pharisees was, like Mark's, inexact.[2] More importantly, however, his reading of the phrase, compared with Matthew's substitution of "Pharisees," reveals significant differences from Matthew in the Lukan understanding of Jewish groups. In Matt., as we have seen, "scribe" is a neutral term. In Lk., however, about the most one can say for a scribe is that he may be better than a Sadducee and may even be right on some issues.[3] And in the rest of the Christian tradition the scribe may be associated with the Pharisees in theological disputes or with the chief priests and elders in political matters, in which case he is a negative figure.[4] It should perhaps be pointed out that even the Pharisees are somewhat less reprehensible in Lk. than elsewhere in the Christian tradition;[5] it is they who

1. The Lukan variants *hoi grammateis autōn kai hoi Pharisaioi* (℞ A Θ *al*) and *hoi Pharisaioi kai hoi grammateis* (ℵ D *al* it sa^{pt} bo^{pt}) attest both the problem and the scribal dissatisfaction with Luke's handling of it.

2. Lagrange, *Luc,* 169 suggests that the wording is designed to retain the nuances of Mark's language without implying that other groups also had scribes of their own. But this is just what Luke's wording *does* imply.

3. Cf. Lk. 20:39 with Mk. 12:28–34. Even here, however, the scribe is a stock figure, introduced because the context requires someone familiar with legal disputes.

4. Note esp. 22:2.

5. Similarly, Israel as a whole; cf. Gnilka, *Verstockung*, 126.

warn Jesus that Herod wants to kill him (13:31f.), and in general they disappear in the passion story.[6]

The charge against Jesus is also slightly modified. For one thing, the Markan note that Jesus *eats* with tax collectors and sinners becomes in Luke the complaint that Jesus' disciples *eat and drink* with them (cf. v. 33). But why the change from *Jesus* to *the disciples*?

Luke knows that this complaint was lodged against Jesus (15:2), and even here it is Jesus, not the disciples, who answers the charge against the disciples' conduct.[7] Many explanations are possible, but the simplest one is purely literary: Having reworded the context of the question to read ". . . murmured *against* his disciples" (cf. Mk. 2:16), Luke is required to include them as well as Jesus in the implied condemnation. One could hardly complain against the disciples for what Jesus alone does! Incidentally, it is impossible to decide on the basis of the Lukan wording whether "you" (v. 30) means the disciples alone[8] or Jesus and the disciples.[9] Two minor literary changes are without significance: Mk.'s *ischyō* becomes *hygiainō*, and *ēlthon* becomes *elēlytha*.[10] But it is the saying itself which is modified in the most important respect: Mark's "I have come . . . to call sinners" becomes "I have come . . . to call sinners *to repentance.*" This purely conventional linguistic change shifts the emphasis with respect to the *sense* in which Jesus "called" or "invited" sinners. The invitation is not, of course, to this or any other specific meal; it is his general invitation, that is, the object of his ministry. But by the rewording the contrast between sinners and righteous men[11] has almost become

---

6. Cf., e.g., Lk. 20:20 with Mk. 12:13; see Conzelmann, *Theology of St. Luke*, 78.

7. Jesus' answer presupposes the Markan, not the Lukan, form of the question.

8. Hauck, *Lk.*, 75: Jacques Dupont, "Vin vieux, vin nouveau (Luc v, 39)," *CBQ* 25 (1963), 286–304 (300).

9. But the natural sense of "them" in the phrase "with them" (v. 29) is that the publicans and others were with Jesus, Levi, *and the disciples* (Lagrange, *Luc*, 169); *autōn* (most witnesses) is to be preferred to *authou* (B* λ *pc*), on the grounds of inherent difficulty as well as attestation.

10. So also 7:33f. (from Q)? Possibly the perfect tense accents *permanence* more than Mark's aorist (Lagrange, *Luc*, 169).

11. The following patristic interpretations of the phrase are clearly to be re-

lost in the expression of Jesus' concern that sinners must repent. In insisting that Jesus' call was primarily a call to repentance, which Luke understands ethically (see below) as the condition of forgiveness, Luke "no longer sees its Messianic significance."[12] Jesus is now thought of not primarily as the one who invites even the outcast to the Messianic banquet but as the one who demands that sinners repent. This change is, naturally, conformable to Luke's special understanding of repentance and sin.[13] Repentance is no longer a general term for the movement of a whole people back to God. It is now a specific term for a once-for-all individual conversion, which must be supplemented by good works (Acts 26:20). Similarly, sin is for Luke primarily an ethical, not an anthropological or cosmic, phenomenon. Hence it is Luke who can suggest (15:7) that some men do not need repentance and forgiveness. In the context of a libertine challenge, this ethical definition of repentance need not represent a fundamental perversion of Jesus' essential message. But the perennial danger of the Christian church is that it will understand "the righteous" as a definition of itself and "sinners" as a good description of others.

2. The Sons of the Bridechamber (5:33ff.; cf. Mk. 2:18ff.; Matt. 9:14f.)

The changes in the Lukan version of this parable are so slight as to be almost insignificant, although in some ways he has rendered the concrete historical setting even more obscure than it is in the Markan version.

In v. 33, for example, Luke defines Jesus' questioners simply as "they." Since he had made vv. 29–39 into a single extended inci-

---

jected: a) it is ironic (Chrystostom, Jerome, Theophylact); b) it speaks of angels (Jobios, Macarius Magnes); c) it refers to those justified by the grace of Christ (Maldonatus); see Jülicher, *Gleichn.*, II, 175; Swete, *Mk.*, 40; Klostermann, *Lk.*,4, 27.

12. Conzelmann, *Theology . . . Luke*, 155, n. 1; 227, n. 2.

13. On this, see Conzelmann, *Theology . . . Luke*, 227–230; Jacques Dupont, "Repentir et conversion d'après les Actes des Apôtres," *Sciences ecclésiastiques* 12 (1960), 137–173; Ulrich Wilckens, *Die Missionsreden der Apostelgeschichte* (Neukirchen: Neukirchner Verlag, 1961), 178–186; R. Michiels, "La conception lucanienne de la conversion," *ETL* 41 (1965), 42–78.

dent[1] (unlike Mark, who introduces a break at 2:18), this should
be "the Pharisees and their scribes" (cf. Lk. 5:30), however awkward this may seem.[2] In his Markan source, however, the questioners are simply an undefined group: ". . . some people came and
said. . . ." Thus Luke renders explicit the hostility of the question,
which in Mk. is at most implied. He also revises the question into
a mere statement,[3] as he does elsewhere (cf. 4:36; 5:21. 33; 8:21,
24, 49, 52; 19:46; 20:37; 22:71).

Mk.'s simple contrast (v. 18) between "fasting" and "non-
fasting" has become much more involved in Lk. (5:33). It is now
a contrast between those who "fast often and offer prayers," on the
one hand, and those who "eat and drink," on the other. Both elaborations make the charge sharper, the contrast greater. Fasting
"often" shows that a general practice, not a specific fast, is at issue,
and for Luke it may carry overtones of hypocrisy as well. The
addition of "and offer prayers" suggests formal practice, perhaps
set forms and occasions, which points in the same direction. It is
not, however, germane to what follows, where fasting alone is
mentioned.[4] Similarly, "eat and drink" in 7:34 is anti-ascetic, but
this motif is absent in this passage; the wording increases the
rhetorical force without actually changing the argument.

Mk.'s statement that the wedding guests *cannot* fast (2:19) is
modified by Luke to a question, "Can you make the wedding
guests fast . . . ?" Neither form will bear strict logical examination.

1. Not only by repeating the phrase "eat and drink" (vv. 30, 33; Lk. only), but
also by recasting the connectives. A similar pattern may be observed in 4:15–30;
5:1–11. Its effect here, as commonly in Lk. (7:36–50, 11:37–52; 14:1–24;
19:1–10; 22:14–38), is to make the whole matter a discussion at the *table.*
2. Note that by making all of vv. 29–39 refer to a single incident, Luke has included the Pharisees in the banquet, although they are scandalized at *Jesus'*
presence there!
3. On Luke's treatment of questions in his sources, see Henry J. Cadbury, *The
Style and Literary Method of Luke* (Cambridge: Harvard University Press, 1920),
81f.
4. It is by no means necessary, however, to think of Luke as preserving the more
primitive form of some non-Markan (Jewish? Jewish-Christian?) source at this
point (vs. Julius Wellhausen, *Das Evangelium Lucae übersetzt und erklärt* [Berlin:
Georg Reimer, 1904], 18f.; Schramm. *Markus-Stoff,* 106f.; Burton Scott Easton,
The Gospel According to St. Luke [Edinburgh: T. & T. Clark, 1926], 72), since
the addition prepares the way for the discussion beginning at 11:1. The scribes
responsible for the variant *ouden toutōn poiousin* (D e) doubtless noticed the
absence of prayer in the subsequent discussion.

Nevertheless, in both the sense is fairly clear: "In this situation it would be absurd to try . . . , etc."

The Lukan rewording in v. 35 is interesting primarily as an example of a comparatively rare phenomenon: He has made Mark's balanced and clear Greek more awkward, not less; the language represents a slight shift in emphasis away from the removal of the Bridegroom toward the reintroduction of fasting.[5] None of this, however, significantly changes the meaning of the parable (which in Lk., as in Mk., is really an allegory). That Luke includes the section, which he could easily have omitted, shows that he has no objection to the practice of Christian fasting in his own day, even though it cannot appeal to Jesus' own custom for support. Quite possibly fasting was so firmly established that he never thought to challenge it. More probably, however, he had, like Moffatt's Paul (Phil. 1:10) "a sense of what is vital." The virtue, unfortunately, has never been universal among his followers.

3. The Patched Garment and the Old Wineskins (5:36–39; cf. Mk. 2:21f.; Matt. 9:16f.)

These two parables are paired, as in Mk., and their interpretations are necessarily so close that they may rightly be considered simply variant expressions of the same point. Yet it is not easy in the case of any one of the Gospels to ascertain precisely what that point is. An examination of the details in Luke will make this clear.

Luke has created his own introduction to the parable of the Patched Garment with the words, "And he also spoke a parable to them. . . ." This formula is common in Lk.;[1] it is often used to introduce a parabolic illustration into a non-parabolic discourse or narrative, although in this case he probably means not that the allegory of the Sons of the Bridechamber was not a parable[2] but simply that the argument is being modified at this point. In any

---

5. On the awkwardness of the Greek, see John Martin Creed, *The Gospel According to St. Luke* (London: Macmillan & Co., 1930), 82; Jülicher, *Gleichn*, II, 183. The translations of Lagrange (*Luc*, 171) and NEB preserve the anacolouthon; RSV, Moffatt, Weymouth, and Goodspeed obscure it.

1. 6:39; 21:39; see also 12:16, 41; 13:6; 14:7; 15:3; 18:1, 9; 20:9, 19.

2. So Jülicher, *Gleichn.*, II, 189.

case, the two parables that follow are reckoned by Luke either a single parable (hence the singular) or two parables on a single theme.

In the first parable Luke has considerably (and not very felicitously) changed the image. In Mk., the foolish practice rejected is the sewing of a piece of unshrunk cloth, perhaps acquired by accident, to an old garment. In Lk., however, the situation is different. Here the new garment is deliberately destroyed in order to provide a patch, and later—presumably at the first washing—shrinkage occurs which tears the (worthless!) patch.[3] Anyway, he adds, almost as an afterthought, the patch will not fit the old cloth —but if this were true, no one would ever patch anything.[4] Like Mark, he is concerned to show the incompatibility of the new with the old. But this strikingly awkward modification of the parable shows that he is also concerned to emphasize the value of the *old*, as in the parable of the Old Wineskins, which follows immediately, and in the puzzling expression of v. 39.[5]

Only one modification of the Markan parable[6] has any significance, the addition of v. 39. While Luke even takes over, in reworked form, the Markan ending of the parable, which speaks of new wine and fresh skins without any mention of the old, he has added v. 39, based perhaps originally on a secular saying.[7] This

3. Logically only the tearing of the new *patch* can be intended. The language permits the view, however, that Luke is thinking of the senseless destruction of "what is new" = "the new garment."

4. It is reasonable to conclude that whatever Luke's vocation was, he was not a tailor. On Thomas' equally unsuccessful—and clearly secondary—version of the saying, see below, chap. 6, sec. 3, n. 3.

5. Schmid, *Lk.*, 105 sees in the Wineskins an emphasis on the new and a complete inconsistency with v. 39; so also Hauck, *Lk.*, 77; Jeremias, *Parables*, 104. Easton, *Lk.*, 71 interprets the saying to imply that a partial reformation is worse than none and that disciples of the Baptist would be harmed rather than helped by adopting the non-ascetic features of Jesus' teaching. He seems not to have noticed the importance of v. 39 for Luke's intention.

6. In v. 38 the rare Lukan form blēteon (which means "*must* be put" and accentuates the folly of the situation) is a random agreement with Matthew (*ballousin*) against Mark (who has no verb). The coincidence, in view of the fact that the Markan source has already used both *epiblēma* and *ballei*, is hardly remarkable. (Vs. Lagrange, *Luc*, 172, who presupposes literary dependence.)

7. Cf. Bultmann, *HST*, 19, 81; Dupont, "Vin vieux . . . ," 286; Schmid, *Lk.*, 105; Creed, *Luke*, 83. Cf. Berach. 51ª, "Is not old wine better?" and the other parallels cited in Wettstein, 689f.

verse may be interpreted in three quite different ways.[8] From one view, he is saying only what the two preceding parables have said figuratively: the old and the new are incompatible. This has the advantage of coinciding with the natural meaning of the preceding parables. But it is not what the Greek really says, since in *both* of its variant forms[9] the statement implies that the old wine is preferable to the new.

A second way of interpreting the verse is to insist that it must teach, like the two parables, "the inability of old tradition to contain new life."[10] With this view, the interpretation of v. 39 is given by the parables, and it means approximately the opposite of what it says: the *new* is better than the *old*. In favor of this view one could argue that its polemic point would be the inability of Jesus' opponents, hindered by adherence to the past—which is, in itself, good—to understand the new age; it would also be of parenetic value in urging Christians to break with mere tradition.[11] Furthermore, one might note that Luke's theology would not allow him to pass along a statement urging the superiority of the old.[12] Again, however, it is hard to see how the Greek can be made to say this.[13] Either of these two views presupposes that Luke used a (secular?)

8. The elaborate analysis of Dupont, "Vin vieux . . ." includes even more subtypes.

9. *Chrēstos* is clearly the more primitive and better attested reading.

10. Creed, *Luke*, 83; Lagrange, *Luc*, 173; Henry Troadec, *Évangile selon Saint Luc* (Paris: Mame, 1968), 93.

11. Dupont, "Vin vieux . . .," gives examples from the history of interpretation of both of these forms of this second view; he notes—rightly, without regret, p. 290—that the "break with mere tradition" interpretation has died out.

12. Schmid, *Lk.*, 105; but see below, chap. 4, sec. 3, n. 14.

13. Dupont, "Vin vieux . . .,'" 298f. attempts to deny the obvious force of v. 39 by breaking it into two parts: "No one prefers new wine to old" (an observable fact which confirms the incompatibility of the old and the new, v. 39a) ". . .because he says, 'The old wine is good' " (his justification for his conduct, but irrelevant for *evaluating* anything "old" in our context, v. 39b). In the absence of any context, the superiority of old wine to new is self-evident and rests on proverbial wisdom. Applications, however, are multiform. Note, e.g., Rabbi Jose b. Judah (*Pirke Aboth* 4:26): "He who learns from the young . . . is . . . like one who . . . drinks wine from his wine-press. He that learns from the old . . . is like one that . . . drinks old wine!" F. Hahn, "Die Bildworte vom neuen Flicken und vom jungen Wein! (Mk. 2.21f. parr)," *EvTheol* 31 (1971), 357–375 understands the original parable to teach the danger of the new to the old and believes that the Lukan modifications point instead to the danger to the new. This view requires him to understand v. 39a as a warning against giving up the new for the sake of the old, which is milder and more pleasant (p. 374). And this in turn really reduces v. 39 to a melancholy observation about human frailty.

saying from another context without noticing its inappropriateness, perhaps because of a catchword connection.

The third possibility is that Luke in some sense urges the incompatibility between the old and the new and at the same time insists on the superiority of the *old*. This must have been what Marcion and others[14] understood Luke to mean. On anti-Jewish grounds they omitted the whole phrase. So long as one interprets the saying as exonerating some group in the original dispute (John's disciples? Jesus' disciples? Unbelieving Jews?) this interpretation must be mistaken; it is hard to imagine any "older" group that Luke might consider superior to a "newer" group. But if the possibility be granted that Luke has now passed rather suddenly from historical concerns to the issues of his own day, it is quite easy to find a situation in which he might, after pointing up the lesson in his source, go on to urge the superiority of the old.[15] This would not be an unusual view, in either the Lukan world[16] or the Lukan theology.[17] He is not averse to insisting that some early Christians kept the Law (Acts 21:24; 26:5), and he never hints that Judaism is *bad*. On the contrary, Christianity is for Luke the fulfillment of Judaism. On this basis, the verse could well be primarily a judgment on some kind of Christian innovators, possibly ascetic in character,[18] who understood the incompatibility of the old and the new in so radical a way as to abolish, or threaten to abolish, the old altogether. Support for this interpretation, naturally, could come only from the context of Luke's theology as a

14. The verse is omitted by D it Marc Iren Eus. But its presence in Thomas (Saying 47) confirms its originality, which on textual grounds is clear in any case. The saying in Thomas comes *before* the parable proper, evidence (whatever else it may mean) that Thomas probably knew our Lk.

15. A. T. Cadoux, *The Parables of Jesus* (London: James Clarke & Co., Ltd., 1931), 128f. thinks of the old wine as the OT, the new as either oral tradition or apocalyptic books, an interpretation which hardly fits either Jesus' teaching or Luke's.

16. Cf. Mk. 1:27; Tacitus, *Dialogus* 18 (Loeb, p. 62); Justin, *Apol.* I.44, 59f.; *Dial Tryph.* 7; and, probably, Ign. *Phil.* 8:2. (I am grateful to Prof. Margaret Schatkin of Boston College for bringing the references in Tacitus and Ignatius to my attention.)

17. Acts 17:19ff.; hence Luke's stress on *tēn asphaleian* of the Christian teaching (Lk. 1:4).

18. Cf. I Tim. 4:1–3; 5:23, where anti-asceticism and the (mis)conception of heresy as *innovation* are combined.

whole, although it has at least the obvious meaning of v. 39 in its favor.

The key question here is what Luke really intends by v. 39. If he has used a secular saying which does not really fit the context,[19] the first alternative is more probable. It is much more likely, however, that he means v. 39 in its evident sense, in which case something like the third alternative must be his meaning. In spite of much contemporary rhetoric to the contrary, there are occasions when this flat rejection of innovation is the sole Christian response. The parable itself (without v. 39) teaches, however, that such occasions are far less numerous than religious people generally suppose.

4. The Beelzebul Parables (11:14–26; cf. Mk. 3:22–27; Matt. 12:22–30, 43ff.)

The analysis of this patently composite section is complicated by the fact that Luke has apparently tried to weave materials from both Mk. and Q into one continuous discourse, perhaps extending as far as v. 36. Yet on the whole his sources are reasonably clear and his modifications comprehensible.

Luke, following Q (but unlike Mark), introduces the whole Beelzebul controversy by a specific healing (11:14). The crowd responds in three ways: 1) some marvel (v. 14, probably Q), 2) some accuse him of casting out demons by Beelzebul (v. 15, probably both Mk. and Q), while 3) some test him by demanding a sign.[1] Certain awkwardnesses in the account are evident: he has not observed that (in Q) it is the *demon* who is dumb, but after the healing it is the *man* who speaks.[2] More importantly, however, he has used the saying about seeking a sign (which he cites later, v. 29) in its proper Q position to create this third group among his hearers. This has the effect of providing a structure to

---

19. Wellhausen, *Lk.*, 19.
1. The additional charge that he has a demon (Mk. 3:22) is omitted.
2. Lagrange, *Luc*, 329. This is not, however, completely foreign to the ancient mode of thought; cf. Plutarch, *De def. orac.* 438b (Loeb, *Moralia*, V, 499).

the section: vv. 17–26 oppose the second group, while vv. 29–32 oppose the third. But he uses the Q phrase, "knowing their thoughts," to introduce his reply to the second group, as if the third had not spoken; when he returns to their demand (v. 29) he provides a new introduction (v. 29a). Literarily, then, the smoothness of the reconstructed scene is somewhat artificial.

Two brief theological notes might be added. The conception of the people as divided into different groups represents the people as potential disciples in varying stages of unbelief. It is also probable that the purpose of putting the demand for a sign at this place (v. 16) instead of later, at its Q position in v. 29 (cf. Matt. 12:38), is "to shew that Christ's healings of the possessed have the force of a sign to those who can read them aright" (v. 20).[3]

In the first section of the reply (vv. 17–23), Luke is completely dependent upon Q. Vv. 17f. elaborate in different ways the brief thought that a divided kingdom is laid waste. Luke's "and house falls upon house" implies that "house" means "building" and probably suggests the desolation of cities.[4] V. 18 then applies the same principle to Satan, arguing that his kingdom would be similarly endangered by disunity. The latter part of the verse (18b) is created by Luke on the analogy of Mk. 3:30, which he omits, and makes the transitions smoother.

The next two verses (19f.) are, as commonly noted, incompatible, in both Q and Lk. The former shows the absurdity of the charge by pointing to Jewish exorcisms.[5] V. 19b, "they *shall* be your judges," most naturally has an eschatological reference in Greek, as in vv. 31f.; in view of Luke's relative disinterest in the Last Judgment, however, it is also possible that he sees such judgment as taking place in that (rhetorical?) moment when the question of the motives behind his accusers' double standard is seriously posed and impartially resolved: Jewish exorcists become

---

3. Creed, *Luke*, 159f.; cf. also Jülicher, *Gleichn.*, II, 216; Loisy, *ES*, I, 701.
4. So Jülicher, *Gleichn.*, II, 222; Creed, *Luke*, 106, supplies *diameristheis* and understands the phrase as "a house divided against itself falls."
5. "Your sons" has no clear reference in Lk. and is best taken as referring to Jews in general. Easton, *Luke*, 181 suggests "men like you."

witnesses for the defense.[6] The next verse (20) argues rather that
exorcisms by Jesus are unique, a sign of the presence of the Kingdom—in the very works which his opponents see as proof of collusion with Beelzebul.

The parable of the Strong Man (vv. 21f.) forms part of the
same controversy in all three Synoptic Gospels. But the Matthean
form of the parable is so completely assimilated to the Markan
language that the Q form, if any, is unrecoverable. And we may
suspect (but hardly prove) that an early form of the parable has
been elaborated, by either Q or Luke.[7] The "house" of Matt./Mk.
is now a "palace,"[8] and the "anyone" (i.e., the houseowner)
is now described as "one stronger than he," i.e., as an armed lord
(v. 22). Further, the Lukan (Q?) form seems to be elaborated
on the basis of Isaiah 49:24b, 53:12 (LXX),[9] and these elaborations seem to represent a small step in an allegorical direction.[10]
That Luke understands the Stronger One who falls upon Satan
and completely conquers him as Jesus is quite clear,[11] although
the stages of his defeat (binding, disarming, plundering,[12] etc.)
seem to have no explicit chronological or christological reference.[13]

With the parable of the Strong Man (vv. 21f.) Jesus' answer to
the charge of collusion with Satan is complete. Yet this historical
setting, which for Mark is the focus of attention, has receded for
Luke (as it had already begun to do in Q); the addition of v. 23

6. Lagrange, Luc, 331.
7. Loisy, ES, I, 707 thinks of an early parable about a Strong Man and a Stronger
One (originally: God or Jesus) who binds him. The contrast is weakened in
transmission when the parable becomes an allegory.
8. As Jülicher notes (Gleichn., II, 227), the owner does not guard a palace.
9. S. Légasse argues that the reminiscence of Is. 53:12 (LXX) is much clearer
than the more commonly cited Is. 49:24; see his "L' 'homme fort' de Luc xi
21–22," NovTest 5 (1962), 5–9, esp. 6f.
10. As Haenchen points out (Weg, 148), the armored strong man envisages a
Greek readership; so also A. Oepke, "panoplia," TDNT, V, 295–302 (300).
11. The original reference may have been to God (so Creed, Luke, 161). The
phrase "in which he trusted" has a biblical ring (cf. Prov. 11:28; Ps. 49[48]:7),
but Luke does not allegorize the details.
12. Diadidonai elsewhere in Luke-Acts refers to distributing goods to the poor
(Lk. 18:22; Acts 4:35). It is possible that this common Lukan motif here has
an indirect christological reference: Christ plunders Satan, but for the sake of the
poor, not for his own benefit; see Légasse, "L' 'homme fort,' " 9.
13. The reference to the harrowing of hell, popular among patristic commentators,
is impossible, as Schmid, Lk., 204 notes.

(Q) shows that the victory of Christ over Satan, reflected in various ways in the whole preceding section, demands a response rather than merely neutral observation: "He who is not with me is against me."[14] In a sense, to be sure, the stress on Christ's victory is a comfort to the beleaguered post-resurrection church.[15] More importantly, however, Luke's parenetic interests now come to the fore: his concern in vv. 24–28 is the faithfulness of the church, not in the past, but at all times.

This emphasis is apparently central in the obscure parable of the Unclean Spirit Seeking Rest (vv. 24–26). Both the meaning[16] and position of this parable in Q are uncertain. But even if Matt. 12:45c be attributed to Matthew rather than Q, it is probably best to view the Matthean (not the Lukan) position as the Q version; the parable would then be the concluding judgment on Jesus' generation. In this case, Luke has moved it from its original position (following 11:32) in Q and inserted it after v. 23, so that it serves to illustrate both the necessity of the decision and the extreme danger of not persevering in it.[17] That this is Luke's intention is indicated by vv. 27f., which can only be understood as a Lukan (and individualistic) blessing on those who hear *and keep* the Word of God (cf. also 6:47f.; 8:15). If the reference to Jesus' own generation is relatively unimportant now for Luke, it is not allegorizing to point out that what had happened to the Jewish people has become, for Luke, a possibility for every man. A house, once swept and put in order, is not in itself guaranteed against further incursions of the demonic. And a response, even a positive response, to the Word of God, permanently eliminates the option of merely returning to an earlier neutral state. Luke's general tendencies suggest that he understood the parable neither of a particular generation nor of the church as such but of individuals.

14. Lagrange, *Luc*, 330. Quite generally: any indifference to the one who is gathering God's flock is equivalent to scattering that flock and thus opposing God; Schmid, *Lk.*, 205.
15. So Conzelmann, *Theology . . . Luke*, 188, n. 4.
16. Bultmann, *HST*, 164 cites Arabic parallels, which however provide no sure guidance.
17. Jülicher, *Gleichn.*, II, 238: the section, viewed as a single parable, asks, "Who is your Sovereign—God or the Devil?"

5. The Sower (8:4–8, 11–15; cf. Mk. 4:1–9, 13–20; Matt. 13:1–9, 18–23)

The Lukan form of this parable is almost a textbook example of his general tendency to smooth out, vary, and improve Mark's somewhat rambling style. Close attention to these literary changes will, therefore, aid perceptibly in judging his literary habits as well as his theological intentions.

Among the many changes that seem to be primarily literary in motivation we may mention the following: the parable, the "hardening theory," and the explanation are all substantially abbreviated.[1] Mark's "rocky shelf" becomes simply "the rock" (v. 6), and the fate of the seed sown on it is so highly abbreviated that the reader must himself supply the explanation for its withering away[2] —especially since Luke's own appended explanation ("because it had no moisture") is really as elliptical as Mark's "it had no root." But Mark's over-aoristic "when the sun rose" (which would imply a single day's sunshine!) is eliminated for a much simpler and more logical expression, "and as it grew up it withered" (v. 6), a form that also removes the tautological "it was scorched and . . . it withered." Luke uses a synonymous term for "choke"[3] and omits Mark's superfluous "and it bore no fruit" (v. 7), which properly occurs in the explanation (Mk. 4:19). Even in the use of prepositions the Markan style is polished: Mark's repetitious *para-epi-eis(epi?)-eis* becomes *para-epi-en mesō-eis.*[4] Mark's simple *kai elegen* (4:9) becomes more formal, *tauta legōn ephōnei* (v. 8).[5] Even the connectives show the tendency toward greater polish and complexity: Mark's 23 *kai's* in the parable are reduced to 10 by both Luke and Matthew. In these changes, as in the similar

1. This abbreviation results, inevitably, in the minimizing of minor allegorical traits in the Markan *Vorlage*, not because they are allegorizing but because they are unclear or redundant; Schramm's attempt to postulate a non-Markan variant tradition (*Markus-Stoff*, 118–123) is quite unconvincing.
2. The allusion to Jer. 17:8 (LXX) is perhaps clearer in Luke than in the parallels; McNeile, *Matt.*, 188; Swete, *Mk.*, 70.
3. *Apopnigō* for *sympnigō*, which however reappears in the explanation (v. 14).
4. In the explanation, Mark (followed by Matthew) uses *para-epi-eis-epi*, Luke *para-epi-eis-en*, clear evidence that Luke interprets the Markan interpretation, not his own version of the parable.
5. Is this "he called out" not Luke's way of including Mark's solemn introductory "Listen"?

tendencies in the explanation,[6] probably no theological tendency is to be discerned, any more than the (rare) anacolouthon created by Luke in v. 12 (but avoided in vv. 13–15) reflects anything theologically significant.

Many changes, however, seriously modify the central concern and the teachings of the parable. Of these, perhaps the most important are changes in the context. These verses are now part of 8:1–9:50, in which Jesus in the course of his travels preaches the Kingdom of God, which for Luke is the typical object of Jesus' preaching.[7] In returning to his Markan source, which he left at 6:19 (cf. Mk. 3:10), Luke omits some material[8] and postpones some,[9] then takes up the Markan narrative with the parable itself (Mk. 4:1–9=Lk. 8:4–8). For this he provides a new setting (8:1–3), in which he notes that in his itineration Jesus is accompanied by the twelve and by several women (Mary Magdalene, Joanna, Susanna, and others), who provided for them; he thus assures the presence of many faithful Galilean witnesses to this important section of Jesus' preaching. Following the parable, Luke omits the Markan Seed Growing Secretly (which does not fit his new theme) and the Mustard Seed, which he uses later (13:18f.) in its Q form (and place?), paired with the Leaven (13:20f.). In the course of these modifications Luke has also removed the Markan setting at the sea[10] and substituted the mere note that Jesus is engaged in travel. While this eliminates the difficulty in the Markan text created by the mention of private conversation (in the boat?) at 4:10, it requires that a boat be reintroduced in 8:22 (Mk. 4:35) before the Stilling of the Storm. The Stilling of the Storm, in turn, serves to introduce a new section of the narrative ("One day . . ."), not, as in Mk., another incident on the same day.

---

6. In v. 14 Mark's *akarpos ginetai* becomes *ou telesphorousin*. For a suggestion as to the theological purpose behind the change, see below.
7. 8:1. See also the programmatic verses, 4:18 (the fulfillment of Scripture) and 4:43; cf. 9:2; Acts 2:12; 19:8; 28:23, 30f.
8. Mk. 3:20f.; he substitutes Q material for 3:22–30.
9. 3:31–35, which he uses *following* the Sower, at 8:19ff.
10. As well as the "house" of Mk. 3:20.

In short, as these changes and others to be seen within the text show, Luke has taken what Mark organized around the themes of parables and private teaching and reorganized it around the theme of Christian preaching.

The difference between the Markan and Lukan concepts is reflected even in the differences in the way the parable itself is portrayed. In Mk. (4:2) the parable is said to be one among many. Luke, however, omits this note (cf. also 20:9), restricts the disciples' question to this single parable (v. 9), and omits the Markan suggestion that the understanding of this parable is related in any specific way to the understanding of the others (Mk. 4:13). He also omits the comment that Jesus spoke only in parables (Mk. 4:33f.; Matt. 13:34). He thus eliminates not only the rebuke implied in Mk. 4:13 but also Mark's overall theory of esoteric teaching. The elimination of these themes, in turn, gives him freedom to expand the Markan parenetic interest (especially in the explanation) into a commentary on the church's ministry of the Word of God.

A similar, though certainly less obvious, indication of the same shift in emphasis may be seen in the elimination of Mark's "Listen" (4:3) before the parable itself, although the point should not be pressed, since it probably lies behind the phrase "he called out" in v. 8.[11] Luke certainly intended men to listen seriously to the church's preaching, the central theme of this section.

In v. 5, as again in 8:11, Lukan modifications show his special concern for the Word of God and the de-emphasizing of the sower. In the former verse the sower is said specifically (and somewhat redundantly) to have sown "his seed," while Mark's "The sower sows the word" becomes explicit: "The seed is the word of God" (8:11). The literary and theological connection with 8:21, the concluding verse of this section in Luke, is clear.[12]

An interesting minor variant occurs in v. 5, in which Luke

11. It is also surely reflected in the saying, "He who has ears to hear, let him hear" (Mk. 4:9 = Lk. 8:8b).

12. Those who hear and do the Word of God are Jesus' mother and brother; so also 11:28. Cf. 5:1 ("while the people crowded around him to hear the word of God") and Acts 4:31; 6:2, 7; 8:14; 11:1; 12:24; 13:5.

notes that some seed fell along the path "and was trodden under
foot." This expansion does not seem to fit Palestinian agricultural
customs[13] or improve the picture, since birds are *less* likely to get
the seed after it has been trampled than (as in Mk.) before.[14] We
might note that both "tread under foot" and "birds of the heaven"
(8.5) may be for Luke terms of eschatological destruction.[15]
Since he omits the phrase "trodden under foot by men" from the
Q parable of the Salt (Matt. 5:13=Lk. 14:35),[16] where Luke's
stress is on radical obedience, unreserved discipleship, it is possible that an eschatological judgment is implied here (the seed is
lost) which would be inappropriate in a different context.

Finally, in the parable itself the harvest is differently described.
Mark's progressively higher yield, "30-, 60-, and 100-fold" has
become simply "a hundredfold" (8:8). This is, of course, the
highest of Mark's figures, as we should expect, since throughout
Luke-Acts the inexorable advance of the Gospel in the face of
obstacles is so important.[17] But the use of the single figure shows
that the greatness of the harvest is not the central theme in Luke.
No figure of any kind is given in the explanation (v. 15; cf.
Mk. 4:20).

For in Lk., as many small linguistic phenomena illustrate, the
center of attention rests on the interpretation, not the parable, and
this interpretation (vv. 11–15) is actually an interpretation, not of
the Lukan parable, but of the Markan interpretation.[18] It spells
out in rather elaborate detail what it means to be a disciple.

V. 12 contains several interesting modifications. Mark's "Satan"
becomes "the devil," a somewhat more conventional Christian

13. See Loisy, *ES*, I. 735; Schmid, *Mk.*, 92; *Lk.*, 130.
14. Creed, *Luke*, 114; in the next verse, on the other hand, if *to petrōdes* were
simply *rock*, as Luke interprets it, the birds would have eaten this seed as well.
15. So Robinson, "Preaching . . . ," 134. The texts (Lk. 9:58; 13:19; Acts 10:12;
11:6) are not, however, unambiguous on the point.
16. Where Luke *adds* (or includes from Q), "He who has ears to hear," etc.
17. Luke's theology clearly explains his words; vs. Hauck, *Mk.*, 51, who holds
that Mark's threefold harvest is a secondary allegorization, and Schramm, *Markus-
Stoff*, 115, whose similar views presuppose both the primacy of the Lukan form
and Matthew's familiarity with it—neither of which is likely.
18. The grammatical details are given clearly in Robinson, "Preaching . . . ," 134,
138, n. 27.

expression, and he is said to take away not "the word which is sown into them" (Mk. 4:15) but "the word from their heart." Luke also omits Mark's characteristic "immediately," substituting "then" for it—from which the modern preacher may conclude that the devil is subtle: he may shrewdly wait until the man in question feels himself secure.[19] The really important addition in this verse, however, is 8:12b, "that they may not believe and be saved." The language here is conventional, not specifically Pauline,[20] but it illustrates an important modification of Mark's thought. In Mk., Satan shares the responsibility for unbelief with God, who has hardened men's hearts; here he shares that responsibility with man.[21] More importantly, Luke has apparently inserted here the equivalent of the clause he omitted from Mk. 4:12, "lest they should turn. . . ."[22] He is concerned for those who do not hear, and their fate can be spelled out clearly. Earlier, however, in his treatment of Mk. 4:10ff., he is concerned only with the "great crowd," some of whom are potential believers and for whom consequently the "hardening theory" is inappropriate. The translation into the categories of individual belief and unbelief is reflected with unusual clarity in his addition of this key phrase.

The second unsuccessful group are also described somewhat differently. They "receive the word," but these "temporary" hearers (Mark) "believe for a time" (Luke) and then apostatize.[23] The shift in emphasis here is striking. In Mark their lapse is occasioned by "tribulation or persecution on account of the word." In

19. So Jülicher, *Gleichn.*, II, 526.
20. Vs. Ernst Haenchen, *Die Apostelgeschichte* (13 . . . Aufl., Göttingen: Vandenhoeck & Ruprecht, 1961), 310, n. 3; Lagrange, *Luc*, 241; cf. Loisy, *ES*, I, 754. Note the Lukan emphasis on faith in vv. 12f.: "The first response to make to the Word of God is to believe it!" (Jacques Dupont, "Le chapitre de paraboles," *NRT* 89 [1967], 809).
21. Jülicher, *Gleichn.*, II, 526.
22. Schmid, *Lk.*, 131; Robinson, "Preaching," 134. Surely the Markan *hina*, reinterpreted in connection with the hardening theory (8:10), shows up again here?
23. *Aphistēmi* is Lukan in the Gospels (Matt. 0; Mk. 0; Lk. 4; Acts 6). Luke says that some plants "have no root," not, as in Mk. 4:17, "have no root in themselves." But it is over-interpreting to see this omission as Luke's way of emphasizing "more strongly than Mk. or Mt. the fact that what matters is not man himself but his rooting in the soil outside." (So Christian Maurer, *"hridsa, ktl.,"* *TDNT*, VI, 988.)

Lk., however, the thought of persecution *for the word* is completely abandoned, while *thlipsis* is here, as elsewhere in Lk.,[24] "de-eschatologized" into temptation, *peirasmos*, which he probably thinks of as daily spiritual temptations.[25] Again the elaboration of the parenetic element is clear.

In his description of the third unsuccessful group of hearers Luke does not go sensibly beyond his Markan source. Nevertheless, he has eliminated Mark's "of the world" (*tou aiōnos*), with its implied contrast between this age and the next, and substituted *bios*, daily "lived" life. He has also reworded Mark's language about the "entering (in)" of the evils that choke the word to imply that the seeds are choked *in the process of growth*.[26] Thus he avoids suggesting, as Mark and Matthew do, that the Word is choked, a concept unacceptable to Luke and foreign to his whole emphasis in this section. For the same reason he omits the Markan note that the Word remains fruitless (v. 14).

The successful seeds, similarly, are described in such a way as to illustrate Luke's understanding of discipleship. They "bring a good and honest heart to the hearing of the word" (NEB), "hold it fast," and bring forth fruit "with patience" (v. 15). "Hold it fast" suggests continued action, and in conjunction with *hypomonē* suggests "a persistent holding fast."[27] The term *hypomonē* in this context reflects "typical persecution terminology which has no parallel elsewhere"[28] and implies not merely patience, but endurance, steadfastness, perseverance.[29]

---

24. On the Lukan usage of this term, see Conzelmann, *Theology . . . Luke*, 98f.; Lucien Cerfaux, "Fructifier en supportant (l'épreuve), à propos de Luc, viii, 15," *RB* 64 (1957), 481–491 (487).

25. McNeile, *Matt.*, 194; Cerfaux, "Fructifier," 487f.; cf. 9:23 with Mk. 8:34.

26. Cf. Jülicher, *Gleichn.*, II, 529. NEB: "Their further growth is choked"; RSV: "as they go on their way they are choked."

27. McNeile, *Matt.*, 194. Goulder, "Characteristics," 63f. finds "no less than five small additions [in the interpretation of the Sower which] emphasize the moral of faithful endurance by the Christian."

28. Donald W. Riddle, "Die Verfolgungslogien in formgeschichtlicher und soziologischer Beleuchtung," *ZNW* 33 (1934), 271–289 (274).

29. Cerfaux insists, probably correctly, that in Lk. the word already implies "endure under testing" ("Fructifier," 481–491). It is thus already moving in the direction of the technical term, which it becomes in martyrological literature (Riddle, "Verfolgungslogien"). It is used only here and in 21:19 in the Gospels.

To sum up, this section defines the meaning of true discipleship: to know the secrets of the Kingdom of God (v. 9), to hold fast to the Word of God (vv. 11, 15) even in testing, and to do it (v. 21),[30] bringing forth fruit with steadfastness (v. 15). The judgment on unbelieving hearers, which may once have been of some importance in the parable itself, has almost totally disappeared. Now the individualistic, ethical, and parenetic emphases predominate.

6. The Wicked Husbandmen (20:9–18; cf. Mk. 12:1–12; Matt. 21:33–46)

This parable, as both its Lukan position and its Lukan wording attest, rests on Mk. 12:1–12.[1] In Lk., as in Mk., it is preceded by the unfriendly question about the source of Jesus' authority, which he counters with the (unanswerable) question about the authority of John the Baptist. It is followed, again as in Mk., by the unfriendly question about paying tribute to Caesar. Its main force is thus largely negative in both Gospels.

In Lk., however, this brief bit of *Heilsgeschichte* has a larger meaning as well. It is now told against the scribes and high priests (the elders, cf. v. 1, have dropped from sight by the end of the story) and in their presence, but it is told *to* the people (20:9). It is thus, for Luke, part of Jesus' general teaching and preaching of the gospel (in the Temple: 19:47; 20:1, 19). The Lukan modifications reflect in various ways his special understanding of that teaching.

The first notable modification occurs in v. 9, in which Luke reduces—for all practical purposes, obliterates—the reference to

---

30. The positive affirmation of discipleship, not anti-family polemic, is central in vv. 19–21 (vs. Conzelmann, *Theology . . . Luke*, 48f.).

1. Cadoux, *Parables*, 40 argues that Luke preserved the Q form of the parable, but there is little to suggest this. Some have held that the Lukan form is more primitive (see the discussion of vv. 10–12, below), but it is on all counts more probable that Luke has improved and to some extent de-allegorized Mark's text; see Werner G. Kümmel, "Das Gleichnis von den bösen Weingärtnern," *Aux Sources de la Tradition Chrétienne* (Neuchâtel/Paris: Delachaux & Niestlé, 1950), 124ff. (= *Heilsgeschehen und Geschichte*, 210ff.); Martin Hengel, "Das Gleichnis von den Weingärtnern Mc 12:1–12 im Lichte der Zenon-papyri und der rabbinischen Gleichnisse," *ZNW* 59 (1968), 4, n. 19; John Dominic Crossan, "The Parable of the Wicked Husbandmen," *JBL* 90 (1971), 451.

Is. 5:2, patent in Mk.[2] This is doubtless at least partially literary, since the hedge, the winepress, and the tower are of no significance in the story. A theological purpose of some kind could also be present, however, since the details of the Isaiah passage omitted by Luke suggest the *care* lavished by God on his people and contrast it with the people's ingratitude and lack of fruitfulness;[3] the passage also says explicitly (Is. 5:7) "the vineyard of the Lord of Hosts is the house of Israel," which does not fit the course of action in the parable.

In the description of the landowner, Luke notes that he went into another country "for a long time."[4] Naturally, he must be some distance away to send servants instead of coming himself, but Luke stresses the time rather than the distance involved. In itself, this item makes little sense. Even if several harvests are involved—and the action of the landowner is so peculiar that we cannot rule out a priori the possibility that it was several years before he took action—the times are fixed by the agricultural data: from planting to harvest (probably, though not necessarily) in a few years.[5] Consequently the item is most naturally explained as a reflection of the delayed Parousia,[6] not perhaps completely consistent (God, the Owner, has not gone away, in Luke's thought or any other), but clear enough to suggest that the delay is executing judgment is by no means permanent.

The description of the various groups of servants, unlike the minor modifications of Mark's language, are of central importance. All the evangelists reflect, though in different ways, the well-known form-critical "rule of three." Matthew has two groups of servants, then the son. Mark has a series of three servants, the last of whom is killed; followed by a general category, "many others"; followed by the son. Luke, on the other hand, has a series of three

2. Of the eight Gr. words Mk. shares with the LXX, only two (*ampelōn* and *phyteuō*) are retained by Luke.
3. So Jülicher, *Gleichn.*, II, 387.
4. *Hikanos* is Lukan in the Gospels (Matt. 3; Mk. 0; Lk. 16; Acts 6) and is used of *time* by him only among the evangelists.
5. See below, chap. 6, sec. 13.
6. Hauck, *Lk.*, 242; Easton, *Luke*, 292 suggests "the long period since the covenant with Moses," but this is hardly a Lukan conception.

individual servants, followed by the son. Furthermore, Luke alone of the evangelists portrays a steady rise in the mistreatment of the servants and then of the son.[7]

Some interpreters[8] see the Lukan form as more primitive than that of the other evangelists, though not necessarily identical with the earliest form of the story. Certainly it is not impossible that so clearly anti-Jewish a parable would have proved useful, and thus survived, for decades in the oral tradition, and we must grant that it was a striking surprise to find in Thomas (Saying 65) something like the very parable Dodd had suggested years before as lying behind all the synoptic accounts. Furthermore, the Lukan form is at this point less obviously allegorical than Matthew. Yet certain literary questions make this possibility much less appealing than it seems at first sight. Luke 20:11 is evidently a revision of Mk. 12:4, with *derō* substituted for the very difficult and quite possibly erroneous Markan *kephalioō*.[9] The omission of Markan details from v.1 (=Lk. 20:9) may have been due to the factors mentioned above, while Mk. 12:5b is exactly the kind of adventitious Markan material which Luke usually omits. Furthermore, the gradation in the treatment of the servants in Luke is more plausibly explained as a refinement of Mark's rather vague expressions than an earlier form of them.[10]

In addition, the position of the incident in Lk. makes it quite certain that he actually had the Markan text before him as he wrote, whereas the possibility that he also knew the story in a simpler form (is it really simpler, or just stylistically refined?) is at best a guess. Finally, it is hard to escape the feeling that recent

---

7. As Hauck notes (*Lk.*, 242), Mk. corresponds more closely with the historical course of the fate of the prophets, Lk. with psychological probability and dramatic necessity. Goulder, "Characteristics," 61 has correctly seen these changes as only one example among others of Luke's tendency toward "de-allegorization." Thomas preserves the rule of three in the portrayal of a) a badly beaten servant, b) a beaten servant, and c) a murdered Son (Saying 65), but without the gradation evident in Lk.

8. Jeremias, *Parables*, 67–77 (later editions of this work see the form in Thomas as confirmation of a non-allegorical original); Hengel, "Weingärtnern," *passim*; Crossan, "Wicked Husbandmen," *passim*.

9. On this, see below, chap. 6, sec. 13, n. 8.

10. Jeremias himself admits (*Parables*, 72, n. 84) that vv. 10, 12 reflect an unusual number of peculiarly *Lukan* expressions.

attempts to urge a primitive form quite different from that given in *any* of the Gospels reflect a strongly apologetic attempt to minimize the difficulties in accepting the authenticity of the whole. On balance, then, Luke is best understood as having rewritten his Markan source for his own purposes without any other sources, written or oral, for the story.

Following the mistreatment of successive groups of servants, the owner considers the matter carefully[11] and decides to send his (beloved: Mk., Lk.) son, saying, "Perhaps they will respect my son." This hesitant form, a modification of Mark's flat assertion, "They will respect my son," is patently theologically motivated: since the father is God, he would be mistaken if he made an erroneous assertion[12] and morally reprehensible if he deliberately sent his son to death. It is a Lukan attempt to maintain both the parabolic setting and the doctrines of divine providence and omniscience.

When the decision is made, the son is promptly killed and thrown out of the vineyard. (In Lk. [v. 15], as in Matt. [v. 39], the order is reversed.) This shameful act is then followed (v. 16) by the promise of the owner's coming to destroy the tenants and to give the vineyard to others. To this promise the people (not the leaders) reply in horror "God forbid!" A straightforward reading of the account might suggest that the people see themselves condemned and are horrified only by the promised judgment, not by the crime itself.[13] In Luke's thought, however, the crowds are by no means at one with the officials. That they should here reject both the act and its consequences—i.e., all of vv. 9–16—is really a Christian response, and this favorable description of the crowds is, as Jülicher noted long ago, *"echt lucanisch."*[14]

The crowd's response also provides a transition to the scriptural citation which Luke adds in v. 17. (Cf. 19:25 for a similar transi-

---

11. The monologue style is characteristic of Luke: 12:17f.; 15:17ff.; 16:3f.; 18:4f.
12. See Jülicher, *Gleichn.*, II, 392.
13. So Lagrange, *Luc*, 510; Easton, *Luke*, 293.
14. *Gleichn.*, II, 400.

tion.) Jesus looks at the crowds and cites the rejected-Stone saying from Ps. 118[117]:22f. Luke, however, uses only the first part of the quotation as given in Mk. (v. 17) before adding (in v. 18) "everyone who falls on that stone," etc. Quite possibly he has abbreviated the former quotation on literary grounds: he wants to add the second "stone" saying immediately, without introducing any new idea to separate the positive (v. 17) and negative (v. 18) functions of the Stone.[15] Theological reasons, however, may also be adduced. What is eliminated from Mk. (". . . it is marvelous in our eyes . . .") would most naturally be understood as an elaboration not of individual judgment (so v. 18) but of the resurrection, the Gentile mission, and the rise of Gentile Christianity—themes which Luke clearly wishes to reserve for the book of Acts. The second quotation, v. 18 (Lk. only), is probably due to Luke himself, and is apparently something like a very free reminiscence of Is. 8:14[16] or perhaps a free composition based on such passages as Is. 8:14f.; 28:13; Dan. 2:34f., 44f.; etc.[17] or even the confused desposit of early Christian use of scriptural texts dealing with Christ as Stone.[18] The effect of the saying, in any case, is to reintroduce the Son into a central place (unlike the parallel accounts) and *individualize* the Judgment.[19] It provides scriptural and christological support for Luke's insistence on the inevitability and immutability of God's purposes for history[20] and the sure and certain success of the Word against all would-be opponents.

The same theme is expressed in the Lukan form of the conclusion: the scribes and chief priests tried[21] vainly to lay hands on

15. So Lagrange, *Luc*, 511.
16. Bonnard, *Matt.*, 317
17. So Loisy, *ES* II, 314; Schmid, *Lk.*, 297; Lagrange, *Luc*, 511.
18. Creed, *Luke*, 246; cf. Acts 4:11; 1 Pet. 2:7; etc. Jülicher, *Gleichn.*, II, 401 thinks Lk. rests on an apocryphal addition to Is. 28:16c; Lagrange, *Luc*, 511f. suggests an authentic saying of Jesus.
19. Jülicher, *Gleichn.*, II, 402.
20. Siegfried Schulz, "Gottes Vorsehung bei Lukas," *ZNW* 54 (1963), 104–116 (115) points to the crucial significance of 22:22 in Luke's thought: Mk.'s "as it is written" (14:21) becomes "as it has been determined"!
21. Neither a single attempt (Lk.) nor repeated attempts (Mk.) on Jesus' life were actually made, as Luke (v. 20) points out.

him "at that hour." But it was the wrong hour. Since God foreknew not only *that* Jesus must suffer but *when*, even his opponents could put him to death only when their hour had come (22:53).

Of this brief parable of *Heilsgeschichte*, then, Luke has made something like a theology of history: the Jews will be rejected for their rejection of the prophets and God's Son, and the gospel will be given to others. All of this is part of God's plan, however, for the rejected Son, become the head of the corner, will eventually destroy not the wicked tenants alone, but everyone who opposes him.

7. The Fig Tree as the Herald of Summer (21:29ff.; cf. Mk. 13:28f.; Matt. 24:32f.)

This brief parable comes, as in Mk., toward the end of the apocalyptic discourse. In both the context and the wording, however, Luke has made significant changes which greatly affect the interpretation.

In Mk. 13, Jesus speaks to the disciples, especially to the first four disciples, privately, seated on the Mount of Olives after having left the Temple (13:1–4). But Luke has changed all of this. The teaching is now *in* the Temple,[1] and it is neither private nor intended especially for the disciples. The context seems to be, as often in Lk., what it was in 20:45: he speaks to the disciples in the hearing of the people. The reference is thus to all disciples of whatever period. And the teaching is understood as typical of his daily Temple teaching (21:37), to which "all the people" come.

The details also reflect the broad Lukan understanding of Jesus' message. Mark's "learn the parable (lesson) of the fig tree" becomes "And he spoke a parable to them, 'Look at the fig tree. . . .' " The effect of this brief introductory phrase is to loosen up somewhat the connection with what immediately precedes,[2] since vv. 20–24 are now understood purely historically and vv. 25–28

---

1. 19:47–20:1; cf. 21:27f. The very awkward expression in 21:5, "some were talking about the Temple . . ., and he said . . ." results from Luke's omitting Mk. 13:la.

2. So also at 5:36; see above, chap. 4, sec. 3, n. 1.

purely eschatologically, while Luke (v. 32) does not wish to restrict the reference to these events alone. His addition of "and all the trees," though doubtless the result of his non-Palestinian situation,[3] is not entirely happy: in losing the special place accorded the fig tree, he has also lost some agricultural accuracy, since trees do not all come out in leaf[4] at the same time. Yet whatever precise phenomenon Luke had in mind, he thought that from it men could see for themselves and know that "the summer is already near." The significance, if any, of Luke's revising Mk.'s "near" to "already near" is uncertain; since the phrase is not repeated in v. 31, it may not be very significant. On the other hand, it could represent a certain sharpening of the apocalyptic symbolism, since for Luke the eschatological harvest may be portrayed apocalyptically when (as here) it is thought of as purely future.

The most significant variation, however, occurs in v. 31. Mark's statement that Jesus' hearers will then know that he (i.e., the Son of Man, 13:26) is near, "at the very gates," becomes in Lk. the saying that "the kingdom of God is near." Both the consolation and the precision implied in Mk.'s "at the very gates" have been removed. The "kingdom of God" is now de-eschatologized, in keeping with Luke's general tendency to think of the Kingdom as the content of Christian preaching rather than that which has drawn near.[5] The nearness of the Kingdom, especially the nearness of the Kingdom as such, plays little role in Luke's theology.

The complexity of Luke's conception of the Kingdom should not be underestimated. But in general, it may be said that in Luke-Acts the Kingdom of God is the ordinary object of Christian preaching, whether of Jesus (Lk. 4:43; 8:1), his disciples (Lk.

---

3. Lagrange, *Luc*, 533.
4. *proballō* can also mean "produce fruit" (Epictetus, *Discourses* I.xv. 7 [Loeb, I, 106]), but the fruit comes forth in the middle of summer, not at its beginning; furthermore, most trees do not bear fruit.
5. "The phrase *euaggelidsesthai tēn basileian tou theou* is the typically Lucan, non-eschatological form of the proclamation of the Kingdom, a substitute for the original form *ēggiken*." (Conzelmann, *Theology . . . Luke*, 40; see also pp. 113f.) Exactly the same impulse lies behind 21:19 (cf. Mk. 13:13), where the original *eschatological* reference has given way to the general virtue of steadfastness under adversity of any kind, at any time. Cf. Wilhelm Ott, *Gebet und Heil* (Munich: Kösel-Verlag, 1965), 137ff.

9:60; Acts 8:12), or even Paul (Acts 19:8; 20:25; 28:23, 30f.). The thought that it has drawn near is occasionally removed by Luke from his sources (9:2=Matt. 10:7, Q; Mk. 1:15), while at 21:8 one of the signs of the false Messiahs to come is that they will say not only "I am" (Mk., Lk.) or "I am the Christ" (Matt.) but also "the *kairos ēggiken*" (Lk. only!). Often connected with healing (9:2; cf. Matt. 10:7; 9:35; added by Luke to his sources at 9:11), it may even, in connection with healing, be spoken of as *near* (10:9 [=Matt. 10:7, Q?]; 10:11). Yet of its nearness, especially its *immediate* nearness, in general, there can be no thought, as 19:11 makes clear.

In our parable, then, the "nearness" of the Kingdom of God at some future time is substituted for the teaching that the signs mentioned portend the nearness "at the very gates" of the Son of Man. That Luke's thought, in spite of his use of apocalyptic material, is really anti-apocalyptic, is shown by his revision in the verses which immediately follow. Mark's "all these things" (v. 30) becomes simply "all things"[6] (v. 32), so that the emphasis shifts from the apocalyptic details of the preceding discourse to the entire Plan of God. In this context, v. 32 does not really fit; in Luke's thought, therefore, "this generation" has lost its temporal reference and must refer to all things (as in v. 33, "heaven and earth") or perhaps "mankind in general,"[7] an unnatural interpretation which the words can hardly have had originally. The following verse in his Markan source (Mk. 13:32, the "day nor hour" saying) is problematic, not only for Luke's Christology but also for his eschatology, and he simply omits it.

The key to the whole is thus provided by Luke's general eschatological thought and by the immediately preceding verse, 21:28: when these things begin to happen (not the apocalyptic signs

---

6. The inferior readings *tauta panta* or *panta tauta* (D Ψ Φ pc 1) come from the parallel accounts.

7. Schmid, *Lk.*, 314; Conzelmann, *Theology . . . Luke*, 105, n. 2. The attempt to take "this generation" in its normal sense but to refer the "all things" merely to the historical events of Luke's time (so Erich Klostermann, *Das Lukasevangelium* [2. Aufl., Tübingen: J. C. B. Mohr ((Paul Siebeck)), 1929], 204; hesitantly, Creed, *Luke*, 258) minimizes the universal reference of the Plan of God in Luke's theology.

alone, for their discerning requires no special insight, but all the acts by which God fulfills his Plan and brings his Kingdom), learn from the fig tree and all the trees when they begin to bud that then—not now, not immediately, but whenever God so intends—your redemption is drawing near!

8. The Waiting Servants (12:35–38; cf. Mk. 13:34–37)

Thus far our study has concentrated on the Lukan redaction of those parables which both Luke and Matthew have taken from Mk. In addition to these parables, however, Luke has one brief parable which Matthew has not used from Mk. (The Waiting Servants), and five that occur in both Q and Mk.: The Beelzebul parables, discussed above;[1] the Mustard Seed, which in Lk. is apparently taken entirely from Q, without reference to Mk., and thus is not directly relevant to our study of the Triple Tradition;[2] and the parables of the Salt, the Lamp and the Bushel, and the Manifestation of What Is Hidden. The latter three parables, as well as the Waiting Servants, are important enough to discuss separately.

The best explanation of Lk. 12:35–38, from the literary point of view, is that it is a Lukan revision and elaboration of the Waiting Servants (Mk. 13:34–37). It is the only Markan parable which is not in Markan order in Luke's account, yet the common themes in both Gospels—wakefulness in the light of the master's absence, as well as the division of the night into "watches"[3]—make it clear that it is the same parable.

---

1. See above, sec. 4.
2. Briefly, on the Mustard Seed (13:18f.): a) the inclusion of the Gentiles, implied in Mk.'s use of Dan. 4:21, is no longer a problem for Luke (or his tradition); and b) by including this parable in the same context as 13:1–9 (the Barren Fig Tree), 13:22–30 (the Few and the Many in the Kingdom), and esp. 13:17 ("And as he said this, all those who opposed him were put to shame, and all the people rejoiced at all the splendid deeds being done by him") he has emphasized the success-motif more than consolation as such.
3. The Jewish division of the night into three watches (Judg. 7:19; cf. Ex. 14:24; 1 Sam. 11:11; Ps. 90:4; Lam. 2:19; Ber. 3b; Job 35:10?) is used here by Luke; the Roman division into four watches is used by Mark (13:35; cf. 6:48), by Matthew (14:25), and later by Luke himself (Acts 12:4).

In chapter 12, Luke uses Q material (12:22–31, 33f., 39f.) which is strongly eschatological, and he uses it in a parenetic sense. In the midst of this material (12:35–38) he has inserted his version of Mk. 13:34,[4] carrying through in a fairly consistent way the (pre-Lukan) resolution of the problem of the delayed Parousia. When he then comes to fashion his own version of the end of Jesus' teaching, however, Luke cannot use Mk. 13:34 again. So he uses most of the other material of Mk. 13, adding the parable of the Pounds (19:11–27), which is very similar in emphasis, perhaps from the ending of Q,[5] and creating (in 21:34ff.) his own version of the closing words of the final public discourse in Mk. (13:33–37).

The parable itself, as both the (Lukan) introduction ("be like men who . . .") and the details make clear, is not a genuine parable, but a highly allegorical comparison. In v. 35, a double symbolism introduces the exhortation: Let your loins be girded[6] and your lamps alight (a symbol of wakefulness). The quality suggested by these expressions is readiness, preparedness (cf. v. 40), a quality demanded not only of the few (vv. 41ff.) but also of all Christians; as in Mark, the stress is parenetic, not anti-hierarchic, on the obligations of watchfulness for all, not the failures or potential failures of a few appointed watchmen.[7] His primary concern is the exhortation to all Christians not to wakefulness as such, which cannot be long continued, but to readiness, defined in v. 47 as "acting according to his (i.e., the master's) will."

---

4. There is little evidence that Luke knew the parable of the Ten Virgins [Matt. 25:1–13] (vs. Jülicher, *Gleichn.*, II, 459; Loisy, *ES*, II, 461f.; Troadec, *Luc*, 148). His free use of Mk. and Q adequately accounts for the literary phenomena: v. 37a,b = v. 43a,b = Matt. 24:46, Q; v. 37c = Mk. 13:37; v. 37d = Lk. 17:8; etc.

5. A fixed catechetical *Schema*, according to which teaching about the Last Things comes last, may be reflected in Q, Mk. 13, etc.; so Hans Conzelmann, "Geschichte und Eschaton nach Mc 13," *ZNW* 50 (1959), 210–221 (211f.).

6. This biblical symbol may be used of preparation for battle, both literal (Is. 5:27) and figurative (Job 38:3, 40:7; Eph. 6:14; 1 Pet. 1:13?); for travel (Ex. 12:11; 1 Kgs. 18:46; cf. 1 Kgs. 4:29; 9:1); for work (Jer. 1:17); etc.; cf. also Is. 59:17.

7. Schmid, *Lk.*, 223. Lagrange, *Luc*, 368 defends the historicity of the insertion in v. 41, but neither this verse nor the similar ones which he cites (11:27, 45; 12:13; 14:15; 17:5, 37) prove anything more than that Luke utilizes the literary devices of dialogue and interruption. The parable is probably addressed to the disciples (v. 22; cf. v. 41), not the multitudes (v. 54); so Gnilka, *Verstockung*, 127.

V. 36 is not so clearly allegorical. The master returns from a wedding, which seems not to be his own wedding[8] or any sort of eschatological symbol, but simply an ordinary nuptial festivity, prolonged enough to account for his arriving at an uncertain hour. The wedding itself is of no great importance; all the stress is laid on the master's arrival, not on his leaving the festivities.

With v. 37, however, the allegorical traits again become prominent. Even assuming that the master was in the proper physical and psychological state to prepare a midnight (?) meal for his servants, there is no plausible reason for their not having already eaten or for his willingness to do so; such a practice is not merely uncommon—it is unthinkable.[9] This is, however, no ordinary master: "This master is he who came to serve" (22:27).[10]

Finally, the influence of the theological point on the symbolism is evident in the mention (in the best texts) of the second and third watches but not the first. The explanation of this can hardly be that he was still at the wedding during the first watch.[11] The omission is rather a clear reference to the delayed Parousia: the first watch is already long past.

In its present form, then, this brief section reflects Luke's use of eschatological materials in Christian parenesis: Christians are to be prepared (i.e., to do the will of God) in a continuing world until the return of the master; the solemn "truly I tell you" (v. 47b), so inappropriate in a story of an ordinary return from a wedding, becomes (like the unusual promise given to the "ready" servants) explicable in a Parousia context. But disentangling the traditional elements in the wording would be an unrewarding and probably unachievable task.

8. So, rightly, Alfred Plummer, *A Critical and Exegetical Commentary on the Gospel according to S. Luke* (5th ed., Edinburgh: T. & T. Clark, 1922), 330. From his own wedding he would not return alone or (quite probably) quietly; so Jülicher, *Gleichn.*, II, 163; Schmid, *Lk.*, 222.

9. Jülicher, *Gleichn.*, II, 165; Schmid, *Lk.*, 222. The omission of the phrase *kai parelthōn diakonēsei autois* in ℵ * probably came about when an early scribe noticed the incongruity.

10. Lagrange, *Luc*, 367. Julius Wellhausen, *Das Evangelium Lucae übersetzt und erklärt* (Berlin: Georg Reimer, 1904), 67 thinks that the service motif is imported from 22:27ff., where it is more appropriate. Jeremias, *Parables*, 54, on very inadequate linguistic grounds, holds that v. 37b is not only secondary but pre-Lukan.

11. Plummer, *Luke*, 331.

Is there, however, some genuine parable behind these Lukan materials? Jülicher thinks there is,[12] arguing that the allegory is incomplete, since disciples cannot be servants and be like servants at the same time and that the language, with minor modifications, is fully compatible with the teaching of Jesus. But the argument is not convincing. The incompleteness of the allegory is characteristic of practically all allegories, especially the biblical ones. Both Jülicher's moral interpretation of the story's meaning and his general description of Jesus' eschatological teaching miss what is genuinely distinctive about Jesus' message, namely, the call to repentance on the basis of the inbreaking power of the Kingdom (not the injunction to be patient no matter how long the consummation is delayed). So while it is conceivable that some form of this parable, now lost to us, could have come from Jesus, its details and its interpretation in Luke seem to presuppose the problem of the delayed Parousia. In Luke's theology this problem is met not merely by moral exhortation but by the promise of blessedness, of being set over all the master's possessions (v. 44), to him who knows his master's will and in readiness for his coming acts according to it (vv. 47f.).

9. The Savorless Salt (14:34f.; cf. Mk. 9:50; Matt. 5:13)

The Lukan form of this saying may be taken as roughly identical with Q,[1] although the introductory "Salt is good, but . . ." is probably taken over from Mk. Special Lukan interests are shown in the wording and the context.

The introductory "therefore" ties the saying to what immediately precedes, the paired parables of the Tower Builder and the King Going to War (vv. 28–32). These parables, in turn, are embedded in the larger section, vv. 25–35, whose apparent intent is to provide instruction on the nature and requirements of true discipleship. V. 25 characteristically[2] says that the words are directed to large crowds, here understood as potential disciples. A nom-

---

12. See *Gleichn.*, II, 166, 171.
1. Creed, *Luke*, 195; Schnackenburg, "Salz," *passim.*
2. Cf. 12:1; 18:6; 19:3; 20:45; 21:38.

inal faith, a partial renunciation, Luke says, is a contradiction in terms; it is like salt that has lost its savor.[3] It is useful neither now (on the land) nor in the future (in the dunghill). It will be thrown out.[4]

We may be sure that Luke's understanding of agriculture is reflected in the wording, but unfortunately we do not know whether he intended to say that: 1) salt is used for manure[5] or 2) unlike other kitchen waste, which could be used as fertilizer, spoiled salt would only ruin the land (Judg. 9:45) or the manure pile and should therefore be thrown on the street.[6]

But to what does the "imperfect renunciation"[7] refer? The general idea is quite clear: just as the Tower Builder and the King must count the cost and make certain they have the resources to complete what they have begun, lest they find themselves faced with a shameful end, so the disciple must be sure he intends to carry out the arduous task of being Jesus' disciple lest he too suffer a shameful fate.

Yet in this form the parable is more Stoic than Christian, as the parallels show.[8] The Tower Builder and the King do not really renounce anything; they are merely examples par excellence of prudent judgment followed by heroic perseverance. Even the provision of an eschatological context of sorts by the addition of the stereotyped "He who has ears . . ." (v. 35; cf. also 8:8=Mk. 4:9) does not give these parables the sharpness we may assume they had for Luke. Hence two more specific suggestions have been made.

3. Luke's kai is probably emphatic in v. 34: "But if even salt . . ." (Jülicher, Gleichn., II, 68).
4. A veiled allusion to the Judgment: Hauck, Lk., 195.
5. Creed, Luke, 196 speaks of "a well-attested practice for Egypt and Palestine, both in ancient and in modern times"; but Lohmeyer/Schmauch, Matt., 98 and Cullmann, "Salz," 195 dispute this.
6. So Schmid, Lk., 249.
7. Cullmann, "Salz," 197 suggests sacrifice, suffering, and complete self-denial, but these are not the same, and none of them are quite identical with hating father or mother (v. 20) or bearing one's own cross (v. 27).
8. Epictetus, Discourses, III.5.9 (Loeb, II, 102); Philo, de Abr., 105 (Loeb, VI, 56).

Loisy,[9] noting that the preceding discourses are dominated by the theme of Israel's reprobation and the calling of the Gentiles, suggests that Luke uses this traditional saying as a comment and warning based on Israel's failure to persevere. Lagrange,[10] however, rejects this "violent" interpretation and prefers to restrict the application to the disciples, as a solemn warning that an ex-disciple would be no better than stale salt. Surely the latter interpretation is more probable, although we should perhaps stress the importance in Luke's mind of the application to disciples of his own day.[11] A ruined builder, a conquered king, spoiled salt—these are the unpleasant pictures Luke uses to illustrate the situation of a disciple who from discouragement[12] or any other cause draws from the profession he has once made.

10. The Lamp and the Bushel (8:16; 11:33; cf. Mk. 4:21; Matt. 5:15)

This brief parable, perhaps originally a secular wisdom-saying,[1] and used in different forms by both Mark and Q, occurs twice in Lk.[2] in nearly identical form, at 8:16, immediately following the explanation of the Sower, and at 11:33, where it follows the Jonah-saying (vv. 29–32) and precedes a brief section opposing the Pharisees and scribes (vv. 37–54).

The latter passage may suitably be discussed first, since here, in

9. *ES*, II, 137; so also I, 555f. Jeremias, *Parables*, 169 also understands a primary reference to Israel, citing 14:25 in support.

10. *Luc*, 414.

11. On this basis, 14:28–32 forms a unity. See Wellhausen, *Lk.*, 80 (". . . decisive commitment"); Dodd, *Parables*, 141 (". . . the heroic virtue of the true Christian"); Cullmann, "Salz," 196; Schnackenburg, "Salz der Erde," 182, n. 14.

12. Lagrange, *Luc*, 413; in the modern world, this is probably a rather insignificant cause, as even a superficial reading of the church's critics will show.

1. Bultmann, *HST*, 98 (probably). Jülicher, *Gleichn.*, II, 80 holds that the variety of forms tells against the existence of such a secular wisdom-saying, an inconclusive argument. Joachim Jeremias, *New Testament Theology I* (London: SCM Press, 1971), 20, 39 argues rather that the saying, which shows Aramaic influence, is characteristic of Jesus' method of teaching. Note that form-critical analysis yields *two* primitive forms, roughly identical with Mk. and Q.

2. On this saying in Thomas, see Heinz Schürmann, "Das Thomas-evangelium und das lukanische Sondergut," *BibZeit* 7 (1963), 254; Schneider, "Lampe," 206ff.; and esp. Wolfgang Schrage, *Das Verhältnis des Thomas-evangeliums zur synoptischen Tradition und zu den koptischen Evangelien-übersetzungen* (Berlin: Alfred Töpelmann, 1964), 81–85.

its position in Q, there is no Markan influence on the meaning or the interpretation. A comparison of all forms of the saying makes it clear, in spite of the minior textual problem,[3] that Luke has modified the Q wording. He has added—as in 8:16—the flat statement that no one lights[4] a light. Whether a question or (more probably) a statement originally stood in Q, and whether Luke has introduced the synonym *to pheggos* for *to phōs* at 11:36[5] are of no special importance for understanding Luke's literary or theological interests. Of special significance, however, is the phrase, "that those who enter may see the light" (v. 33c), which Luke has inserted both here and at 8:16.[6] Since the purpose of a lamp is not, as Luke says, to be *seen*, but rather (as Matthew has it) to *give light*,[7] we may be sure that the damage to the parable results from the importance of the phrase in Luke's understanding of the theological point.[8] Addressed to the crowds (v. 29), whom Luke views as potential disciples, it may be presumed to have a parenetic, contemporary purpose for Luke in addition to its obvious, negative sense.

But how is this positive sense to be understood? A reference to

---

3. *oude hypo ton modion* is omitted by p[45, 75] L≡0124 λ 700 *al* sy[s] sa. In spite of Jülicher's learned protest, however (*Gleichn.*, II, 81f.; so also Schneider, "Lampe," 205; Schramm, *Markus-Stoff*, 25, n. 1; B. T. D. Smith, *The Parables of the Synoptic Gospels* [Cambridge: Cambridge University Press, 1937], 120; cf. Creed, *Luke*, 163), and Luke's well-known antipathy to foreign loan-words, the phrase should be seen, not as an interpolation from the Matthean parallel, but as original at this place: the external attestation is very strong, and Matt. 5:15 suggests that the words stood in Q.

4. *haptō* occurs in this sense only in Luke-Acts. *kaiō* ("burn") surely represents the same original (McNeile, *Matt.*, 56).

5. External attestation slightly favors *to phōs* (p[75] ℵ D Θ [λ] Φ *al*) over *to pheggos* (ℛ W 33 *pm*), but internal considerations, especially Luke's own preference for synonymic variation, make the *lectio difficilior to pheggos* more probably original.

6. The words are omitted at 8:16 by p[75].

7. Hence the scribes responsible for ℵ 33 *pc* modify (as a comparison with 8:16 makes clear) *blepōsin* to *blepousin*.

8. Not (vs. Schmid, *Lk.*, 160) from his use of a *Sonderquelle* at this point. The commonly noted difference in customs reflected (in Palestine, farmhouses have no cellars or hidden corners and only one room, elsewhere a lampstand is placed in a vestibule [see Dodd, *Parables*, 143, n. 1; Joachim Jeremias, "Die Lampe unter dem Scheffel," ZNW 39 ((1940)), 237–240 ((=ABBA [[Göttingen: Vandenhoeck & Ruprecht, 1966]], 99–102))]) does not explain the peculiarities of Luke's wording here.

the "light within"[9] is excessively interiorized, while the equation
of the "light" with Christian doctrine or Christ himself[10] is an allegorical (and non-Lukan) refinement. The general sense must be
given by the thought that the light is to be *seen* by those who
enter.[11] It is not (as in Matt. and Q) a source of illumination for
those already in the house. A general reference to missionary
expansion[12] (not specifically to the acceptance of the Gentiles)[13]
fits the language used, while the parenetic intent of what follows
(vv. 34ff.) is clear.[14] Somehow older Christians are to "bear light"
or "be light," to "hear and keep the Word of God" (11:28), thus
making available to others in the "house" the light originally
brought by Jesus.

The same parenetic use is evident in the use of the saying at
Lk. 8:16, its position in Mk. (4:21). In Mk. the connection with
what precedes (the explanation of the Sower, vv. 13–20) is not
very close; the saying is introduced by "And he said to them. . . ."
The omission of this phrase by Luke, however, as often elsewhere,[15] serves to attach the saying immediately to the context.
The similar omission at v. 18 (=Mk. 4:24) and the very brief
introduction used in v. 19 (cf. Mk. 3:31) have the effect of connecting all of vv. 16–21 with the explanation of the Sower, so that
hearing and holding fast to the Word of God is the characteristic
of seed on good land (v. 15), i.e., Jesus' true relatives (vv. 19–21).

9. The Gospel of Thomas (Saying 33b; cf. 24c and 50) implies something like
this.
10. So Lagrange, *Luc*, 339; Schmid, *Lk.*, 208; Schnackenburg, "Salz," 197;
Schneider, "Lampe," 204f. For these and other equivalents among the Fathers,
see Jülicher, *Gleichn.*, II, 84.
11. Not, as Easton rightly notes (*Lk.*, 116), "that those who see the light may
enter. . . ."
12. McNeile, *Matt.*, 57; Jeremias, *Parables*, 121, 164; Gnilka, *Verstockung*, 125.
13. Rightly, Jülicher, *Gleichn.*, II, 86.
14. C. Spicq, "La vertu de simplicité dans l'Ancient et le Nouveau Testament,"
RSPT 22 (1933), 5–26 (15–18): the lamp is the doctrine of Christ or Christ
himself, the "single eye" that which enables one to see straight, purity of intention, simplicity. Conny Edlund, *Das Auge der Einfalt* (Copenhagen: Ejnar Munds-
gaard, 1952), 113–117 restricts the meaning in 11:33 to a condemnation of
Jewish unbelief; but the parenetic application to Christians seems obvious in the
present context.
15. Cf. Lk. 9:4 with Mk. 6:10; Lk. 9:27 with Mk. 9:1.

In so interpreting the saying in 8:16, Luke has departed from his Markan source in several respects. The secrecy motif has disappeared completely. Mark's "put under a bushel" (v. 21) has become "... covers it with a vessel" (Lk. 8:16), a modification of no great importance, since both expressions imply that the light is thereby hidden.[16] He has replaced Mark's rhetorical question with a simple statement that no one lights a lamp and hides (or extinguishes) it, although it is hardly plausible to see in this a shift from the centrality of the lamp to the centrality of the lamplighter,[17] since in both cases (though with different emphases) two situations, not two objects or actions, are contrasted: a lamp-under-a-bushel and a lamp-on-a-stand. A fortiori the correction of *hypo tēn klinēn* to *hypokatō klinēs* is a characteristically Lukan improvement in style[18] without any particular significance. What is important is that the Markan distinctive has been quietly removed and the saying transformed here (from Mk.) as well as at 11:33 (from Q) into a commentary on a central Lukan theme: the true hearing of the Word of God. That he has thereby reinterpreted the tradition in the light of his own understanding of that Word is evident. His conception of orthodoxy not only allowed such retranslation; it seems positively to have required it.

11. The Manifestation of What Is Hidden (8:17; 12:2f.; Mk. 4:22; Matt. 10:26)

This saying, like the Lamp and the Bushel, also occurs twice in Lk., and (presumably) at the positions determined by Mark and Q, though in both cases with characteristic modifications.

Again, it may be well to begin with the Q-form, 12:2f., in which no Markan influence is apparent. The context is patently Lukan:

16. A. Dupont-Sommer, "Note archéologique sur le proverbe évangélique: Mettre la lampe sous le boisseau," *Mélanges Syriens*, Festschrift Dussaud (2 vols., Paris: Paul Geuthner, 1939), II, 789–794 suggests, with great plausibility, a *modius* with legs (illustrations in the text), which would cover but not extinguish the light. (Schneider, "Lampe," 189 n. 29 is sympathetic to the suggestion, although he notes that the vessels portrayed by Dupont-Sommer are not called *modii*.)
17. Vs. Gnilka, *Verstockung*, 125.
18. The Semitic use of the article here (see Jeremias, "Lampe," in *ABBA*, 100) is Grecized by Luke.

The saying follows both the "woes" of chapter 11 and a summary saying (11:53f.) about the repeated efforts of the scribes and Pharisees to trap Jesus in his preaching. The address to the disciples in the presence of great multitudes makes it evident that Luke intends the verse to be understood as part of Jesus' general preaching of the Kingdom—negatively, against hypocrisy, but also positively, as a promise that what is now hidden (v. 2) or said privately (v. 3) will some day be made public.[1] The nature of Pharisaic "hypocrisy" is not spelled out,[2] nor is it clear just when or how judgment on such hypocrisy will be executed. (Within history or beyond history?) Luke himself has probably created the anti-Pharisaic context of the saying,[3] and given the Lukan stress on the disciples and the friendly crowds, it could only mean, in its negative sense, something like "One day—presumably at the Judgment—hypocrisy will disappear, and all the secrets of men's hearts will be revealed."

But this assumes that the key to Luke's intention is given by v. 1. If it is connected instead with what follows, however, with the "housetops"-saying of v. 3 and with vv. 4–10, the verse speaks not of hypocrisy or even (like Matt. 10:27) of fearless proclamation, but of promise, of the success of the Word (in spite of hypocritical opposition), of God's care for those who avoid hypocrisy (12:1f.), trust God and fear not (vv. 4–7), confess Jesus even in despair (vv. 8–12), and avoid covetousness (vv. 13–20) and care (vv. 22–31)—for those, in other words, who accept the promise, "Fear not . . . , for it is your Father's good pleasure to give you the Kingdom" (12:32, Luke only).

That this parenetic concern is central for Luke is evident in the other form of the saying, 8:17. Here Luke has, to be sure, retained the phrase ". . . that shall not be known" from Q (cf. Matt.

1. Jeremias, *Parables*, 221, n. 66.
2. Hints have already been given in the Q material in chap. 11. That their teaching reflected a fraternal system, "almost a secret society," or involved esoteric teaching (Troadec, *Luc*, 145) is more explicit than Luke intends here, though perhaps not far from what he says in 15:1 and 16:14f.
3. Vs. Taylor, *Mk.*, 264, who thinks that Luke's version and setting are more probably original than Matthew's; *per contra*, see Creed, *Luke*, 170.

10:26f.), which destroys both the rhythm and the balanced parallelism of the saying,[4] but essentially his wording is a modification of Mk. The Markan hina-phrases in v. 22 have vanished, and the secrecy-theory with them. Mark's "Take heed what you hear" has been ethicized to "take heed how you hear" (v. 18a), and the first of the two contradictory principles of repayment urged by Mark (vv. 24f.) has been eliminated, so that emphasis is given to the promise for him who has. Furthermore, we may presume that Luke is not aware of (or not in sympathy with) the eschatological meaning v. 18 doubtless had in its earlier use by Christian prophets as a "sentence of holy law" and has, as often, understood the phrase gnomically.[5] It would agree with the wording in 8:17 and with Luke's general theological interests to see here a precise reference to the success of the Word (the time of relative hiddenness contrasted with the time of successful proclamation)[6] or a statement opposing esoteric tendencies in some Christian circles, although this is uncertain. What is clear is that Luke has made all of vv. 16–21 into a literary unit, an elaboration of the explanation of the Sower (vv. 11–15). Thus both the secrecy-motif (Mark) and the promise of Judgment (Q, Matthew) have receded, and the warning that a Day of revelation is coming is fitted into the context of a new promise: those who hear the Word of God and do it (v. 21) are truly related to Jesus. Because this is his theme, Luke does not, like Matthew, append new parables after using Mk. 4:21–25; instead he interprets what he takes over in a new parenetic, ethicized fashion. In his thought an inseparable connection exists between ethics, Christology, and the Word of God.

4. Luke has frequently weakened antithetic parallelisms, no doubt because "he felt this Semitic mode of speech to be unattractive" (Jeremias, NT Theology, I, 17).
5. So Käsemann, "Anfänge," 17f. (= NT Questions, 98f.).
6. Gnilka, Verstockung, 126.

PART
THREE

THE
MARKAN
PARABLES

Chapter Five

THE MARKAN THEORY
OF THE PARABLES

(4:10ff.; cf. Matt. 13:10–17; Lk. 8:9f.)

Several times in the course of this work reference has been made to the Markan "hardening theory." It is now time to discuss in detail just what this theory is and how it illuminates Mark's purpose in chapter 4. This chapter includes many awkward features which point to a combination of tradition and redaction: the situation varies between the presence and absence of the crowd; the phrase "those who were around him with the twelve" is quite obscure; the disciples' question (v. 10) is answered twice (vv. 11, 14f.) without actually being answered at all; and v. 33 cannot be harmonized with v. 34.

The last point is particularly important. In v. 33 Jesus speaks many parables, "as they were able to hear." This implies that the parables are an aid to understanding. And if, as seems probable, the four explanations given in the synoptic tradition (the Sower, the Tares, the Net, and the Things That Defile) are all to be assigned to the tradition and not to Jesus, the original clarity of the parables may almost be taken for granted. No one reading v. 33 alone would ever imagine that a parable needed or even tolerated an appended explanation.[1]

---

1. "Hear" in v. 33 = "hear and understand," a probable Semitism (Black, *Aram. Approach*[2], 235). The best explanation of v. 33 is that it reflects pre-Markan tradition. But Mark must have read the verse as if it meant something like "insofar as they were able to understand" (Willi Marxsen, "Redaktionsgeschichtliche Erklärung der sogenannten Parabeltheorie des Markus," *ZThK* 52 [1955], 255–271 [263] or "(only) insofar as they were able to hear (but not to understand)" (Heinz-Wolfgang Kuhn, *Ältere Sammlungen im Markus-evangelium* [Göttingen: Vandenhoeck & Ruprecht, 1971], 133); the latter is more in keeping with Mark's overall theological intention.

Yet this is precisely what v. 34 asserts: *everything* Jesus said was parabolic, and private explanations were given solely to the disciples, who without such explanations would have been as bewildered as the crowds.² We are thus led to expect that not only the parable of the Sower but all the parables were explained clearly and unambiguously, although Mark has recorded only one of the explanations. This presupposes that parables are obscure, not—as in v. 33—clear. It is impossible to believe that Jesus or Mark or any other single individual held both of these conceptions at the same time.

It should also be noted that an ambiguity exists in the use of the word "parable" itself. In the disciples' question (v. 10) only the narrow literary meaning, the parable as a form of indirect statement, is possible.³ In v. 34, however, he cannot mean that all of Jesus' teaching was of this literary form, since he has himself already included in his Gospel many non-parabolic statements. What he must mean in this passage is that a "parable" is any statement that includes an element of indirection, perhaps even of obscurity, and hence demands explanation. Furthermore, this obscurity resides in the statement, not in the heart of the hearer, since even those to whom the secret of the Kingdom has been given do not understand without an (unambiguous) explanation.

But what does the Markan question mean? Matthew (13:10) interprets it to mean, "Why do you speak to them in parables?" If this were the question, it might mean either "Why do you use this strange teaching method?" or "Why do you speak only in

---

2. While the disciples often do not understand Mark's Jesus, presumably they understand individual parables once they have been explained (or the explanations would have been omitted). It is thus most artificial to see the disciples as simple models of Mark's own opponents. On the other hand, if the "explanations" were simply a device to point up the paradoxical nature of revelation, they could well have been given to everyone.

3. The Heb. *māšāl* (Aram, *matlā'*) may mean "parable," "metaphor," "fable," and even "riddle." (Jeremias, *Parables*, 16, n.22. E. F. Siegmann, "Teaching in Parables . . . ," *CBQ* 23 [1961], 161–181 [174ff.] wrongly denies that *māšāl* ever means "riddle.") The same breadth is reflected in Greek-speaking Judaism, as the phrase *en ainigmasi parabolōn* in Sir. 39:3 shows; cf. also 47:16. In Greek and rabbinic thought parables are perspicuous and serve as illustrations. Elsewhere, esp. in apocalyptic, they are, in varying degrees, obscure. Texts and discussion are to be found in G. Minette de Tillesse, *Le secret messianique dans l'évangile de Marc* (Paris: Éditions du Cerf, 1968), 201–216.

parables instead of using both parables and other forms of discourse?" But there is no evidence that the use of parables was a strange teaching method (or that Mark thought it was), while the specific data of all the Gospels are against the view that Jesus taught solely in this particular way. On the other hand, Luke's restriction of the question to this one parable, ". . . what this parable might mean . . ."[4] is excluded by the Markan plural in both v. 10[5] and v. 11. The Sower is, to be sure, the longest Markan parable, and it may have held some place of priority in his mind.[6] But it is at most a good example of a universal phenomenon: Jesus' teaching as a whole—not merely the parables—is obscure. The repeated emphasis on explanation and private teaching to the disciples (but no others) makes it legitimate to add that this obscurity *could* have been removed by direct explication if Jesus had so chosen.

This, then, is the proper context for examining the notoriously complex problems in vv. 10–13: The Markan meaning in these verses must show either that Mark has imposed a theory of obscurity (v. 34) on a tradition of clarity (v. 33) or the other way around; and only the former alternative squares with the repeated emphasis in redactional passages on private teaching. The view that the parables are clear, consequently, is traditional.[7] V. 33, which teaches it, looks like the original ending of the discourse in Mark's source.[8] Hence—regardless of what some parts of vv. 10–13

---

4. 8:9. It is probable that this is also what was included in Mark's source, which would then be followed immediately by the explanation (vv. 14ff.).

5. The plural is, on both external and internal grounds, clearly to be preferred to any of the singular forms attested in the manuscript tradition.

6. "Do you not understand this parable? How then will you understand all the parables?" (4:13). G. H. Boobyer, "The Redaction of Mark iv. 1–34," *NTS* 8 (1961/62), 59–70 tries to relate v. 13 to vv. 10f. Although this attempt is based on the correct insight that v. 13 is redactional (cf. 7:17f.) and that a "parable" for Mark can be a story, an aphorism, or even an event, it shatters on the obvious fact that what is explained in vv. 14–20 is the "parable" of vv. 3–8, not the "hardening-parable" of vv. 10ff.

7. That v. 34 forms a perfect (chiastic) counterpoint to v. 11 means only that Mark created v. 34 on the basis of v. 11, not (vs. Minette de Tillesse, *Secret*, 177f., 183) that he created *both*.

8. Branscomb, *Mk.*, 77; Kuhn, *Ält. Samml.*, 134f. (and n. 58); Minette de Tillesse, *Secret*, 181 speaks of a *"quasi-unanimité des exégètes"* on the point.

may have meant in the pre-Markan tradition—we should interpret the details of these verses in Mark in the light of the following:

a. Any implication that the parables are clear is non-Markan.

b. The view that the parables are obscure is Markan, although it may also have been part of his tradition.

c. The theory of private explanations to the disciples (v. 34) is Markan, although this too may have been part of the stuff of his tradition in some form.

Another key to separating tradition from redaction in chapter 4 is found in v. 10: the question about the parables is asked by "those who were around him with the twelve." This phrase, which occurs nowhere else in the NT, must be the result either of Mark's adding the twelve to an originally anonymous tradition[9] or, conversely, of his adding others to a source that originally spoke only of the twelve.[10] In favor of the first view we might note that movement from the indefinite to the definite is rather well-attested in the tradition, especially in the post-biblical tradition. And in favor of the view that the pre-Markan material spoke only of the twelve one could point to the parallel in 7:17 and urge that the church of Mark's own day is surely in the author's mind,[11] so that he adds others to the twelve to include the preachers of his own time.

---

9. Bultmann, *HST*, 325, n. 1; Ernst Lohmeyer, *Das Evangelium des Markus* (17. Aufl., Göttingen: Vandenhoeck & Ruprecht, 1967), n. 1.; Haenchen, *Weg*, 164; Eduard Schweizer, *Das Evangelium nach Markus* (12. Aufl., Göttingen: Vandenhoeck & Ruprecht, 1968), 51; Siegmann, "Teachnig," 166, n. 10; Kuhn *Alt. Samml.*, 137. Charles Masson, *Les Paraboles de Marc IV* (Paris: Delachaux & Niestlé, 1945), 23f., 29 thinks that both phrases are pre-Markan, one originally associated with v. 11 and one with vv. 10, 13; but this is unnecessary.

10. Loisy, *ES*, I, 742; Marxsen, "Red. Erklärung," 261 leaves the question open. Johnson, *Mk.*, 89 merely suggests the possibility of conflation, without attempting to separate the earlier from the later reading. Grammatically, one would expect in this case "the twelve and those around them. . . ." Minette de Tillesse, *Secret*, 175–179, 187, in a very careful discussion of the problem, seems to side with Marxsen (see next note) on Mark's intention while ascribing the phrase largely to Mark. R. P. Meye, "Mark 4:10: 'Those about Him with the Twelve,'" in *Studia Evangelica* II, ed. F. L. Cross (Berlin: Akademie-Verlag, 1964), 211–218 cuts the Gordian knot by interpreting the phrase as "some belonging to the twelve," but I cannot make the Greek say this, nor am I persuaded that Mark knows of only and precisely twelve disciples, as Meye suggests.

11. So (or similarly) Loisy, *ES*, I, 742; Lohmeyer, *Mk.*, 83; Marxsen, "Red. Erklärung," 267; *per contra*, Gnilka, *Verstockung*, 29, n. 4, who finds this detail historical on the grounds that Mark considers the church of Jesus' day *representative* of his own church.

53097

On balance, the former view is more probable, since any mention of the twelve anywhere in early Christian tradition probably implies that someone thought their authority had been somehow communicated, whether "others" are mentioned in connection with them or not. And although Mark is very reserved about the use of the term "apostle" (3:14; 6:30), he freely adds the twelve to his sources.[12] What is quite certain is that Mark intends vv. 10–13 as a private communication; while he might not have wished to restrict the hearers to the twelve, he cannot have wished the entire "very large crowd" (v. 1) to hear. This is made explicit in the insistence that Jesus and his hearers were "alone." When this or similar expressions occur in Mark[13] they intend a contrast between disciples and crowds; this contrast and the esoteric teaching which it implies provide another note by which Markan redaction may be separated from pre-Markan tradition.

As for the saying itself (vv. 11f.), the important elements include the "secret of the Kingdom" (v. 11), the contrast between the disciples and outsiders, and the purpose clauses introduced by "in order that" (*hina*, v. 12a) and "lest" (*mēpote*, v. 12c). An analysis of these elements makes it clear that the saying in vv. 11f. comes from pre-Markan tradition, not from the evangelist.

The "secret" (*mysterion*) of the Kingdom is not elaborated here; it is merely some secret that outsiders, whose hearts are hardened,

---

12. For evidence that the well-attested words "whom he also named apostles" are original in Mk. 3:14 and a careful discussion of the relationship between the "apostles" and the twelve in the theology of Mark, see Haenchen, *Weg*, 247–250; cf. also Günter Klein, *Die zwölf Apostel: Ursprung und Gehalt einer Idee* (Göttingen: Vandenhoeck & Ruprecht, 1961), 202–210. Kuhn, *Ält. Samml.*, 137 (incl. n. 64) notes that of the dozen or so occurrences of the "twelve" in Mk., at least four (4:10; 9:35; 10:32; 11:11) are clearly redactional. (Several others could be, as well.)

T. A. Burkill, "St. Mark's Philosophy of History," *NTS* 3 (1956/57), 142–148 (148) rightly insists that "although [the disciples] . . . cannot understand the divine word when it is communicated to them, they can retain it as authentic tradition and can thus equip themselves for their future role as apostles and pillars of the church."

13. 7:17–23; 8:27–30; 9:28f., 33ff.; 10:10ff.; 12:35ff.; 13:3—such passages are clearly redactional. I also agree with Minette de Tillesse, *Secret*, 175 vs. Gnilka *Verstockung*, 58f. that both *kata monas* (4:10 only) and *kat' idian* (all other instances) are Markan, in spite of the *"discordance criante"* (Minette de Tillesse, *Secret*, 186) between 4:10 and Mark's own introduction to the whole section (4:1, 2).

do not have. The term itself, much discussed,[14] is of uncertain significance. One possible meaning is "hidden or esoteric teaching," something that is not so much obscure as unknown to those without the interpretive key.[15] This kind of teaching is given secretly, primarily to protect its holiness from outsiders, and it may be unequivocally explained. Such an interpretation would fit well with what we have described above as Mark's intention in v. 34. But this motif is comparatively rare in the Scripture.

A more common view, especially in Paul (Rom. 11:25; 1 Cor. 4:1; 15:51; and 18 other occurrences in Paul and the deutero-Paulines) is that, as in apocalyptic,[16] a "mystery" is too profound *in itself* for human understanding; it is thus something that is grasped, if at all, by revelation, not by explanation from initiate to non-initiate. This meaning clearly squares better with the wording of v. 11 than the first, since this secret has already been given to the disciples.[17] Hence we may tentatively conclude that while

14. See, *inter alia*, J. Armitage Robinson, *St. Paul's Epistle to the Ephesians* (London: Macmillan & Co., Ltd., 1903), 234–240; Günther Bornkamm, "*mysterion myeō*," *TDNT*, IV, 802–828; D. Deden, "Le 'Mystère' paulinien," *ETL* 13 (1936), 405–442.

15. So E. P. Gould, *A Critical and Exegetical Commentary on the Gospel According to St. Mark* (Edinburgh: T. & T. Clark, 1896), 71; McNeile, *Matt.*, 189; Alfred Loisy, *L'Évangile selon Marc* (Paris: Emile Nourry, 1912), 131f. and *ES*, I, 741; cf Johnson, *Mk.*, 89f.; Branscomb, *Mk.*, 79. The verb *myō*, from which *mystērion* ultimately derives, meant originally "to shut" (the eyes, the mouth, etc.); cf. *prin mysai* "in the twinkling of an eye": cited in the supplement to Liddell and Scott's lexicon, 102.

16. It is used in the technical sense of "secret rites" in Wisd. 14:15, 23 but of "Gods secret purposes" in Dan. 2:18f., 28ff., 47; Wisd. 2:22; 6:22; 8:4. For texts in apocalyptic and Qumran, with discussion, see Minette de Tillesse, *Secret*, 195–200.

17. Opposed to the "mystery" in v. 11 is *ta panta* (ℵ D Θ omit *ta*), a Semitism which implies not "everything in the world" but only "everything that has been given to the disciples." This would be primarily the understanding of Jesus' true nature as Messiah (Bornkamm, *TDNT*, IV, 819; William Wrede, *Das Messiasgeheimnis in den Evangelien* [1901; 3. unveränd. Aufl., Göttingen: Vandenhoeck & Ruprecht, 1963], 58f. [ET: 57ff.]; Hauck, *Mk.*, 54; Schmid, *Mk.*, 95; C. E. B. Cranfield, *The Gospel According to St. Mark* [Cambridge: Cambridge University Press, 1959], 153, 157) or the dawning of the Kingdom itself (Jeremias, *Parables*, 16; Conzelmann, *Theology . . . Luke*, 103 seems to think of this as the Markan meaning) or (for Mark) "the secret of the revelation itself, i.e., the Word of the Cross" (Eduard Schweizer, "Die theologische Leistung des Markus," *EvTheol* 24 [1964], 337–355 [346]) or, still more generally, the presence of the Kingdom "hidden to the world but revealed to faith in the person of Jesus, in his words and in his acts" (Masson, *Paraboles*, 21f.) or simply "the entire economy of the Kingdom" (Minette de Tillesse *Secret*, 188).

Since this mystery implies knowledge of the Kingdom already inaugurated, not a special source of knowledge for the intelligent, it is, as Bonnard suggests (*Matt.*,

Mark understood the text to imply esoteric teaching, the saying itself does not. If it arose in the pre-Markan tradition (or with Jesus) it would have implied, as in the rest of the NT, a kind of "knowledge" gained through revelation. As such it is not primarily cognitive.

Those who have received this gift are distinguished from others who are described as *hoi eksō,* literally, "those who are outside." *hoi eksō(then)* (= *hoi ektos,* etc.) is a quasi-technical term used among many religious groups for those who are outside the society,[18] and the avoidance of the term by both Matthew and Luke could imply that they recognized and rejected its technical use, although this is uncertain. But there is no need to understand the term in a specifically esoteric sense in the Markan tradition; *some* expression for the non-disciples is required. Mark himself may either have modified the wording at this point or understood it in a more technical sense than his tradition intended (i.e., "outside the church").[19] On the other hand, it is certainly a very strong term to imagine on the lips of Jesus, and it is instructive to note that Jeremias[20] can affirm the authenticity of the saying only by ascribing it to "the period [!] of the secret teaching of Jesus." In sum, this phrase cannot have come from Jesus and need not have come from Mark; it is best understood as having arisen in the post-dominical but pre-Markan tradition.

The "purpose" clauses are more difficult. The text clearly implies a "hardening theory," i.e., that God (or Jesus) did not intend all

---

193, n. 1) of the Matthean usage, "at once both more radical and more open" than the "gnostic esoterism" of such passages as 1 En. 1:2ff. and 1 Q H 2:13. A. E. J. Rawlinson, *St. Mark* (London: Methuen & Co., Ltd., 1925), 51f. notes that Mark's Gentile readers might well have mistakenly understood the term to imply that Christianity was a mystery-religion.

18. Johannes Behm, "*eksō,*" *TDNT,* II, 575f. See Sir. Prol. 5; 1 Cor. 5:12f.; Col. 4:5; 1 Tim. 3:7; 2 Clem. 13:1; Thucyd. V. 14.3 (Loeb, II, 26: "Those beyond the border" = "those who had escaped"); Lucian, *On Salaried Posts* 21 (Loeb, III, 446). For the rabbinic usage of *haḥisonim,* Gentiles or heterodox Jews, see Billerbeck II, 7; III, 362.

19. Erich Grässer, "Jesus in Nazareth (Mark vi.1–6a): Notes on the Redaction and Theology of St. Mark," *NTS* 16 (1969/70), 1–23 (21) rightly notes that 6:1–6 serves "as a retrospective confirmation of the term to iv.12, the impenitence of those who are standing 'outside.'" The people of Nazareth show by their unbelief that they are "outsiders." It is apparent (vs. Masson, *Paraboles,* 26) that at every stage the phrase means more than "outside the house."

20. *Parables,* 18.

men to heed and thus hardened the hearts of some. This is the obvious meaning of both *hina* ("in order that") and *mēpote* ("lest"). Many commentators, however, read *hina* as a kind of shorthand for *hina plērōthē*, "in order that (the Scripture) might be fulfilled," suggesting that the action of speaking in parables (or granting the secret to some and withholding it from others) serves as a fulfillment of the scriptural quotation (Is. 6:9f.) which follows.[21] But this elaboration of the text is not only without supporting examples in Markan usage and thought;[22] it is also contrary to the primary meaning of *mēpote*, which is "lest." And the attempt to translate *mēpote* as "lest perhaps" or "unless"—which suggests a theoretical possibility of eventual conversion—is grammatically unlikely and contextually impossible: this "optimistic" interpretation of *mēpote* is elsewhere always clear in the context, while in this instance it would rob the scriptural quotation of its force.[23] Other weakening translations[24] are open to similar grammatical objections. Writing long after the Jewish rejection of Jesus was an accomplished fact, Mark cannot have had any objection to describing the *result* of Jesus' ministry or any aspect of it as identical with its *intention*. It is perhaps best, therefore, to see this hardening theory as simply one aspect of his whole theology of discipleship: those who refuse to believe find their hearts hardened and their unbelief confirmed by God.

If, then, the "secret" of the Kingdom may be pre-Markan, since its evident meaning does not bear the special Markan esoteric

21. M.-J. Lagrange, *Évangile selon Saint Marc* (Paris: Librairie Lecoffre, J. Gabalda et Cⁱᵉ, 1947), 95; Jeremias, *Parables*, 17; Siegmann, "Teaching," 176 ("Today it is admitted quite generally . . ."!). Minette de Tillesse, *Secret*, 192ff. holds to this as the pre-Markan meaning, although he seems to retain it as an element in Mark's interpretation as well.
22. Alfred Suhl, *Die Funktion der alttestamentlichen Zitate und Anspielungen im Markusevangelium* (Gütersloh: Gütersloher Verlagshaus [Gerd Mohn], 1965), 149, 166–169 and *passim* casts doubt on the basic premise of the argument: Promise and fulfillment are not a central Markan theme. But Suhl's own view, that the *hina* is consecutive (". . . and so . . .") and that Mark himself created vv. 11f. (see 145–152), has little to commend it.
23. Gnilka, *Verstockung*, 28.
24. Such as that *hina* may be the equivalent of *hōste* or *hoti*, as in later Greek (Lohmeyer, *Mk.*, 84): on this, see Hans Windisch, "Die Verstockungsidee in Mc 4,12 und das kausale *hina* der späteren Koine," *ZNW* 26 (1927), 203–219.

emphasis, and if both the "outsider" phrase and the "purpose" clauses need not be interpreted as including such an emphasis, it is probable that the saying in vv. 11f. is pre-Markan and implies hardening but not esoteric teaching. Its Semitic elements attest its antiquity: the reverential passive, antithetic parallelism, the redundant demonstrative *ekeinos*, the use of a participle plus a finite verb (an attempt to express in Greek the emphatic Hebrew infinitive absolute), the peculiar (Semitic) expression *ginetai en* (Aram. *hᵃwa lᵉ bᵉ*), and above all the fact that the quotation agrees with the Targum against both the MT and the LXX.[25] These details also indicate a *Palestinian* and not merely a *Semitic* milieu for the origin of the saying. Somewhere in Mark's tradition —and apparently not in his immediate tradition—the saying arose, circulated independently, and was inserted by Mark in its present place.

Does this tradition extend back to the historical Jesus? Many commentators insist that it does, naturally in Aramaic, not Greek. But the various arguments urged in support of this contention are by no means convincing. It is of course true that the saying should be completely dissociated from parabolic *speech*.[26] While Mark

---

25. The text may conveniently be found in J. F. Stenning, *The Targum of Isaiah* (Oxford: Oxford University Press, 1949), 22f., 180f., 192f.

26. The following points should all be noted: a) the Markan question is vague; b) the question is answered twice (vv. 11, 13); c) Markan *hapax legomena* include *mysterion, dedotai* as a circumlocution for the divine action, *hoi exō, ta panta*, and *epistrephein* for conversion (Jeremias, *Parables*, 15); d) an inconsistency exists between 4:11a and such passages as 4:34 and (in a different way) 6:51f.; 8:17, 32; e) the present tense *kai legei autois* (v. 13), as in 7:18, though not simply a continuation of the conversation (vs. Gnilka, *Verstockung*, 24, nn. 2, 3), is indicative of the way Jesus answers a question (never *elegen*, impf.) and involves a slight shift to a new thought; it does not begin a new section, a purpose for which Mark ordinarily uses *kai elegen autois* (note: this is just what one could expect if the present tense is pre-Markan and *kai elegen autois* comes from Mark himself—so Kuhn, *Ält. Samml.*, 167; cf. M. Zerwick, *Untersuchungen zum Markus-Stil* [Rome: Pontifical Biblical Institute, 1937], 38, 67–70); f) the composite nature of the whole section is clear, while the explanation (to the *crowd*, not merely to the disciples!), which immediately follows (vv. 13–20), almost certainly comes from a time and place different from that of the parable proper; g) the strongly Semitic character of the saying contrasts sharply with the Hellenistic Gospel as a whole; h) the best place to insert a discussion of this kind is after an obscure parable but before the explanation of it, which is just where we find it. The pre-Markan text of 4:10 thus probably read, ". . . about the parable [sing.] . . ." and continued with v. 13—so, *inter alia*, J. Wellhausen, *Das Evangelium Marci übersetzt und erklärt* (1. Aufl., Berlin: Georg Reimer, 1903; 2.

doubtless saw a connection with parables, the only connection in the text is the single phrase, "in parables." Here *parabolē*, a word of notoriously broad meaning, implies only an enigmatic, indirect quality of some kind, and the phrase may best be translated as an adverb, "enigmatically" or "in riddles." Further, the Greek verb *ginetai* must have stood either for some Aramaic verb implying "happen" or "come about"[27] or for the simple copula. Hence the saying most naturally refers to the enigmatic nature of some aspect of Jesus' ministry, not to parabolic speech as such; if the latter had been intended, the saying would have read "all things are spoken in parables," which is exactly what it does not say.[28] It is perfectly legitimate, therefore, to urge that the statement originally had nothing to do with teaching in parables (as a literary form) and that consequently the well-known objections to the authenticity of the saying are of little force insofar as they rest on such modern assumptions as "Jesus could not have used parables to conceal his meaning."

The rest of the linguistic details, however, do not strongly encourage the view that the saying itself is authentic. Essentially, most of those who ascribe the saying to Jesus hold that not only its parabolic context but also its interpretation in Mk. are entirely different from what they were originally (in Aramaic). But most of the proposed Aramaic reconstructions currently in vogue are, in varying degrees, unconvincing.

This may be illustrated by the retranslation of *hina* and *mēpote*, the crucial terms in Mark's "hardening" theory.[29] One suggestion is that *hina* is a mistranslation of the Aramaic *dᵉ*, which is actually

---

Aufl., 1909), 33; Marxsen, "Red. Erklärung," 260f.; Haenchen, *Weg*, 161, n. 2, 168. Schmid, *Mk.*, 93 notes that the reproach (v. 13) suggests that the original question referred to a single parable.

27. Gnilka, *Verstockung*, 24–28 argues persuasively for "happen" or "become" ("*geschehen in*" or "*wird zu*"), not merely "are." Masson, *Paraboles*, 20ff. and Minette de Tillesse, *Secret*, 188: "*Arriver*," "*devenir*," i.e., "*tout se passe en paraboles.*" This is surely correct *for Mk.*

28. Vs. Günther Bornkamm, *Jesus of Nazareth* (New York: Harper & Bros., 1960), 201, n. 11, who sees both halves of the verse as giving instruction; cf. Schmid, *Mk.*, 94: "*die Lehrtätigkeit Jesu überhaupt.*"

29. For the discussion see Billerbeck, I, 663; Jeremias, *Parables*, 15ff.; Gnilka, *Verstockung*, 24–28; Taylor, *Mk.*, 256ff.

used in the Targum and could be rendered "who." V. 12 would then be epexegetical and read, "those who are without, who . . . ," etc. Even if we were certain of the equation $hina = d^e$, however (which we are not), we should still have to take account of the fact that the use of a relative particle so far from its antecedent is unlikely (though by no means impossible), and the translation of d^e as "in order that" is perfectly acceptable, though less common than the relative. The cumulative force of these reservations, then, cannot but raise serious questions about this interpretation of the saying as a whole.

Similar difficulties attend the suggestion that $m\bar{e}pote = dilm\bar{a}'$ should be rendered not "lest" but "unless." Evidence for this is supposedly provided by the fact that rabbinic exegesis (at least in the four examples cited by Billerbeck) understood Is. 6:10b as a promise, not a threat, holding open the door to Israel's eventual repentance. But this argument is even more precarious than the other. For one thing, these traditions are not very early.[30] Further, the same interpretation of Is. 6:10 can be found in the LXX, and there it is an interpretation of (not the Aramaic but) the *Hebrew* text! The obvious conclusion is that the rabbis' views rest, like those of the LXX translators, on theological convictions about Israel's election, not on ambiguities in the Aramaic language. In short, "unless" is an impossible translation of the Hebrew and an unlikely translation of the Aramaic.[31]

What we seem to be left with, then, is the choice between a hardening theory that goes back to Jesus and one that does not, since a mediating (Aramaic) understanding of the statement which would not imply "hardening" has been shown to be unlikely.[32] But it is difficult to ascribe any such theory, either in

---

30. The earliest is R. Eleazar b. Jose (c.180).

31. The polemic in the last passage cited in Billerbeck (Seder Elij R 16 [82]) includes specifically the comment that the concluding words of the passage *seem* to assert that God does not will Israel's penitent conversion. This meaning is denied, however, not on the basis of any linguistic ambiguities (Hebrew or Aramaic) but on theological grounds.

32. For various unsatisfactory explanations of the Greek text which would eliminate the hardening theory, see Jülicher, *Gleichn.*, I, 131–145.

general or with reference to the parables, to Jesus, not on a priori grounds[33] but on the basis of the data. For there are no parallel texts to support the theory. And it is clearly eliminated by Jesus' concourse with ordinary, unsophisticated people and by the central theme of his message: the eschatologically based call to repentance.[34] A statement of this kind presupposes a situation in which rejection of the message has already taken place, not in the mind and intention of God, but within the ongoing context of history. Even the Isaiah passage cannot be used as a historical example, since as Hans-Walter Wolff has shown, on form-critical grounds the personal call of the prophet and his message must be separated, while the central message in the prophetic calls to repentance is promise, not threat.[35] Theological reflection, not actual prophetic calls, creates the view that God's messenger is called and *simultaneously* warned not only that the people will not hear but the God does not intend them to hear.

In early Christian tradition, then, vv. 11f. represent the theological solution to the problem of unbelief: God has hardened the unbelieving heart (cf. Rom. 9:18–29; 10:16–21; 11:8ff.). To this Mark (or his immediate tradition) has added two new elements: a) the whole ministry of Jesus, especially the teaching in parables, is intended to do this, and b) the disciples share, though to a lesser degree, in the general blindness. That both Markan elements, like the hardening theory itself, conflict to some extent with Jesus' intention that men heed this message and understand his mission is evident.[36] But it is a dangerous assumption that the Markan text is consequently a simple misunderstanding of little

---

33. "If he had not wished them to hear and be saved, he should have kept quiet, not spoken in parables." (Chrysostom, *In Matt. hom.* 45, n. 2. [Migne PG 58, 473].)

34. It is impossible to evaluate such suggestions as that Jesus spoke in irony or that Isaiah "hoped to shock his hearers into obedience" (Johnson, *Mk.*, 90).

35. Hans-Walter Wolff, "Das Thema 'Umkehr' in der atlichen Prophetie," *ZThK* 48 (1951), 129–138.

36. Vs. Kingsbury, *Parables*, 51. Kingsbury speaks, to be sure, of Matt. 13:10–17, not Mk. 4:10ff., and he is quite right that Matthew, like Jesus, uses the parables in a way befitting the situation. But this does not mean, as Kingsbury suggests, that a conflict between Jesus and *any* form of the hardening theory is a mere "postulate."

theological value. Preaching always includes both a yes and a no. And Mark gives a serious theological judgment on a lamentable fact. Is his hardening theory uncongenial to us because we understand Jesus better than he? Might it not also be so because we are not quite so serious? Or even (God forbid!) because our own understanding of the parables as limpid illustrations allows us to explain the "mystery of unbelief" in simplistic intellectual or moral terms?

Chapter Six

THE MARKAN PARABLES

Although the precise definition of a "parable" is notoriously difficult—and, for our purposes, not very important—it seems likely that about sixteen Markan passages should be classified as parabolic. These sixteen passages are discussed below. It would perhaps be more nearly consistent if only those parables modified by both Matthew and Luke (as., e.g., the Wicked Husbandmen) were treated here, since then every text could be seen in its threefold form. For the sake of completeness, however, all the Markan parables are discussed below, whether they occur in all three Gospels, in only Mk. and one other Gospel, or in Mk. alone. This chapter thus amounts to a complete study of the Markan parables.

1. The Physician (2:15ff.; cf. Matt. 9:12f.; Lk. 5:31f.)

The saying, "Those who are well have no need of a physician, but those who are sick do" is probably a secular *māšāl* of uncertain application[1] which may or may not have been used by Jesus himself.[2] In its Markan setting, it is somehow directed against "the scribes of the Pharisees," a very awkward phrase[3] which in Mark's mind must have been intended to represent the scribes who belonged to the Pharisaic party, or (perhaps) who had Pharisaic

---

1. Schmid, *Mk.*, 65 notes that similar sayings are common among the philosophers to justify consorting with "*schlechten Leuten.*" See, e.g., Pausanias and Aristippus in Plut. *Moralia* 230F (Loeb, III, 382).

2. Cf. McNeile, *Matt.*, 119; Haenchen, *Weg*, 111; Bultmann, *HST*, 81, 104f.; Creed, *Luke*, 181f. For a brief (and not entirely convincing) defense of the view that secular proverbs can plausibly be fitted into Jesus' eschatological teaching, see Appendix xi in W. D. Davies, *Setting*, 457–460.

3. The variants "scribes of the Pharisees" ($\aleph$ bo^{pt}) and "the scribes and the Pharisees" in slightly different forms (C $\aleph$ A D Θ *pl* sy^p sa^{pt} bo^{pt}) are easier (and secondary) variations of *hoi grammateis tōn Pharisaiōn* (B W sa^{pt}).

sympathies. The phrase is unusual—and so is the setting: Mark seems to think of these opponents as present, either at the actual meal (which they would hardly have countenanced) or at least in or near the house where the meal was taking place.[4] But once Mark's intention becomes clear, this problem, like others in the narrative, becomes comprehensible.

What Mark has done is create an artificial scene out of materials, including an apothegm (vv. 16–17b), that probably had at least minimal scenery of its own. He has tried to do so with familiar groups of people for opponents and familiar surroundings for the dialogue: In 2:13 Jesus is beside the sea (a detail omitted by Matthew and Luke), which is the place Mark ordinarily puts Jesus when he is instructing the people, however little contextual sense it may make here.[5] In 2:15ff., however, Jesus is with several of his disciples (probably more than the five whose call has been described, but not very many more, since there is a limit to the hospitality of small villages toward large crowds of guests)[6] in Levi's[7] house. In Mk., the house is the place of private fellowship

---

4. A scholar "should not take a set meal (i.e., recline) in the company of ignorant persons (i.e., the *am ha-aretz*)" because "perhaps he will be drawn into their ways" (Ber. 43b). Creed suggests that the scribes may have made the actual complaint somewhere else, after Jesus had left his unacceptable table-fellows (*Luke*, 82) and Lagrange thinks of the next day or even later (*Matt.*, 182).

5. Karl Ludwig Schmidt, *Der Rahmen der Geschichte Jesu* (Darmstadt: Wissenschaftliche Buchgesellschaft, 1969 [repr. of 1919 ed.]), 82f. argues that v. 13 does not fit very well with what immediately follows. The reason for this is probably that Mark is editing some kind of (brief) collection, so that the "seams" show; if he had created the entire context for *all* the individual elements in chap. 2, the difficulties would not be so evident. (So, rightly, Kuhn, *Ält. Samml.*, 86. B. M. F. Van Iersel, "La vocation de Lévi (Mc., II, 13–17, Mt., IX, 9–13, Lc., V, 27–32)," in I. de la Potterie et al., *De Jésus aux Évangiles* [Gembloux/Paris: J. Duculot/P. Lethielleux, 1967], 212–232 [220] also insists that v. 13 is redactional.) Rudolf Pesch, "Das Zöllnergastmahl (Mk. 2, 15–17)," in *Mélanges Bibliques en hommage au R. P. Béda Rigaux* (Gembloux: J. Duculot, 1970), 63–87 (esp. 68f., 72, 78) translates *hoi grammateis tōn Pharisaiōn* simply as "*die pharisäischen Schriftgelehrten*" or "*die Schriftgelehrten der pharisäischen Laiengenossenschaft*" and explains the fact that the Pharisees "saw" Jesus' action (at a meal at which he grants that they could not have been present) as quite in accord with form-critically recognizable rules of story-telling.

6. Haenchen, *Weg*, 110.

7. It is not clear whether Mark intends the house of Jesus (Lohmeyer, *Mk.*, 55, citing Matt. 4:15 and Jn. 2:12; Jeremias, *Parables*, 227, n. 92; Gould, *Mk.*, 41) or of Levi (Loisy, *Mc.*, 91; Rawlinson, *Mk.*, 28; Swete, *Mk.*, 38; Taylor, *Mk.*,

and esoteric teaching; outsiders do not belong here. Hence Mark describes the tax collectors and sinners who are seated with Jesus as followers.[8] And the opponents, who are near enough to observe but not near enough to converse with Jesus directly, speak to the disciples; Jesus, overhearing them,[9] replies.[10]

Mark's theological understanding of places thus becomes the real explanation of the very unusual fact that the Pharisaic question[11] is directed to the disciples, not to Jesus himself,[12] even though it is Jesus' action against which the complaint is lodged and Jesus who replies—an abnormality that not only calls into serious question the authenticity of any presumed pre-Markan controversy-story[13] but also raises the possibility that Mark's materials were not really "apothegmatic" in form. In the next section (2:18–22), however, he is no longer in the house, so the people come to him and question him directly. Once assume that the

---

204; Haenchen, *Weg*, 108f.; Walter Grundmann, *Das Evangelium nach Markus* [2. Aufl., Berlin: Evangelische Verlagsanstalt, 1959], 61; Johnson, *Mk.*, 61, who however thinks the pre-Markan tradition may have understood it differently and cites v. 1 as evidence; D. E. Nineham, *St. Mark* [London: Penguin, 1963], 99).

8. The subject of *ēkolouthoun* is ambiguous. But Markan usage makes it clear that those in the house cannot include Jesus' opponents. It is generally recognized that v. 15c is Markan and was created to explain the abrupt introduction here of Jesus' disciples, who have not yet been mentioned; but this does not (vs. Pesch, "Zöllner," 65) necessarily presuppose all of v. 15ab in the pre-Markan tradition. More probably all of v. 15 is redactional; cf. Van Iersel, "Vocation," 220, 225, who correctly notes the important function v. 15 plays in the transition from a specific call (v. 14) to the whole of Jesus' ministry (vv. 16–17).

9. Or, hearing of the charge from others (*akousas*).

10. To them, not to the people in general; the textual evidence for the omission of *autois* is (vs. Taylor, *Mk.*, 207) extremely weak. It is also highly improbable that Jesus is portrayed as hearing the *disciples* (see previous note) and responding to them (so Van Iersel, "Vocation," 222), although this would obviate the difficulty of the atypical form of controversy-discourse.

11. The *hoti* could be *recitativum*, introducing a simple (accusatory) statement (Hauck, *Mk.*, 36); but it is more probably interrogative (= *ti hoti*). The use of the third person singular in reproaches in common: Mk. 2:7, 16; 3:21, 22 (*bis*), 30; 4:41; 6:2f., 14ff.; 7:37(?); cf. Van Iersel, "Vocation," 217, n. 10.

12. The view that they did not attack Jesus directly out of respect or fear (McNeile, *Matt.*, 118; Swete, *Mk.*, 40; Haenchen, *Weg*, 109; Loisy, *Mc.*, 92ff., who however sees a *progression* in the degrees of hostility reflected in subsequent Markan incidents) takes insufficient account of the hostility implied in the question addressed to Jesus only a verse or two later (v. 18) and again in 2:24 (cf. also 3:2).

13. Van Iersel, "Vocation," 222 grants that vv. 16–17a do not simply reproduce some historical discussion.

overall scene is a Markan construct[14]—although elements of the
pre-Markan framework may show through in minor details—and
the problem becomes unreal. Similarly, we need not wonder why
Levi leaves his position at the tax office instantly, unhesitatingly,[15]
nor how, having done so, he is any longer able to afford such a
banquet. It is also fruitless to seek a literary or catechetical unity
in vv. 13–17, since the connections are unclear and since some of
the material probably comes from a pre-Markan collection in any
case.

The Markan meaning, however, is generally quite clear. As in
most double-edged sayings, the emphasis lies on the second member of the clause:[16] "[Not those who are well but] those who are
sick need a physician; I came to call [not the righteous but] sinners."[17] Mark's intention is thus both to justify Jesus' action in eating with sinners (and the theology implied in such an action)[18]
and to condemn those who oppose it on principle; it is no part of
his intention here to insist that sinners must repent.[19] One hardly

14. Van Iersel, "Vocation," 217ff. argues that Mark's tradition contained a nearly
perfect apothegm (vv. 16–17a), to which v. 17b was added. This is inherently
plausible, and it has the great advantage of separating the two halves of v. 17
and thus of minimizing the problems of ascribing v. 17b in its present context to
Jesus. If the pre-Markan tradition did contain an apothegm, however, v. 17a
(which contains problems in any case) is a very unusual and atypical ending.
Furthermore, the scenery is so condensed and problematic that no pre-Markan
apothegm is really recoverable from our text. On balance, then, it seems best to
assume that Mark received both v. 17a and v. 17b from his tradition (possibly
with some narrative setting), while he is largely responsible for the present context himself. On these grounds v. 17a and v. 17b are really best thought of as a
single composite saying for Mark.
15. Porphyry notes the psychological improbability of this and suggests Matthew's
mental weakness; Jerome counters with Jesus' personal magnetism (Swete, Mk.,
38); Schmid, Mk., 64 speaks of "the extraordinarily moving force of Jesus' word
and personality. . . ." For Mark, however, it is self-evident that when the Son of
God calls, men abandon all other security and respond without hesitation. Cf.
1:18, 20 as well as Lk. 5:11, 28 and see Van Iersel, "Vocation," 222.
16. The pattern "not a but b" is used esp. to emphasize the *affirmative* statement;
see Heinz Kruse, "Die 'Dialektische Negation' als semitisches Idiom," VT 4
(1954), 385–400.
17. The addition of *eis metanoian* (C 𝔄 *al* a c r' [vg] sa^pt bo^pt) is surely due to
Lukan influence on the textual tradition, as is the similar addition in Matt.—in
many of the same texts!
18. On this, see Lohmeyer-Schmauch, Matt., 174 and the works of Ernst Fuchs,
esp. his "Bemerkungen zur Gleichnisauslegung," *Zur Frage nach dem historischen
Jesus* (Tübingen: J. C. B. Mohr [Paul Siebeck], 1960), 136–142.
19. The elaborative additions in Just. *Apol.* I.15 ("For the heavenly Father wills
the sinner's repentance, not his punishment") and the passage from Ps. Clem II
Cor 2 cited by Swete (*Mk.*, 40) are homiletic applications but nothing more; see
also Jülicher, *Gleichn.*, II, 177.

needs to add that it is absurd to force this text into the doctrine
of total depravity, so that the "righteous" really become the "self-
righteous."[20] This completely extraneous idea would carry the
corollary that Jesus should have spent his time eating with Pharisees! Even less plausible is the use of the text to show that in
Jesus' day some naturally just men really did exist.[21]

But does the saying originate with Jesus, with the pre-Markan
tradition, or with Mark himself? We may somewhat hesitantly
eliminate the first possibility, even for v. 17a (and, more strongly,
for v. 17b). While there is no insuperable obstacle to accepting a
general wisdom-saying like v. 17a nor any conclusive argument
for denying that Jesus could have used it in just this kind of context,[22] it should be pointed out that wisdom-sayings are not in any
way distinctive of Jesus, they do not reflect the eschatologically
based call to repentance which formed the heart of his message,
and there are no sayings of this type so indubitably authentic that
they can carry less certain sayings over with them. The attached
"I have come" saying (v. 17b), though not necessarily originally
part of this context, is similarly a reflection of christological
thought in the apostolic age rather than of Jesus' own understanding of his vocation.[23] It goes far beyond the sense of a prophetic
call, and although it does not necessarily imply preexistence,[24] it
reflects a specific dogmatic conviction of somewhat Docetic tendencies. Apart from these general considerations, however, the say-

20. A recurrent view in the history of criticism; cf. Taylor, *Mk.*, 207 and the
patristic material cited above, chap. 4, sec. 1, n. 11.
21. Lagrange, *Mc.*, 40 rightly rejects this example of older anti-Protestant polemic.
Pesch, "Zöllner," 80 thinks the term can only have arisen before *dikaioi* became
a Christian technical term; it must therefore refer to the Jewish *ṣāddîqîm* and must
have originated in a Palestinian-Jewish milieu.
22. Haenchen, *Weg*, 111; Van Iersel, "Vocation," 223 is noncommittal. On the
other hand, as Lohmeyer rightly points out (*Mk.*, 56), the question of eating with
publicans and sinners is already settled for the Pharisees. It is a real question only
for a Jewish-Christian community. But the context is admittedly a Markan construct, and v. 17a may originally have had nothing to do with Jesus' table-
fellowship.
23. Loisy, *Mc.*, 93; Bultmann, *HST*, 92, 155; Nineham, *Mk.*, 98; Dodd, *Parables*,
118; cf. also Kuhn, *Ält. Samml.*, 94. Per contra, Pesch, "Zöllner," 79ff., who insists
that many of the *ēlthen*-sayings are secondary, but that the *ēlthon*-sayings are
authentic; and esp. the long footnote (25) on p. 223 in Van Iersel, "Vocation."
24. Lagrange, *Mc.*, 40 so understands it; he also accepts its authenticity. So also,
hesitantly, Cranfield, *Mk.*, 106.

ing itself assumes the Pharisaic division[25] between "righteous men" and "sinners," which Jesus did not.[26] Furthermore, Peter cannot have known of so clear a defense of Jesus' conduct in eating with those who did not keep the Law (Gal. 2:12).[27]

On the other hand, neither part of the statement (apart from a few unimportant elements in the context) is particularly characteristic of Mark, either. He does not (like Q) often portray Jesus as a wisdom-teacher.[28] And his special christological views are not implied in either half of the saying.

It is quite probable, then, that (whether v. 17a arose in the secular world or the early church) v. 17b was attached to the Jesus-tradition before Mark, quite possibly in *written* form as a commentary on 2:1–12. Jesus' thought and practice had clearly included a call[29] to those who did not keep the Law, not so much because he found them more congenial than his more observant

---

25. The Pharisaic definition of "sinners" includes not only the '*am ha-aretz* and immoral people (like adulterers, harlots, murderers, robbers, traitors, etc.) but also (by virtue of their occupation) gamblers, shepherds, weavers, physicians, camel-drivers, butchers, and many others; "publicans" are linked (though not identified) with "murderers" and "robbers" in Baba Kamma 113a. See esp. I. Abrahams, *Studies in Pharisaism and the Gospels* (Cambridge: Cambridge University Press, first series, 1917; second series, 1924), I, 54–61; Joachim Jeremias, "Zöllner und Sünder," ZNW 30 (1931), 292–300.

26. Bonnard, *Matt.*, 131 denies this; yet he admits that in the presence of Jesus the distinction breaks down. Pesch, "Zöllner," 73–76 and *passim* tries a) to ascribe the words "and sinners" in vv. 15f. to the developing tradition, as an elaboration of "publicans" (but cf. Matt. 11:19 = Lk. 7:34, Q, which Pesch cites [79] *without* the last two words!); b) to defend as authentic Jesus' use of the term and concept "sinners"; c) to accept v. 17b as the original ending of the (historical) controversy; and d) to interpret v. 17b as an indication that Jesus intended to accept *both* "righteous men" and (esp.) "sinful men." All four arguments can hardly be correct; a) and b) in particular are really mutually exclusive, while c) becomes more improbable the less likely b) becomes; d) rests on a misinterpretation of "dialectic negation," which (unlike the "historical Jesus"— on this, Pesch is completely right) says nothing positive in 2:17 about the "righteous."

27. If Peter had had so clear a guide as this from *Jesus* on the matter, he would not have withdrawn out of fear of *James*! (Vs. Taylor, *Mk.*, 204.)

28. Even though *didache* is his characteristic term for the essence of Jesus' powerful ministry; see Ed. Schweizer, "Anmerkungen zur Theologie des Markus," in *Neotestamentica et patristica [Cullmann Festschrift]* (Leiden: E. J. Brill, 1962), 35–46 (= *Neotestamentica* [Zürich/Stuttgart: Zwingli Verlag, 1963], 93–104 [95f.]) and J. Delorme, "Aspects doctrinaux du second Évangile. Études récentes de la rédaction de Marc," in I. de la Potterie et al., *De Jésus aux Évangiles*, 74–99 (84–97).

29. In Mark's theology, the call is specifically to discipleship, as its position (following vv. 13–15) shows.

co-religionists (although this may well have been true) as because of his understanding of God's love and concern for them.[30] The opposition to Jesus' practice of associating with such people—surely historical—is also known to Q (Matt. 11:19=Lk. 7:34) and used to good advantage by Luke in his introduction to the parable of the Lost Sheep (15:1f.) and in the wording of the Zacchaeus incident (Lk. 19:7). Even if this particular "I have come . . ." saying does not go back to Jesus, therefore, it represents genuine reminiscence of his intention and practice. It could be used in later controversies over the *disciples'* conduct,[31] and it was patient of a wide variety of homiletic application, as both Luke (5:32) and the history of interpretation show. Exactly which "sinners" are to be the object of the church's special solicitude in any time and place the text does not specify. But a church that is not accused of unholy commerce by righteous men is failing at a key point to follow Jesus, who originally raised the issue by his conduct and concern.

2. **The Sons of the Bridechamber (2:18ff.; cf. Matt. 9:14f.; Lk. 5:33ff.)**

This brief and deceptively simple parable (the third conflict-story in this chapter) seems to teach merely that Jesus' disciples, unlike certain other pious Jews, do not fast, just as people[1] ordinarily do not fast at a wedding. Later, the text goes on, the bride-

---

30. It should not be forgotten that keeping the Law was profoundly important to Jesus' opponents and that "Jesus' reply as given by Mark, thought-provoking and profound as it is, does not really answer their question" (Nineham, *Mk.*, 96).

31. Esp. within the church; cf. Acts 11:3; Gal. 2:12. The controversies between Jewish and Gentile Christianity are consequently, the most likely *Sitz* of the saying in v. 17b, although it is not certain (vs. Kuhn, *Ält. Samml.*, 94f.) that the problem of table-fellowship in the primitive church was a problem solely of Eucharistic fellowship between Jewish and Gentile Christians. See also Pesch, "Zöllner," 83f. and esp. Van Iersel, "Vocation," 218, n. 16.

1. The Semitizing *hyioi tou nymphōnos* can only mean "wedding guests," although the phrase was not always so understood in the ancient church. Cf. the Old Latin *filii sponsi* (= *hyioi tou nymphiou!* as in sa[pt] bo), a reading that practically guaranteed extensive allegorizing in the Latin church's exegesis of the parable. See Franz Gerhard Cremer, " 'Die Söhne des Brautgemachs' (Mk 2.19 parr) in der griechischen und lateinischen Schrifterklärung," *BibZeit* n.F. 11 (1967), 246–253; Karl Th. Schäfer, " '. . . und dann werden sie fasten, an jenem Tage' (Mk 2,20 und Parallelen)," *Synoptische Studien. Alfred Wikenhauser zum siebzigsten Geburtstag . . . dargebracht* (Munich: Karl Zink Verlag, 1953), 124–147 (127ff.).

groom will be taken away,[2] and then the disciples will fast. This simplicity, however, does not correspond either to the tangled history of the tradition or to the awkwardness of Mark's language and intentions.

First of all, the questioners are given by Mark as simply "the people,"[3] and they contrast the actions of Jesus' disciples with those of the disciples of John and the disciples of the Pharisees. Matthew specifies that the questioners were the disciples of John, which would coincide accidentally with the view, repeatedly set forth,[4] that they may have been the original participants in the dispute. In favor of this view one could point out that the Pharisees, who are so sharply attacked elsewhere in the Gospel tradition, are only incidentally involved here; the disciples of John are mentioned only rarely elsewhere, so their participation here has an inherent plausibility (although this argument cuts both ways); and the *association* of the two groups of disciples corresponds so little to the historical relationships as we otherwise know them that it is a reasonable surmise to suggest that originally only one group was involved. These difficulties may also be used, however, to point up the inadequacy of Mark's knowledge about the true state of the relationships, while the sharp distinction between John's disciples and the disciples of Jesus points not only toward a

2. The term *apairō* does not in itself imply a violent death (McNeile, *Matt.*, 121; Schäfer, *Syn. Stud.*, 133), but the context, as well as the fact that *airetai* is used in Is. 53:8 (LXX), makes it clear that the word is a thinly veiled allusion to the Crucifixion (Bonnard, *Matt.*, 133; Swete, *Mk.*, 43; Taylor, *Mk.*, 211; Kuhn, *Ält. Samml.* 66, n. 87). As Jülicher notes (*Gleichn.*, II, 184), in antiquity it is the guests, not the bridegroom, who leave when the wedding-feast is over—and they do not *mourn* after leaving, either—so the allegorical interpretation is evident. G. Quispel, "The Gospel of Thomas and the New Testament," *VigChr* 11 (1957), 189–207 (192) suggests that the term "go away" in the Venetian Diatessaron and in Thomas (Saying 104) reflects a primitive and non-theological tradition, but the parable in Thomas is certainly not primitive.

3. No other translation is adequate. On Mark's impersonal verbs, which Matthew and Luke commonly modify, see C. H. Turner in *JTS* 25 (1924), 378–386.

4. Lagrange, *Matt.*, 183 (a correction of his views in earlier editions of his Mark commentary); Loisy, *Mc.*, 94; Hauck, *Mk.*, 37; Rawlinson, *Mk.*, 30f.; Taylor, *Mk.*, 209f.; cf. Klostermann, *Mk.*[4], 25, 27 (originally *no* subject; Pharisees added later). Some interpret this view as presupposing a difference between the disciples of John, who had lost their master—either through death (Rawlinson, *Mk.*, 31) or imprisonment (Loisy, *ES*, I, 498, n. 2)—and the disciples of Jesus, who had not. But this not only eliminates the Pharisees; it also renders meaningless the surprise implied at the conduct of John's disciples. In any form, however, this interpretation requires that Jesus' answer be referred solely to his own presence, not the presence of the Kingdom.

118 THE PARABLES OF THE TRIPLE TRADITION

period later than the beginning of Jesus' ministry[5] but equally toward the period following the crucifixion. The form of the question in Mk. also suggests that Mark's historical information is somewhat limited. The phrase "disciples of the Pharisees" is singularly inexact (although Luke, with perhaps no greater knowledge than Mark, reproduces it),[6] since the term "disciples" implies "teachers," and the Pharisees were a party, not a school. It is an illegitimate extension of the text to add the paraphrastic explanation, i.e., "the pupils of Pharisaic rabbis."[7]

Again, the situation implied is somewhat obscure. Mark does not follow here the typical pattern of the controversy-discourse: no specific situation and no specific questioners are involved. Yet he is clearly trying to create a concrete situation in v. 18: "And the Pharisees and John's disciples were fasting. . . ." But assuming that he intends to refer to a specific fast, the reference is by no means clear. The regular fast on the Day of Atonement[8] may be immediately excluded; surely Jesus kept that particular fast, or at least did not publicly and openly refuse to do so. The recurrent suggestion that the fast was a fast of mourning for the death of John the Baptist may be rejected out of hand as pure conjecture: he is not mentioned in either the question or the reply, and such a fast would in any case have required that the Christians ignore it or join it, not oppose it![9] Some kind of special fasts could well be implied: the Jewish fasts occasionally specified for the second and fifth days of the week,[10] priestly fasts adopted, like other priestly

5. So Taylor, *Mk.*, 208.
6. Mark's *hoi mathētai tōn Pharisaiōn* (a *hapax legomenon*) does not differ materially from Luke's *hoi tōn Pharisaiōn*. The reading *kai hoi Pharisaioi* (θ *pc* a ff[2]) in Mk. is either a scribal attempt to avoid the problem (A 544 omit the phrase entirely) or an (unconscious?) insertion of the Matthean wording.
7. Swete, *Mk.*, 41. A better explanation is literary: the phrase provides a transition from the scribes (2:1–12) to the Pharisees (2:18–3:6); so Wellhausen, *Mk.*, 19.
8. Lev. 16:29; Num. 29:7; Acts 27:9 (*hē nēsteia*).
9. See Haenchen, *Weg*, 118; Branscomb, *Mk.*, 53; Alistair Kee, "The Question about Fasting," *Nov Test* 11 (1969), 161–173 (164); vs. Loisy, *Mc.*, 96.
10. Lk. 18:12; Did. 8:1. See also Johannes Behm, "*nēstis, ktl.*," *TDNT*, IV, 924–35; Billerbeck, II, 242f., IV, 77–114. Emil Schürer, *Geschichte des jüdischen Volkes im Zeitalter Jesu Christi* (3 vols., 4. Aufl., Leipzig: J. C. Hinrichs, 1901–09), II, 573 suggests that some Pharisees fasted throughout the year on Monday and Thursday but that the practice was not universal.

practices, for Pharisaic laymen, or any of the special fasts for seasons of disaster[11] known to later rabbinic writers.[12] It seems clear that if Mark had anything specific in mind—and his language does not require this, perhaps because he intends a generalizing of the issue—we can no longer deduce what it was, beyond of course the general principle that fasts are for mourning, not for joyous occasions,[13] which fact alone explains the contrast between joy and (not mourning but) fasting.

The question, doubtless intended in an unfriendly sense, provokes a counter-question in the form of a parable: "Can the wedding guests[14] fast in the presence of the bridegroom?" (v. 19a). The latter phrase (literally, "while the bridegroom is with them") even taken alone without v. 19c implies two things. It implies that the presence of the bridegroom makes fasting anomalous, and it suggests that this state of affairs is temporary.[15]

In its Markan context, the effect of this addition is doubtless to spell out what is only implied in the original statement, that the crucifixion of Jesus will be followed by a period of time during which fasting will be reintroduced. The peculiar oscillation between "days" and "day" in v. 20[16] is probably to be attributed to Mark, whatever the ultimate origin of the thought, since "days"

11. Most of the fasts mentioned in Ta'anith are of this kind.
12. For other conjectures, see Lagrange, *Mc.*, 41.
13. It is illegitimate, however, to eliminate fasting, of which mourning was a sign, and make mourning itself the concern of the passage (vs. Rawlinson, *Mk.*, 31; Taylor, *Mk.*, 211; Schäfer, *Syn. Stud.*, 140f., 146f., and *passim*), and esp. to reduce "fasting" to "mourning," on the grounds that the same Aramaic word may be used for both (vs. A. Feuillet, "La controverse sur le jeune [Mc 2,18–20; Mt 9.14–15; Lc 5,33–35]," *NRT* 90 [1968], 113–136, 252–277 [120]; J. O'Hara, "Christian Fasting. Mk. 2:18–22," *Scripture* 19 [1967], 82–95 [92ff.]), which Mark certainly and Matthew possibly did not even know; its significance in the *pre*-Markan tradition would in such a case be very general: cf. the Indian proverb (cited, Klostermann, *Mk.*[5], 28) "Who eats gruel on Divali-day?" and see Bultmann, *HST*, 102, n. 2.
14. On the meaning of this phrase and its Aramaic equivalent *šôš^ebînê*, see Jülicher, *Gleichn.*, II, 181; Alex. Pallis, *Notes on St. Mark and St. Matthew* (new ed., London: Oxford University Press, 1932), 6f.; Taylor, *Mk.*, 210; for the Heb. *b^enê haḥuppâ*, see Lagrange, *Mc.*, 42.
15. But not necessarily *brief*; such celebrations could go on for a long time; see Judg. 4:12; Tob. 8:19ff. Cranfield, *Mk.*, 109 rightly insists that "while" be taken seriously (vs. Dodd, *Parables*, 115f.; Jeremias, *Parables*, 42, n. 82): it emphasizes the *end* of the celebration, not the fact that it has begun.
16. The reading *en ekeinais tais hēmerais* (ℛ al it [vg] sa bo) is palpably a secondary correction.

must apply to the whole period following the death of Jesus; "in that day" must be merely a (typically redundant) variation of the language meaning essentially the same thing.[17] A brief glance at the synoptic parallels as well as at the textual tradition shows both the priority of Mark and the obscurity of the reference: both Matthew and Luke modify the wording so as to eliminate such possible misunderstandings as a reference to a single day or an eschatological intention (since "that Day" is a common technical term for the Last Day).[18] Mark's meaning must have been related to the reintroduction of the practice of fasting, not to a mere quibble over a particular fast.

This brings us to the question of the original *Sitz* of the parable.

17. Redundancy is almost a Markan characteristic; cf. 1:32, 45; 3:7f.; 4:30; 5:3ff., 15; 8:25; 12:41, 44; 13:19; 14:30. That Mark intends by "in that day" the (Christian) Friday fast commemorating the crucifixion (tentatively, Rawlinson, *Mk.*, 30; Loisy, *Mc.*, 97; Klostermann, *Mk.*[4], 28; T. A. Burkill, "Anti-Semitism in Mark's Gospel," *NovTest* 3 [1959], 34–53 [= *Mysterious Revelation*, 132]) is most improbable. In spite of Kuhn's learned defense of this view (*Alt. Samml.*, 61–72) it must be rejected on two grounds: a) we do not know that the Christian practice of fasting twice a week (on Wed. and Fri.) arose as an elaboration of a single weekly (Fri.) fast, as this theory requires; the earliest evidence (*Did.* 8:1; cf. *Herm.* Sim. v. 1) also supports the view that the development began with a biweekly fast as a deliberate modification of the common (but by no means universal) Jewish custom of fasting on Monday and Thursday, while a specific connection with Jesus' death was late and secondary (cf. the texts cited by Kuhn, *Alt. Samml.*, 70); and b) the scene and all of vv. 18–19b must be almost totally (and speculatively) revised to reflect such a Friday fast: it must be reworded into a controversy about not fasting *on particular days*; the "bridegroom" parable must be dissociated completely from all the material presently surrounding it (since only his *death*, not his *presence*, is useful in explaining the purported Christian practice); and something must be inserted to explain the Christian *failure* to fast, since the Bridegroom is no more *present* on certain days of the week than he is *absent* on others. (This difficulty, to be sure, is minimized if one posits a pre-Markan stage in which *aparthē* referred to the Exaltation rather than the Crucifixion—so Kuhn, ibid., 70[71], n. 105—but Mark certainly did not so understand it.) The theory, in short, is improbable for any part of the tradition and clearly impossible for Mark. On the other hand, the view that the apocalyptic "days" are to be identified with the "day" on which Jesus died and on which the disciples fast (Johannes Schreiber, *Theologie des Vertrauens* [Hamburg: Furche-Verlag, 1967], 120–125) rests on a misunderstanding of Mark's theology as well as his language.

18. Matt. 7:22; Lk. 6:23; 10:12 [cf. Matt. 10:15]; 17:30f.; 21:34; Jn. 14:20; 16:23, 26; 2 Thes. 1:10; 2 Tim. 4:8; 1:12; cf. Mk. 14:25; 13:32. The attempt by H. J. Ebeling, "Die Fastenfrage (Mk 2,18–22)," *Theol. Stud. u. Krit.* [108=] n.F. 3 (1937/38), 387–396 to refer the whole passage to the Messianic woes of the Last Day rests on an overinterpretation of this single word. Further, the view that the Messiah will abandon his people at the time of these woes is both unknown in either Judaism (TDan 4:7, *aphistatai ho kurios kai kyrieusei ho Beliar*, is non-eschatological, and so is TAsher 1:8f.) or Christianity and specifically excluded by passages like Matt. 28:20; Rom. 8:35–39; Jn. 14:18–21; cf. Mk. 13:11 par.

Suggestions range from the defense of the authenticity of the whole (vv. 18–20)[19] to the rejection of the whole,[20] with most commentators holding to the authenticity of vv. [18–] 19a and attributing vv. 19b–20 to Mark or early Christian preaching.[21] The real alternatives, as an analysis of the details shows, are the latter two of these three options; the authenticity of the whole is very unlikely. Certainly there is nothing intrinsically implausible in the suggestion that Jesus and his disciples did not keep certain fasts which other pious Jews observed. And the inadequacies of the Markan editorial framework point clearly to the artificiality of the present context, which seems to have been constructed to provide a setting for the parable. But 19a and 19b are, in spite of the commentators' best efforts, simply incompatible in the attitude expressed toward the practice of Christian fasting, so we can hardly attribute the whole saying to Jesus or any other single source. Since neither Mark nor his immediate tradition is Jewish-Christian, in either language or customs, and hence do not provide a fitting context for the expansion of the statement, it is consequently best to attribute the saying from v. 19b on to pre-Markan tradition and vv. [18–] 19a to an earlier stage in Christian development.

But how much earlier? Is any or all of the saying to be attributed to Jesus? The obstacles to this seem to be very great, though perhaps not insuperable:

1. The saying implies a fairly distinct Messianic consciousness. In later Christian thought, as in most of exegetical history to our own day, the equation Christ=the Bridegroom is a familiar conception.[22] But the concept of a Messianic Bridegroom is foreign to

19. Cadoux, *Parables*, 72ff.; Taylor, *Mk.*, 211f.; Cranfield, *Mk.*, 111; Hauck, *Mk.*, 37f. (who suggests a *Sitz* after the death of John the Baptist); O'Hara, "Fasting," *passim*; Schäfer, *Syn. Stud.*, 124–147; Feuillet, "Controverse," *passim*.
20. Wellhausen, *Mk.*, 20; Branscomb, *Mk.*, 53 (who rejects vv. 19–20 but accepts v. 18 as an authentic question).
21. Klostermann, *Mk.*[4], 27; Bultmann, *HST*, 19; B. T. D. Smith, *Parables*, 95; Dodd, *Parables*, 116, n. 2; Jeremias, *Parables*, 52, n. 14; Schmid, *Mk.*, 67; W. G. Kümmel, *Promise and Fulfillment* (2d Engl. ed., London: SCM Press, 1961), 76, 105; and probably Kuhn, *Alt. Samml.*, 62.
22. Matt. 22:2f.; 25:1; Jn. 3:2; 2 Cor. 11:2; Eph. 5:22–32; Rev. 19:7, 9;

both the OT and to Judaism, however familiar in Christian history.[23] Furthermore, while it is theoretically possible that the present text is a circumlocution for "during the wedding" or "during the feast," it is not at all certain.[24] The text speaks of the presence of a person, not a thing (as, e.g., the Kingdom or its power), just as in v. 20 it is the removal of the bridegroom, not the breaking-up of the festivities, that creates a new situation.[25] It is, of course, not self-evident that the very form of the question posed requires the application to Jesus, as in v. 20, but the form of the answer does. And it is an oversimplification to think that such an open Messianic claim is easily conceivable, "especially after the Baptist's death."[26]

2. The saying also implies that Jesus expected the continuance of the disciples as a group for some time after his death.[27] While this is spelled out in greater detail in vv. 19b–20, the phrase would normally be understood to imply a temporary and modifiable situation.[28] Only a phrase like "at a wedding" or (better) "once the wedding has begun" would really fit Jesus' eschatological message, and this is not what the saying suggests, even in v. 19a. The same argument makes even v. 19a a very indirect passion-prediction

21:2, 9; 22:17; used of God in Hos. 2:16, 19f. It is evident that the comparison "makes sense only if it presupposes the application to Jesus" (Lagrange, *Mc.*, 42). This is assumed by Swete, *Mk.*, 44 and defended by Taylor, *Mk.*, 210f., who bluntly insists that this "allegorical" trait implies a "silent" Messianic claim.

23. W. H. Brownlee, "Messianic Motifs of Qumran and the NT," *NTS* 3 (1956/57) 12–30, 195–210 would interpret 1 Q Is[a] 61:10 as evidence that in Qumran the Bridegroom and the Messiah of Aaron are equated. Herbert Braun, *Qumran und das NT*, I, 52, 64 rightly disagrees and so does Joachim Gnilka, " 'Bräutigam'— spätjüdisches Messias-prädikat?" *TThZ* 69 (1960), 298–301. The imagery of Joseph and Aseneth is not really relevant. See further Joachim Jeremias, "*nymphios, ktl.*," *TDNT*, IV, 1094f.; Cranfield, *Mk.*, 110.

24. Jülicher, *Gleichn.*, II, 187; Klostermann, *Mk.*[4], 28. Jeremias suggests this translation on p. 52, n. 14 of his *Parables*; by p. 117, n. 10 he considers the point established! (See also his article in the previous footnote.)

25. The allegory is clear; see Wellhausen, *Mk.*, 20; Lagrange, *Mc.*, 42f.; Loisy, *ES*, I, 497f.; Kümmel, *Promise*, 57. Jülicher, *Gleichn.*, II, 187 feels the force of this objection, but he insists that the emphasis lies on the *hyioi tou nymphōnos*, not on the *nymphios*.

26. Vs. Hauck, *Lk.*, 76f.

27. "The Lord anticipates that fasting will remain as an institution of the Church after the Ascension" (Swete, *Mk.*, 43). On the contrary, such an interest in the post-resurrection practices of the church "would have been very uncharacteristic of him" (Nineham, *Mk.*, 102).

28. "There is nothing in 19b–20 not already to be found in 19a" (Kee, "Question," 166).

(v. 20 is explicit), and since the explicit passion-predictions are probably not authentic, either,[29] the saying must be reckoned doubtful.

3. If we have argued correctly that *en hō* implies a temporary situation, Jesus would here be suggesting that the joy in the presence of the Kingdom is temporary. Since this is not the teaching of Jesus or anyone else in the primitive church, we can only assume that the "temporality" has nothing to do with the Kingdom and refers only to joy or sadness in connection with the presence or absence of Jesus.[30]

4. The incident implies a sharp distinction between Jesus and his interrogators on the matter of fasting and what it represents. Whether this is historical or not depends very much on what originally occasioned the dispute. A distinct difference between Jesus and John on various ascetic practices is attested in the NT (Lk. 7:33f.), and we can easily imagine great differences between Jesus and his Pharisaic opponents over fasting. But we do not know the original reference of the saying. While it is methodologically wrong to deny the authenticity of all sayings whose present context is suspect, it is also wrong to create a plausible context and then assume that the context establishes the saying!

5. The argumentation is not particularly characteristic of Jesus, who in discussion of the Torah ordinarily "carries each issue back to the question of what is the true will of God."[31]

6. Most importantly, so far as we can judge Jesus' attitudes on the matter, it is impossible to attribute to him a defense of fasting (especially in the Jewish-Christian form in which we find it in Matt. 6:16ff.). Any hint that fasting is an acceptable pious prac-

29. Vs., *inter alia*, Feuillet, "Controverse," 255ff. and Taylor, *Mk.*, 211f., who argues only that this particular passion-prediction is placed too early by Mark. On the whole problem, see Georg Strecker, "Die Leidens- und Auferstehungsvoraussagungen im Markus-evangelium," *ZThK* 64 (1967), 16–39.

30. These three objections (and, so to some extent, objection 6 as well) lose much of their force if, with Helmut Merkel, "Markus 7,15. Das Jesuswort über die innere Verunreinigung," *ZRG* 20 (1968), 340–363 (361), we eliminate "while the bridegroom is with them" from the original saying. But the response, "Can wedding guests fast?" is so brief as to be almost incomprehensible, esp. since Jesus' eschatological teaching would not have allowed him to use the symbol of the wedding without any modification whatever.

31. Branscomb, *Mk.*, 54.

tice which God will recognize and reward runs counter to the heart of his teaching about the relationship between God and man.[32] While this argument is conclusive only against vv. 19b–20, it has some force in v. 19a if *en hō* implies a situation which will later be modified. It also suggests a context for the origin of v. 19a: early Jewish-Christian attempts to reintroduce the practice of fasting.[33] As an inner-Christian dispute, the saying makes sense: One group[34] defends the practice of non-fasting (or very limited fasting) on some particular occasion by use of the saying,[35] "Is it not absurd to fast in the presence of the bridegroom?" The other group, which certainly did not begin the practice of fasting on the basis of this text but probably simply continued Jewish fasting practices unchanged, then retorts, "But the bridegroom has been taken from us!" The argument, which from the beginning had to do with cultic practices and with Jesus (which were matters of dispute in the early church) and not with the presence or absence of the Kingdom (which was not) eventually finds its way into our form as fasting becomes so widespread that even Hellenistic communities like Mark's accept it without question. This form justifies a difference between Jesus' custom of not observing certain optional fasts with the church's practice of keeping them in terms of the different christological situation implied before and after the "taking away" of the Bridegroom.

What is implied theologically in the passage depends to some extent on the way one analyzes it literarily. Jülicher notes that

32. So, rightly, Haenchen, *Weg*, 117; Kee, "'Question," 170.

33. Kuhn, *Ält. Samml.*, 228f. (but cf. 82f.) rightly insists that *all* of the controversies of chap. 2 are argued on christological grounds and thus reflect a predominantly inner-Christian discussion.

34. Schäfer is right that we know of no Christian groups in the first century who fundamentally reject fasting or of any Christian controversy over the issue (*Syn. Stud.*, 145; so also Franz Gerhard Cremer, *Die Fastenansage Jesu* [Bonn: Peter Hanstein Verlag, 1965], 5). But we do know of controversies over both keeping the Law and the nature of true piety, so this is not very important. Furthermore, we can no longer assume that all early Christian groups must be reflected somewhere in our surviving texts.

35. Possibly secular in origin (Bultmann, *HST*, 102, n. 2; 105). But Bultmann's view (ibid., 17), to which Kuhn is sympathetic (*Ält. Samml.*, 70, n. 105) that the apothegm (without vv. 19b–20) originated in controversy with the followers of John the Baptist does not sufficiently emphasize the *temporary* implications of the *en hō*.

Calvin understands the passage as basically a justification of fasting and objects that Jesus' intention was rather a moral one.[36] Because Jülicher is reluctant to deny the authenticity of v. 20, however, he understands the section as either a developed form of a simple melancholy reflection on the disciples' character (they will, alas, start fasting again by themselves—a distinction between "prediction" and "commandment" that is without parallel in the Gospels) or as a non-parabolic prediction of his own death.[37] Neither suggestion has much to commend it.

If, however, all or part of the saying comes from the primitive church, it represents various understandings of Jesus' basic intention on the matter of fasting. The rejection of fasting, justified on the grounds of the joy inaugurated by Jesus (though perhaps actually occasioned by the blanket rejection of cultic practices in some primitive communities), is a short-lived and ineffectual protest against the widespread practice of fasting throughout the church. It is instructive to note that *no* party in the original dispute appeals simply to Jesus' own conduct. Neither does the Hellenistic Markan tradition nor Mark himself.[38] Then as now the question, "What would Jesus do?" was the wrong way of putting theological issues. This question can only be asked when the conviction of Jesus' presence as Risen Lord has become so dim that some pattern of conduct, often read into the text, can become a surrogate for that presence.

3. The Patched Garment and the Old Wineskins (2:21f.; cf. Matt. 9:16f.; Lk. 5:36–39)

A generally accepted principle of Gospel study is that the pairing of parables is characteristic of the developing tradition, while

36. *Gleichn.*, II, 188. This might explain Jesus' actions, but not this parable.
37. Ibid.
38. Neither Jesus' conduct nor his teaching as such is crucial for Mark, who never uses either *didaskalos* or *didaskalia*. As Schweizer, "Leistung," 341 points out, Matthew grounds Jesus' authority in the content of his teaching (7:28f.); for Mark, however, this content (repeatable and—for us—historically examinable) is not decisive. What is decisive is that "In Jesus' teaching God Himself has broken into our world." Hence "even when the church returns to the old custom of fasting, the practice is reinterpreted eschatologically as a living memory of the bridegroom" (v. 20). (James M. Robinson, *The Problem of History in Mark* [London: SCM Press, 1957], 47.)

the rabbinic materials show—as we should necessarily assume anyway—that the second of a pair is often later.[1] In the few paired parables of the Gospel tradition, furthermore, we may add that *in particular texts* the paired parables must be interpreted similarly,[2] if not necessarily identically, and that the second often provides an excellent clue to the intention of the final redactor. But although we grant the possibility—in this case, probability—that originally neither of these parables had anything to do with the present context (or, for that matter, with one another),[3] we must also immediately confess that the original reference is completely lost to us.[4] In addition, they are so strikingly similar in language that they must either have arisen together or been so early associated (and thoroughly revised) in the tradition that their original form (and hence meaning) has become irrecoverable.

First, then, the Patched Garment. The central emphasis here seems to be not the danger of damage to the old (it is already damaged) or the loss of the new (since the patch as such is worthless), but the incompatibility of the new and the old.[5] But this motif could imply two quite different things: the worthlessness of the new for saving the old, or the impossibility of saving the old. In the present context, following the Sons of the Bridechamber,

1. See esp., B. T. D. Smith, *Parables*, 39–43.
2. This is true of Mark and thus, a fortiori, of Matthew and Luke, who read the two parables in a single (Markan) text. An admirable summary of the evidence for Markan priority and the independence of Matt. and Lk. in Mk. 2:18–22 parr. is given in Cremer, *Fastenansage*, 1–4. A strong link in the chain of evidence is the peculiar reading *apollytai*, which on internal grounds is the better reading, though supported by only B and a few other texts.
3. The Gospel of Thomas (Saying 47) uses both of the parables but in a different context, associated with different sayings, in reverse order, and with at least two nonsensical and obviously secondary revisions: "Old wine is not put into a new wineskin, lest it spoil it" makes sense only as "lest it be spoiled," while "no one sews an old patch on a new garment, because a rip will result" should be "because there is no reason to do so." W. Nagel's attempt ("Neuer Wein in alten Schläuchen [Mt 9, 17]," *VigChr* 14 [1960], 1–8) to show that both metaphors spring from an original *Doppelzeiler* of which the present synoptic form is a late secondary adaptation, while Thomas more nearly reflects the original is (for this reason among several others) totally unpersuasive. Similar objections must be raised to Quispel, "Thomas and the NT," which arrives at the same result, and to Schramm's attempt (*Markus-Stoff*, 108f.) to show both the independence of Thomas and Luke's use of a non-Markan source.
4. Taylor, *Mk.*, 213; Rawlinson, *Mk.*, 32; Johnson, *Mk.*, 66; Cranfield, *Mk.*, 113; Loisy, *ES*, I, 501.
5. The phrase "the new from the old" (2:21b) is a typical Markan redundancy, stressing their incompatibility, not an insertion; vs. Hahn, "Bildworte," 363.

two specific possible references become plausible. If v. 19a and
21f. were contiguous in the pre-Markan tradition, some kind of
eschatological point is possible; just as fasting in the presence of
the Bridegroom is inconceivable, so the old and the new are incompatible. In favor of this view is the fact that vv. 19b–20 refer
to a comparatively minor difference (between Christian and Jewish fasting), which hardly seems to warrant the sharp contrast
implied in vv. 21f.[6] Possibly, however, fasting is understood as representative of something larger, in which case the contrast goes
far beyond the mere words used.

If, on the other hand, the Patched Garment was originally
attached to all of vv. 18–20, the point would either be the incompatibility between Judaism (represented by its fasts) and Christianity[7] or, less probably, the tolerance of the old practice of
fasting and the inadvisability of trying to modify it.

The Old Wineskins is of some use in restricting these alternatives, at least from that point in the history of the tradition when
it was first attached to the Patched Garment.[8] This parable also
stresses the incompatibility of the old and the new, but it seems to
regret the potential loss of *both* the old (wineskins) and especially
the new (wine).[9] Unless we are to accept the view that v. 22 has
been elaborated, then,[10] it is difficult to ascribe this second parable
to Jesus, whose teaching about the Kingdom implied no such con-

6. Taylor, *Mk.*, 212; so also Hauck, *Mk.*, 38.
7. So, *inter alia*, McNeile, *Matt.*, 122; Swete, *Mk.*, 44f.; Taylor, *Mk.*, 212; Henry
Troadec, *Évangile selon Saint Marc* (Paris: Mame, 1965), 65. On these grounds,
the disciples can receive a new teaching only if they become new men (Lagrange,
Mc., 46), or "a piety appropriate to the New Age inaugurated by Jesus must
create corresponding new forms" (Schmid, *Mk.*, 68). Cadoux, *Parables*, 165f.
denies that the "old" is Judaism; he thinks rather of the Baptist movement. But
this does not yet explain at what stage in early Christianity this movement would
be rejected as "old."
8. Since wine is put into wineskins in Palestine (in Egypt, jars are used; see
Lagrange, *Luc*, 172), it is apparent that the materials of this second parable are
pre-Markan and probably Palestinian.
9. The loss of the new wine is clearly regrettable. Hence the view that the paired
parables teach only the *danger* of the new to the old (Klostermann, *Mk.*[4], 28;
Hahn, "Bildworte," 370f.; Kuhn, *Alt. Samml.*, 71) is inadequate.
10. Perhaps from ". . . if he does, the wine will burst the skins" to the end of
the verse, which could have been constructed as a parallel to v. 22c, "but new
wine is for new skins," which emphasizes the new as such, without any contrast
to the old (so Hahn, "Bildworte," 363).

cern for the old. Jülicher's defense of authenticity seems to rest on a priori grounds[11] and on a somewhat Ritschlian understanding of the "new" element in Jesus' teaching: Not a Messianic consciousness but a "consciousness of innovation" (*Neuheitsbewusstsein*), he suggests, is reflected in this, one of the greatest words of Jesus we possess.[12] But the "new" element in Jesus' teaching is the advent of the Kingdom in Jesus' ministry, not of Jesus himself or his teaching, and it is very difficult to interpret the parable along these lines,[13] since no one ever thought, or could have thought, of the old era and the new as compatible or even comparable. The skins seem to be nearly as valuable as the new wine.[14]

We may, then, reconstruct the history of these sayings very tentatively as follows: Both could originally have been secular proverbs (cf. Job 13:28 LXX).[15] If either or both go back to Jesus, they are related somehow to the advent of the Kingdom, which Jesus and his followers believe and accept but his opponents do not. In the tradition, they are used polemically against the "old" Judaism, represented by fasting, and they reflect a sharp distinction between Judaism and Christianity. Possibly Mark himself, who accepts his Hellenistic tradition in its opposition to Judaism, meant something this general in his use of the sayings. Since he accepts without question the practice of Christian fasting, however (vv. 19b–20), he could be pointing out the rejection of Jewish fasts and the acceptance of Christian fasts.[16] Finally, it is possible

11. Mark, poor in parables, could not have created one so *unerfindbar* as this (*Gleichn.*, II, 199).
12. Ibid.
13. Although Jeremias, *Parables*, 117f. attempts, somewhat unsuccessfully, to do so. Hahn, "Bildworte," 372f. argues that the question of the continuity between the old and the new "*ist hier souverän beiseitegeschoben.*" Alistair Kee, "The Old Coat and the New Wine. A Parable of Repentance," *NovTest* 12 (1970), 13–21 denies completely the contrast between old and new and understands the parable to teach the danger of "inappropriate action and thoughtlessness" (20), i.e., "*metanoeite*" (21). But the repeated use of the terms "old" and "new" in all forms of both parables shows the artificiality of this construction.
14. The omission of the phrase *alla . . . askous kainous* (D it bo^pt) would make the stress on newness less evident, but the reading is apparently due to haplography (Streeter, *FG*, 311, vs. Johnson, *Mk.*, 66; Brown, "Early Rev . . . ," 222).
15. Bultmann, *HST*, 102, although true parallels seem to be missing.
16. Haenchen, *Weg*, 118, n. 7. If he were rejecting fasting as such as Jewish, the parable would read "Do not try to put an old patch on a new garment"—which is exactly what Thomas (Saying 47) does say!

that v. 22 suggests a tolerance-motif on matters of fasting within the Christian church: fasting is acceptable, but it ought not to be required and strict (Jewish-Christian?) regulations of it (the "old") ought not to be reimposed on the "newer" Christian observances. If we knew more about those voluntary fasting practices which the church toward the end of the first century regarded as self-evident,[17] we should be in a better position to evaluate this latter possibility.

In Mark's overall theology, however, these verses (2:18–22) go far beyond the matter of fasting, which to him is apparently an *adiaphoron*. He knows that the joy usually associated with weddings has, for the Christian, begun with the ministry of Jesus; he also knows that the present is also a time of suffering and death. The Christian, standing "between the times," is thus free, regardless of external circumstances, not because he can strive heroically to overcome obstacles, but because in the presence of the Bridegroom such vast new resources are available that the old world no longer holds any ultimate threat for him.

4. The Beelzebul Parables (3:22–27; cf. Matt. 12:22–30, 43ff.; Lk. 11:14–26)

In Mk., 3:22–27 forms a compact section on exorcism, an issue of crucial importance for primitive Christianity, since Jesus' power over demonic forces (with its concomitant, the demons' confession), is prime evidence of his divine powers. It is apparent, however, that this section is itself composite and that it has been tightly knit with another—and different—context involving Jesus' relationships with his family (3:19b–21, 31–35). While the nature of this work requires that we give primary attention to the "parables" of vv. 22–27,[1] the larger context must also be discussed

---

17. Lk. 2:37; Acts 13:2f.; 14:23; cf. also Mk. 9:29 par.; Matt. 6:16ff.; Did. 7:4; 8:1.

1. How many of the sayings are parabolic, in Mark's view, is uncertain; but the House Divided and the Strong Man are here understood as parables. "The collection of parables [chap. 4] has as its prelude the 'parables' of the Beelzebub debate" (J. M. Robinson, *Problem of History*, 50).

briefly to set the whole Markan argument in its propér perspective. The larger context is Jesus' relationships with his family. One understanding of our passage sees it as originating in early Christian protest against the claim of Jesus' family to leadership over the church.[2] On these grounds, vv. 31–35 are primarily intended to illustrate the supreme importance of the will of God over even the closest human relationships (as in Matt. 10:37 = Lk. 14:26, Q). The heart of this section would then be v. 35, with vv. 31–34 an artificially created context for it; while v. 21, though resting on good tradition, would have no necessary connection with the present Markan context.[3]

A somewhat different development, however, is also plausible. According to this view, Jesus' family actually did fail from the beginning to understand him and suggested that he was indeed "beside himself." The issues in vv. 20–35 are, on these grounds, inseparable. Mark, however, represents a rather late stage in the development, softening down the language so that a vague group (*hoi par' autou*) now suspect him of madness;[4] he makes vv. 31–35 into a separate incident, transforming an attempt to call Jesus away from his embarrassing activities into a harmless family visit and rewording v. 35 into such general terms that it becomes an edifying comment, not a rejection of his immediate family.[5] The process begun in Mark is then continued in the other Gospels. While such an interpretation is far from certain, it does at least suggest the care with which Mark has united under a common theme materials originally distinct in meaning and purpose. The

2. Johnson, *Mk.*, 84f.
3. Something like this seems to be implied by Bultmann's analysis, *HST*, 13f., 29f. Schmid, *Mk.*, 81 insists that the situation of v. 22 has nothing to do with that of vv. 20f.; he sees only a catchword connection. Yet he also (84f.) asserts that—in the redaction, not in history—v. 20f. and vv. 31–35 belong together.
4. Klostermann, *Mk.*[4], 36 offers linguistic evidence that the phrase must mean "his family" (so also BAG, 615); Haenchen, *Weg*, 139f. interprets it of his disciples, adherents. Loisy, *Mc.*, 114f. insists that the phrase must imply Jesus' immediate family, but he thinks they fear only Jesus' "exaltation mystique" and try only to protect him.
5. This analysis is taken from Haenchen, *Weg*, 139–143.

entire section then becomes a many-faceted reply to the charge that Jesus was the instrument not of God but of Satan. The extent to which Mark himself is responsible for uniting in a single context and under a single theme what could easily have been unrelated traditions cannot be determined.

A still further complication of the tradition is the possibility, strongly defended by Taylor[6] and others, that the twó charges in Mk. 3:22 were originally distinct: "He has Beelzebul" and "He casts out demons by the Prince of demons." Evidence of a tradition that Jesus was himself considered possessed is provided not only by the present context but also by the Johannine tradition (cf. Jn. 7:20; 8:48f., 52; 10:21f.) and by the evident fact that the two charges of Mk. 3:22 are mutually exclusive: one who is possessed by a demon is the *object*, not the *subject*, of an exorcism. It is impossible to say whether Beelzebul, otherwise unknown to us, was first identified with the Prince of Demons in Q,[7] though we may say with some assurance that Mark, who created v. 30, did not distinguish Beelzebul, the Prince of Demons and Satan.[8] For Mark, vv. 22–30 form a single argument, and the charge that Jesus has an unclean spirit is met by, among other things, the warning against blasphemy in vv. 28f.[9] Furthermore, vv. 31–35 make it seem that vv. 20f. occur back at Peter's house in Capernaum.[10]

Tentatively, then, we may reconstruct the history of this section somewhat as follows: Its basis is the charge that Jesus is a demoniac. If this charge was once made in the context of a specific healing (Q) or some other concrete circumstance, Jesus' reply to

---

6. *Mk.*, 237f.; cf. Lagrange, *Mc.*, 71; Haenchen, *Weg*, 145; Schmid, *Mk.*, 83; Burton Scott Easton, "The Beezebul Sections," *JBL* 32 (1913), 57–73 (60, n. 6).
7. Haenchen, *Weg*, 147.
8. Vs. Taylor, *Mk.*, 244, who interprets v. 30 as evidence for such a distinction. (So also Schmid, *Mk.*, 83.)
9. Schmid, *Mk.*, 84 sees 3:23–27 as an answer to the charge in v. 22b and v. 28f. as a reply to v. 22a. In any case, the bewildering ambiguity of the double accusation is met with the unambiguous clarity of the antitheses, Jesus/Satan and Holy Spirit/unclean spirit; so James M. Robinson, *Das Geschichtsverständnis des Markus-Evangeliums* (Zürich: Zwingli Verlag, 1956), 60.
10. Loisy, *Mc.*, 113; Haenchen, *Weg*, 141.

it would form the original apothegm, to which sayings-like materials like the House Divided and the Strong Man were then added. On the other hand, the House Divided could very well be a secular saying whose relevance for the charge of collusion with the Prince of Demons was early recognized; in this case no "apothegm," properly speaking, exists until the twin charges of demon possession (surely more primitive) and collusion with the Prince of Demons have merged and a scene has been constructed appropriate for the use of the two parabolic sayings in these verses. In either case, the development took place early, before the compilation of Q, and it reflects in both of our written sources a considerable process of development.

The narrower context of vv. 22–27, however, is a specific charge made by "the scribes from Jerusalem." Since scribes do not fit well with *either* group mentioned in vv. 20f., 31–35, Markan composition is evident, and in view of Mark's well-known *Heilsgeographie*, it would be a mistake to find genuine historical reminiscence in the fact that they are said to be from Jerusalem.[11] The function of Jerusalem in the account is to make the charge more official and consequently the victory more glorious.[12] In Q, the charge is made by "some" of the people, and this general description is surely more primitive.

The charge itself fits well with the situation of Jesus' time: exorcism was widely practiced among the Jews,[13] so that his own exorcisms created a serious problem for those who did not hold to his views. The ambiguity of the miraculous as a manifestation of divine power is fully preserved—in first-century terms—by the charge that the supernatural force at work in Jesus' actions is

---

11. Vs. Johnson, *Mk.*, 81, who notes in support of his contention the fact that Pharisaic dominance of the Jews in Galilee did not come about until the second century. Lagrange, *Mc.*, 65 notes 3:6 and 7:1 and suggests "un service d'espionage organisé"! But both passages are redactional.
12. Jülicher, *Gleichn.*, II, 216; Wellhausen, *Mk.*, 27; Hauck, *Mk.*, 48.
13. Jos. *Antiq.* viii.42–49 (Loeb, V, 592–96); *War* vii.185 (Loeb, III, 558); cf. Acts 19:13; Justin *Dial.* 85. Further details in the excursus, "Zur altjüdischen Dämonologie" in Billerbeck IV, 501–535; Heinrich Lewy, "Zum Dämonenglauben" *ARW* 28 (1930), 241–252; Wilfred Lawrence Knox, "Jewish Liturgical Exorcism," *HTR* 31 (1938), 191–203; Marcel Simon, *Verus Israel* (Paris: E. de Boccard, 1948), chap. 12.

really demonic. To explain the healings as psychosomatic was for Jesus' opponents an impossibility; to explain them as irrelevant would have been trifling. And the charge, once it had become current, demanded a serious answer.

The text does not indicate when or how Jesus was supposed to have become aware of the charge. But when he does, he calls his opponents to him (cf. 7:1; 8:34), and, as always in the Gospels when Jesus calls, they come.[14] The Markan form of the reply, involving as it does an elaborate double reference to Satan (vv. 23, 26), a superfluous "and" (v. 24), a redundant homiletical postscript that Satan "has an end" (v. 26)—which mars the parallelism—and a double negative in v. 27, is clearly less primitive than the Q form,[15] which is built on the saying about a divided kingdom. To it is added, perhaps by Mark himself, the parallel note that a divided *house* cannot stand[16] and the evident conclusion is then expressly drawn: if Satan revolts against himself, he too cannot stand. In Mk., though perhaps less clearly than in Q, Satan is thus a special case of the general rule about divided kingdoms. The unity of the demonic world is presupposed, not only by the form of the introductory question, "How can Satan cast out Satan?" but also by the logic of the argument.

Yet the reply is hardly conclusive. Jesus' opponents could have responded either that Satan was allowing Jesus temporary jurisdiction over some of the demons in order to give his victims back even more permanently[17] or even that disagreements among such disagreeable forces were only to be expected from time to time. Parabolic logic is at best illustrative, not apodictic.

The second aspect of the Markan reply, a positive counterpart to the negative thesis in vv. 23–26, is the parable of the Strong

---

14. That they came "little suspecting His purpose" (Swete, *Mk.*, 62) misunderstands Mark's intention, which is to portray Jesus' authority.
15. Vs. Taylor, *Mk.*, 240.
16. That *oikia* is not a building is evident; it is more than "clan," less than "kingdom." Neither Matthew nor Luke has fully preserved the Semitic sense, for which see Gen. 7:1; 12:17. Bultmann, *HST*, 13 thinks these verses reflect a double parable, the Divided Kingdom and the Divided House.
17. Haenchen, *Weg*, 146.

Man (v. 27), which is attached here by the catchword connection with "house."[18] The presupposition of the parable, which may originally have been a secular proverb[19] or a well-known Jewish image,[20] is that Satan cannot voluntarily be robbed of his own any more than anyone else can. The (potential?) fate of the Strong Man thus somehow parallels that of Satan. It is hard to go much beyond this without falling into allegory, and whether the parable was originally an allegory or only made such by the tradition[21] cannot be determined apart from questions which can hardly be put except in allegorical terms: Who is the Strong Man? Who (or what) are his "goods"? Who binds him, and when does he do so?

To the first question, the answer is clear: the Strong Man is Satan. This is evident not only from the Markan context—which need not have been original—but also from hints in the OT text. The LXX of Is. 49:24f. and probably also Is. 53:12 suggests such a usage.[22] The "goods," if they are not simply part of the dramatic scenery, are probably not the demons themselves[23] but the men whom they control.[24]

A much more difficult question is: Who binds the Strong Man, God[25] or Jesus?[26] Some commentators have suggested compromise formulas: "Jesus or . . . the power of God by which He worked,"

---

18. Figurative in v. 25, literal in v. 27. In Aramaic the word may imply a political domain; see Wellhausen, *Mk.*, 26; Rawlinson, *Mk.*, 44.

19. Cf. Ps. Sol. 5:4. See Johnson, *Mk.*, 82.

20. Cf. the eschatological new priest of TLev. 18:2, 12; the angel of Rev. 20:2f.; the binding of Semjâzâ and his associates in 1 En. 10:11, 14 and the hosts of Azazel in 1 En. 54:4.

21. Jülicher, *Gleichn.*, II, 226f.; Dodd, *Parables*, 123.

22. It is also possible, though not very likely, that the expression reflects Satan's claims as a usurper of divine prerogatives, since *ischyros* is a common LXX rendering of *'el* or *haggibbôr* (Swete, *Mk.*, 63; see esp. Deut. 10:17 and Jer. 39 [32]:18).

23. Jülicher, *Gleichn.*, II, 228: Satan's *panoplia*; Loisy, *ES*, I, 708; Gould, *Mk.*, 64; Hauck, *Lk.*, 155; cf. H. J. Holtzmann, *Handcommentar zum Neuen Testament. Erster Band: Die Synoptiker/Die Apostelgeschichte* (2. Aufl., Freiburg i.B.: J. C. B. Mohr, 1892), 136.

24. McNeile, *Matt.*, 177; Lagrange, *Mk.*, 74; Swete, *Mk.*, 67; Manson, *Sayings*, 86.

25. Haenchen, *Weg*, 147, n. 12; Creed, *Luke*, 161; Branscomb, *Mk.*, 71.

26. Loisy, *Mc.*, 119; Schmid. *Mk.*, 82f.; Schniewind, *Matt.*, 159; Troadec, *Mc.*, 83. Rawlinson, *Mk.*, 44 suggests that the Binder is God in Q but Jesus in Mk.; similarly, Klostermann, *Mk.*[4] 37; vs. this, Kümmel, *Promise*, 108f. Hauck, *Lk.*, 155 opts for Jesus in Lk.

"Jesus Himself . . . armed with divine power," etc.[27] The adequacy
of these and other formulas must be decided, for both Jesus and
Mark (or his tradition), in the light of the further question, When
does the binding referred to here take place?

We may, I think, eliminate the view that Jesus himself understood his own exorcisms as acts of a Stronger One, binding Satan
by his own power and authority. If the parable is authentic, it
may have been based originally on the assumption that God has
bound the Strong Man and that Jesus, noting this (cf. Lk. 10:18),
sets men free from Satan's power.[28] This would be fully consistent
with Jesus' understanding of the Kingdom and with the Q statement (Matt. 12:28=Lk. 11:20) in our present context. Nevertheless, it meets the nearly insuperable objection that in the parable
itself (not merely the framework) the binder and the plunderer
are the same.

In the Markan context, however, this creates no problem. The
Christology here is explicit: Jesus[29] has bound Satan and in his
exorcisms is plundering him. It is possible that Mark here alludes
obliquely to the Temptation[30] and quite certain that at least the
initial victory was won there. In our present context, in any event,
the Strong Man is a reply to a charge about the actions of Jesus;
as such it is expressly christological. We must not, however, over-
emphasize the *egō* of the "finger of God" saying or argue on
a priori grounds that without some such consciousness as that
reflected in the Strong Man Jesus would never have entered upon
the work he undertook[31] in order to preserve the authenticity of
the parable; so express a Messianic claim on the lips of Jesus is, to
say the least, unusual. For Mark, however, Jesus' conquest of Satan
is so basic an element of the kerygma as to need no defense or

27. Taylor, *Mk.*, 240ff.
28. So, e.g., Grundmann, *Mk.*, 84; Easton, "Beezebul," 63. For the binding of
the demons and the destruction of Satan at the coming of the Kingdom, see Is.
24:21f.; 1 En. 10:11–14; 54:4f.; Assump. Mos. 10:1; TLev. 18:12.
29. The Spirit is not mentioned. As J. M. Robinson, *Problem of History*, 33f. notes,
the Spirit is presumed in the (Markan) cosmic contexts but never in the exorcisms
themselves.
30. Schniewind, *Matt.*, 159; Bonnard, *Matt.*, 182; Foerster, *TDNT*, VII, 159;
Jeremias, *Parables*, 122f.; cf. Swete, *Mk.*, 64.
31. So Jülicher, *Gleichn.*, II, 228–232.

explanation. Jesus performed his exorcisms by virtue of his nature as Son of God. So while Mark surely did not invent this little parable, there is little in it that does not fit into his theology. The verses which immediately follow this parable (vv. 28f.) are not our immediate concern here. They have often been discussed elsewhere.[32] The sayings are doubtless very early, though probably a product of the early church rather than authentic words of Jesus.[33] While the Q form is Messianic, the Markan form is quite generalized and seems (cf. v. 30) intended primarily as a condemnation of the Jewish rejection of Jesus, particularly in the light of his exorcisms. Possibly it intends also to refer beyond this, to anyone who rejects the Holy Spirit resident in the Markan community which transmitted the saying.[34]

In any case, these verses, originating in quite a different context, serve in Mk. as a solemn warning against the opponents of Jesus, who in their blindness refuse to recognize the power of Jesus over demons as the work of God. Early Christianity, faced with the charge that Jesus was a practitioner of demonic arts, replies with a counter-charge: Since the victory of the Son of God over the spirits, both during his lifetime and in the experience of the church, is both fitting and certain, denying him his rightful place is no mere mistake in judgment; it is an "eternal sin." The exorcisms, like the Crucifixion, can be misinterpreted and misunderstood, but both are for Mark reflections of Jesus' divine nature as Strong Man (3:22–27) and Son of God (15:39).

32. Gottfried Fitzer, "Die Sünde wider den Heiligen Geist," ThZeit 13 (1957), 161–182; Evald Lövestam, Spiritus Blasphemia (Lund: Gleerup, 1968); R. Schippers, "The Son of Man in Matt. xii.32 = Lk. xii.10, Compared with Mk. iii.28," Studia Evangelica, IV (Berlin: Akademie-Verlag, 1968), 231–235; Carsten Colpe, "Der Spruch von der Lästerung des Geistes," Der Ruf Jesu und die Antwort der Gemeinde [Festschrift Jeremias] (Göttingen: Vandenhoeck & Ruprecht, 1970), 63–79.
33. Branscomb, Mk., 74; Johnson, Mk., 84; vs. Wrege, Bergpredigt, 167 and Taylor, Mk., 241, who however admits that the Q form probably betrays later concerns, as well as Colpe, "Lästerung," passim.
34. Suhl, Zitate, 100f., 167 insists that Mark uses this saying in such a way as to identify Jesus with the Holy Spirit, an argument that is, on the whole, unconvincing.

5. The Sower (4:1–9, 13–20; cf. Matt. 13:1–9, 18–23; Lk. 8:4–8, 11–15)

In view of the composite nature of Mk. 4 the Markan understanding of any single parable may be quite different from what his tradition meant by it. Whatever the materials may have meant in the tradition, Mark's editorial hand seems to point in the direction of encouragement and consolation (rather than parenesis). The argument is as follows:

1. In addition to the Sower itself, the parables of the Lamp and the Bushel (v. 21), the Manifestation of What Is Hidden (v. 22), and the Measure (vv. 24f.) all seem to be concerned with parenesis only secondarily if at all, while all are of primary significance in offering encouragement and consolation.

2. V. 34, surely Markan, makes it clear that the disciples were fully instructed in Jesus' meaning; this is of obvious help in pointing out the secure basis of Christian teaching, but its parenetic significance is at best minimal.

3. In vv. 10ff., 13 Mark has modified a question about a specific parable into an inquiry about Jesus' teaching as a whole and inserted into this discussion an assurance that although Jesus' message ("all the parables") may be unclear to outsiders this does not destroy the certainty of the gift of the Kingdom to the disciples. While "encouragement" and "parenesis" should not be too sharply separated and may actually be present in any or all of these parables,[1] it is apparent that the former is more central than the latter to Mark's overall concern in all of these passages.

4. The same must be said of the (pre-Markan) parables of the Seed Growing Secretly (vv. 26–29) and the Mustard Seed (vv. 30ff.), which follow immediately: neither can be rightly interpreted as primarily parenetic for Mark.[2]

---

1. Léon-Dufour, *Études*, 277 rightly notes a double orientation, particularly in the Sower: confidence in certain success and an admonition to be good soil. But the question remains, Which motif is dominant for Mark?
2. Burkill, *Mysterious Revelation*, 97. H. Baltensweiler, "Das Gleichnis von der selbstwachsenden Saat (Markus 4,26–29) und die theologische Konzeption des Markus-evangelisten," *Oikonomia [Festschrift Cullmann]* (Hamburg-Bergstadt:

5. Even the next pericope, the Stilling of the Storm (vv. 35–41), though primarily oriented toward Christology in Mark's account, evinces a strong "encouragement" motif in the dominical miracle as a response to the disciples' obvious lack of faith.[3]

6. An incidental confirmation of the centrality of encouragement in the Markan view is provided by the use of the motif of "hearing" in the present context. It occurs three times, once in the exhortation "Listen!" with which the parable is introduced (v. 3); once at the close of the parable proper (v. 9); and finally, immediately following the Manifestation of What Is Hidden (v. 23). It does not occur either immediately before or after the explanation of the Sower (vv. 13–20), where the parenetic theme is most evident in the whole chapter! In all three Markan instances, then, it is most naturally connected with the "mystery" of Jesus' teaching, which is hidden only in order to be revealed (vv. 22f.) and made known fully to "his own disciples" (v. 34).[4] Obviously, one need not suppose that Mark here intended, like later Gnostic sects, a reference to mysteries known only to the true Gnostic.[5] The expression, "He who has ears to hear, etc.," is widely known in primitive *oral* tradition, as its inclusion in many different contexts shows, while the variety of uses in the NT[6] is so great that

---

Herbert Reich Evangelischer Verlag), 69–75 (75) rightly speaks of a "rekerygmatizing" of the tradition at this point.

3. Kuhn, *Ält. Samml.*, 223f. and *passim* argues that consolation was the theme of the pre-Markan collection and that Mark reworked the material to stress the "hardening" of the Jews and the acceptability of the Gentiles; the data do not seem to me to support either contention. See below, chap. 6, on the Things That Defile and the Wicked Husbandmen, for evidence that the theme of Jewish reprobation was no longer a vital issue even for Mark's immediate tradition, to say nothing of Mark himself. As Schreiber notes (*Th. Vertrauens*, 204, n. 227), the Judgment in Mk. 4:11f. is not merely on Israel but on any who refuse the discipleship of the cross.

4. Christian Dietzfelbinger, "Das Gleichnis vom ausgestreuten Samen," *Der Ruf Jesu [Festschrift Jeremias]*, 80–93 (80) thinks that the formula in v. 9 may have been added in the community when the parable first took on the character of a warning to faithfulness: if vv. 10–12(13) were inserted by Mark into a source in which v. 9 immediately preceded v. 13(14), as held here (and by many other interpreters), its parenetic use in Mark's source is evident by its position just before the explanation. The Markan construction is clearly different.

5. Hippolytus *Haer*, v. 8: "That is, they insist, no one has truly become a hearer of these mysteries except the *gnostikoi teleioi*." See also viii.9.

6. Redaction and the influence of oral tradition are the factors which best explain the agreement of Matt. and Lk. (*ho echōn*) vs. Mk. (*hos echei*) at the end of

no single passage can provide the key to its use anywhere else. For Mark, then, the central point of the Sower (as indicated by his editorial work in the chapter as a whole) is not an exhortation ("What kind of soil are you?"). It is a word of assurance to him who has hearing ears that the mystery of the Kingdom has been given to the disciples: its hiddenness is temporary and divinely intended; the full coming of the Kingdom is not so much great or immediate[7] as *sure*.[8] If this interpretation is correct, the notoriously obscure significance of the progression with which the parable ends (30-60-100) becomes somewhat clearer: the increasing fruit-bearing on the part of those among whom the Word has been sown (*hoi ... sparentes*, v. 20) attests the assurance of a good yield despite any counter-indications in the church of Mark's day. The parenetic question, "What kind of soil are you?" though clearly implied by the explanation as a whole, is not central to Mark's purpose here.

What, then, of the pre-Markan tradition? To this must be assigned a setting (perhaps some form of vv. 2, 10, and 33)[9] and the whole of the explanation.[10] The same well-known arguments that show the inauthenticity of the explanation as a whole[11] also

---

the parable proper (vs. Kilpatrick, *Origins,* 91, who suggests its presence in Q) and of the variety of uses reflected elsewhere in the NT: Matt. 11:15; 13:43; Lk. 14:35 (all three passages redactional); Rev. 2:7, 11, 17, 29; 3:6, 13, 22; 13:9. (In every passage except the last the saying is ascribed to Jesus.)

7. *euthys* (v. 29) says that harvesting is immediate when the grain is ripe; it does not say that the harvest is imminent.

8. Schmid, *Mk.,* 99 specifically denies the centrality of the encouragement-motif and stresses the parenetic. To do this he must point out the *difference* between the explanation of the Sower and the surrounding Markan parables, which shows that he can hardly understand Mark rightly here.

9. Kuhn, *Ält. Samml.,* 137f. has correctly shown that both v. 1 and v. 2 are Markan in language and must not be assigned to the pre-Markan parable collection. This collection, however, must have begun "with at least an introductory sentence" (p. 138). (Similarly, Dupont, "Chapitre," 804 and Minette de Tillesse, *Secret,* 180f.) Gnilka, *Verstockung,* 53–62 attributes vv. 3–8, 10, 13–20, 33–34 to the pre-Markan source, a view that is surely wrong for v. 34 and probably for v. 13; in addition, I would prefer, with Haenchen, *Weg,* 161, n. 2 to see the substance of vv. 11f., 21–25, 26–29, 30ff. as traditional and probably (though not necessarily) from the same pre-Markan collection as the rest.

10. As Marxsen, "Red. Erklärung," 259f. notes, the peculiar position of 4:11f. shows that both parable and explanation are pre-Markan.

11. A spirited but unconvincing defense of probable authenticity is given by Cranfield in "St. Mark 4:1–34," *ScotJTh* 4 (1951), 398–414; 5 (1952), 49–66 and

clearly demonstrate its non-Palestinian provenance: the vocabulary is non-Semitic, more closely related to Paul and Acts than to Jesus or Palestinian models; the allegory is extensive and central, not peripheral, and it does not fit very well with the details of the parable itself; the conditions described in vv. 17ff. (especially "persecution on account of the word") are those of the second and third Christian generation, not of Jesus' day (cf., e.g., Phil. 3:18f.); parabolic explanations in the tradition are without exception inauthentic;[12] the eschatological note characteristic of Jesus' message is largely missing; and the whole situation presupposed is one in which the mixed hearing of the Word has been noted, pondered, and explained. The inevitability, even the necessity and legitimacy, of such attempts to apply the words of Jesus to changing conditions and (external) temptations[13] certainly does not require that we wrongly ascribe them to an earlier and different generation. The explanation points out that from very early times a commitment to Christianity has not in itself guaranteed perseverance in the face of persecution or temptation or changing interests—most of the Western world would be Christian if it did.

The parable itself, however, is a much more complex matter. What is its origin and significance? Taken by itself, the parable is patient of various interpretations, some of which could very well go back to Jesus and some of which probably cannot.

Broadly speaking, the various interpretations of the parable fall into three categories, emphasizing respectively the sower, the harvest, and the soils (or, perhaps more exactly, the seed-and-the-soils).

First, the sower. The most that one can say for this view is that Matthew expressly calls it the Parable of the Sower (13:18),

---

in his commentary on Mark, 158–161. (Similarly, Léon-Dufour, *Études*, 286ff.; somewhat differently, Harald Riesenfeld, "The Parable of the Sower and Its Interpretation," *NTS* 14 [1967/68], 165–193.) Against authenticity, see Bultmann, *HST*, 187; Dodd, *Parables*, 13f.; Branscomb, *Mk.*, 80f.; B. T. D. Smith, *Parables*, 128; Loisy, *ES*, I, 756–759; Rawlinson, *Mk.*, 52f.; Taylor, *Mk.*, 258–262; Masson, *Paraboles*, 37f.; and esp. Jeremias, *Parables*, 77ff.

12. On the explanation of the Tares, see Jeremias, *Parables*, 81–85; of the Net, ibid., 85; of the Things That Defile, below, chap. 6.

13. Bonnard, *Matt.*, 198.

although his interpretation, as we have seen, is not consistently christological. Yet there is little evidence for this interpretation in general, and none in the details of the parable, which speaks of the seed, the soils, and the harvest without once mentioning the sower after the seed is sown. *Wherever* the parable arose, whether in the teaching of Jesus, in the pre-Markan tradition, or even with Mark himself, the christological note is at best indirect and implicit.[14] There is, therefore, no way of judging its origin on the basis of this interpretation or of suggesting a situation in the life of Jesus or the early church to which it could have been the response.[15]

A second, and much more likely, interpretation is that which understands the harvest[16] as central to the parable. Certainly the harvest is the climax as well as the last thing in the story. The concluding admonition to "hear" is certainly compatible with the view that primary attention should be given to the whole series of actions, of which the harvest is the natural culmination. And there is a considerable body of evidence showing that a harvest of even thirtyfold is so striking that the hearers' attention would inevitably be drawn to this factor above all others. On these grounds, the parable would teach that in spite of everything (this negative element is important) a bountiful harvest is sure. In the teaching of Jesus, it could then reflect either the "harvest" in Jesus' own ministry, contrasted with the many failures since the early prophets[17] or, much more probably, the greatness of the Kingdom

---

14. So Eta Linnemann, *Parables of Jesus* (E.T., London: SPCK, 1966), 180, n. 2. Léon-Dufour, *Études*, 284f. and *passim*, prefers, however, to keep the traditional title lest the motif of the Kingdom *in Jesus' ministry* be covered over by the other motifs.

15. Bonnard, *Matt.*, 192, e.g., notes that the failures are central: before the ultimate victory both Jesus and the Kingdom must be "stifled" (Mk. 4:7b). But this is not Jesus' teaching.

16. Technically, the harvest is not mentioned at all—only the yield. (So C. H. Cave, "The Parables and the Scriptures," *NTS* 11 [1964/65], 374–387 [380]; Léon-Dufour, *Études*, 274ff.; cf. Augustin George, "Le sens de la parabole des semailles (Mc. iv. 3–9 et parallèles)," *Sacra Pagina* [2 vols., Paris: J. Gabalda, 1959], II, 163–169 [166].) And Jesus' teaching that the Kingdom *had begun to break in* is a very substantial modification of the traditional "harvest" symbolism. Arguments about what associations Jesus' hearers would inevitably have concluded from his use of this "self-evident" symbol are, consequently, very precarious.

17. Dodd, *Parables*, 182f.; A. T. Cadoux, *Parables*, 154–157; B. T. D. Smith, *Parables*, 126.

inaugurated by Jesus in spite of various appearances to the contrary, most notably the failure of Jesus' hearers to respond to his
message.[18] The many and varied failures of the seed in the story
are then merely dramatic elaborations of comparable failures on
the part of Jesus to win all of his hearers to his preaching.

To this view, however, there are several quite substantial objections. In the first place, it requires us to conceive of Jesus as not
only proclaiming the Kingdom but also defending it. We must
imagine that his preaching (or that of the disciples during his
ministry) met with varied responses and that he discussed the
questions raised by such responses.[19] And we must assume that in
the teaching of Jesus the Kingdom is of such a nature that its
presence (or coming) could be called into question by the ambiguous nature of the response to his preaching of it. In other words,
the parable is dealing with the problem of resolving two contradictory things: the hope of the harvest and the certainty of opposition. The difficulties involved in such assumptions[20] can perhaps
be made clear by pointing to the interpretations of Jülicher, who
thinks that Jesus, far from saying anything about his own ministry, is merely pointing out what *always* happens to the Word of
God,[21] and Loisy, who thinks the parable is intended to explain

18. Jeremias, *Parables*, 150f. and, apparently, Schmid, *Mk.*, 93. Bultmann, *HST*,
200 suggests (in the form of rhetorical questions) several possible original mean-
ings, among them the possibility that it might be "a monologue by Jesus, half of
resignation, half of thankfulness" for the mixed reception of his message. It is the
virtue of Nils Dahl's study, "The Parables of Growth," *StudTh* 5 (1951), 132–
166 that it insists on the relationship between the coming of the great Kingdom
and the beginnings of that coming in Jesus' own ministry. This has the advantage
of squaring our parable with Jesus' eschatological teaching as a whole, the dis-
advantage of minimizing the complex shift in imagery involved when the "eschatological harvest" has in some sense begun. Léon-Dufour, *Études*, 281 sees the
problem and holds that Jesus deliberately omits any mention of the harvest
because the Kingdom is present in Jesus' ministry but the day of harvest is not.
19. "Our Lord reflected on the lack of success in His career" (Cerfaux in *NTS* 2
[1955/56], 246). But that is precisely what we do not know! Dahl, "Parables,"
158 interprets all the so-called parables of growth in this way and notes that "at
least in the case of the parables of growth the original meaning of the words of
Jesus was more, and not less, 'christological' than the interpretation given to them
in the synoptic gospels"(!).
20. Still further objections are raised by Linnemann, *Parables*, 181 [-4], n. 15,
who however is reluctant to deny the authenticity of the parable, admitting only
that we cannot know what it originally meant (185, n. 16).
21. *Gleichn.*, II, 537. Similarly, A. T. Cadoux, *Parables*, 155 and Wellhausen, who
holds that Jesus speaks like the old prophets (*Mk.*[1], 34) or simply as a teacher:
"*Jeder andere Lehrer kann ebenso sprechen*" (*Mk.*[2], 32).

the varied results of Jesus' preaching, and nothing more.[22] In the former case, Jesus is not talking about his own ministry at all, while in the latter, he is talking about nothing else. But both Jülicher and Loisy can only fit this parable into their overall understanding of Jesus' ministry by breaking the fundamental connection in Jesus' thought between his preaching of the Kingdom and the situation in which he preached it—and it is precisely the absence of this connection which forms the basic objection to the authenticity of the Sower.

Furthermore, it is not clear either how the yield is to be computed[23] or just how great a "hundredfold" harvest really was. Many interpreters[24] find a tenfold harvest normal or even quite good, in which case the figures cited would have about the same force as (in American terms, for corn or wheat) "300, 600, and 1000 bushels to the acre." If this reasoning is correct, anyone familiar with Palestinian agriculture—i.e., practically all of Jesus' hearers and many readers of Mk.—would immediately be struck by this astonishing, even miraculous yield. On the other hand, many interpreters[25] think of a hundredfold yield as merely good or even average, in which case the harvest would be the climax but not

22. *ES*, I, 759.

23. Linnemann, *Parables*, 117 and K. D. White, "The Parable of the Sower," *JTS* n.s. 15 (1964), 300–37 (301f.) insist that what is meant is not the proportion of harvest to seed but the yield from individual seeds, the number of seeds on each stalk (or ear). Jeremias, in his reply to White ("Palästinakundliches zum Gleichnis vom Saemann (Mc iv: 3–8 par.)," *NTS* 13 [1966/67], 48–53 [53]) denies this.

24. Jeremias, *Parables*, 150 and again in "Palästinakundliches . . . ," 53. Lagrange, *Mc.*, 92f. contains a good deal of information on the matter and notes that Arab *claims* of fifty to one are exaggerated. Texts and discussion are given by White and Jeremias (see previous note); see also next note.

25. White, "Sower," *passim*; Swete, *Mk.*, 71 (who cites Gen. 26:12 as well as Wettstein and J. Lightfoot *ad loc.*); Schmid, *Mk.*, 193; Johnson, *Mk.*, 88f. (for the plain of Gennesareth near Capharnaum); Lagrange, *Luc*, 238 cites evidence that 50 for 1 is a good yield on the shores of Lake Tiberias. The texts in Wettstein, though taken from many lands in different centuries and thus not conclusive for first-century Palestine, do not provide much support for the view that a 100-fold harvest is unusual; see esp. Strabo, *Geog.* XV.iii.11 (100 or even 200 for 1 in Susis); Theophr. *Hist. plant.* VIII.vii.4 (50, or with care, 100 for 1 in Babylon, 4th cent. B.C.); Sib. Or. III.264 (100 for 1). Dr. Sprenger, "Jesu Säe- und Erntegleichnisse, aus den palästinischen Ackerbauverhältnissen dargestellt," *Palästinajahrbuch* 9 (1913), 79–97, esp. 83–87 notes that a 300-fold or even 400-fold return from single kernels may be expected under good conditions and explicitly rejects the possibility that these modern results are much different from those to be expected in the first century.

necessarily the central point of the story; the parable would then speak of the certainty of the harvest in the face of obstacles or indications to the contrary but not (directly) of its greatness. It should be noted, however, that there is nothing in the rest of the parable which would suggest to the original hearers the centrality of a spectacular harvest at the end.

A third possible interpretation of the parable is one in which the soil—or, since the soil itself is hardly mentioned, the fate of the seed in different soils—is central. In this interpretation the nature of the harvest and even the certainty of its coming are relatively unimportant, while attention is focused on the different (and largely negative) responses to the sowing.[26] In this case the author of the parable stands not at or near the dawning of the harvest but in the midst of different kinds of soils, urging his hearers to be the kind of soil which will prevent external dangers (birds, sun, thorns) from destroying the seed—although interestingly enough just what is required to be this kind of soil is not spelled out.[27] If this was the original emphasis, the allegorizing of the differing fates of the seeds is almost inevitable. But was it?

Two factors in the Markan text seem to indicate that it was. In the first place, five verses of the parable are devoted to the seeds and the different kinds of soils (vv. 4–8), while only part of the last verse speaks of the harvest.[28] Secondly, there is a clear progression in the description of the hearers, so that different seeds are lost, not only in three different ways (which would be inevitable in storytelling) but also at different stages of growth; the dramatic scenery is not only logical but also rather highly developed.[29] The common argument that the allegorical explana-

---

26. Schniewind's explanation, "The normal result (Erfolg) of the Word of God is failure (Misserfolg)" (Mk., 74) over-interprets this point.

27. "So the allegory remains dramatic, satanological, rather than psychological or pietist" (Bonnard, Matt., 198).

28. Lohmeyer/Schmauch, Matt., 198; George, "Semailles," 167.

29. Riesenfeld, "Sower," 186f. notes that some factors (rain, for example) are omitted because they are unnecessary for describing the fate of the seed; similarly, C. F. D. Moule, "Mark 4:1–20 Yet Once More," Neotestamentica et Semitica [Matthew Black Festschrift] (Edinburgh: T. & T. Clark, 1969), 94–113 (111). George, "Semailles," 165f., on the other hand, finds in the progression of the parable proper an "optimism" that is not very prominent in the explanation, a

tion in vv. 14–20 represents a *fundamental* shift in emphasis from that in vv. 3–9 becomes persuasive only as we postulate a much simpler original form of the parable itself,[30] a possibility that form-criticism allows for but certainly does not require.

Could such a parable, in its present form or a simpler one, go back to Jesus? Emanuel Hirsch[31] argues that the parable and explanation stand or fall together, and since the explanation is inauthentic, the parable must be also. Jülicher,[32] on the other hand, argues just the reverse: since parable and explanation belong together, both must go back to Jesus. Both cases are overstated. Of course the explanation allegorizes the details given in the parable; a high degree of correspondence is therefore to be expected and does not in itself guarantee identity of origin. On the other hand, the fact that not all the details of the parable are allegorized (cf. the Tares) is hardly proof that the parable and explanation were originally, in some simpler form, non-allegorical. The fate of the seeds is so naturally described that we may safely accept it as a true parable, not an allegory, although one which by its concentration on various types of soils lent itself naturally to allegorical elaboration. In view of the linguistic evidence of late provenance for the explanation, we need have little hesitation in viewing vv. 14–20 as a late—though pre-Markan—allegorization of the original parable, while the description of Palestinian agriculture[33]

---

difference that is particularly clear in comparison with the similar (late first-century) parable in 4 Ezra 8:41f.: "They that are sown . . . shall not all be saved."
30. Jülicher, *Gleichn.*, II, 537ff. thinks of a simpler form of both parable and explanation, Haenchen, *Weg*, 169–186 (esp. 185f.), of the parable alone.
31. *Frühgeschichte des Evangeliums* (I², Tübingen: J. C. B. Mohr, 1951), I, 29.
32. *Gleichn.*, II, 532ff. Riesenfeld, "Sower," 192 (cf. also 187) also believes that "the parable and the interpretation fit each other as hand fits glove."
33. Sowing before ploughing (bSabb. 73b; Jub. 11:23); the rocky ledge covered with thin soil (v. 5, "a characteristic feature of the cornlands of Galilee," Swete, *Mk.*, 69); cf. Theophr. *De causis plant.* III.20.5. Philo, *De Abr.* 134 (Loeb, VI, 68) notes that the land of the Sodomites, later called Palestinian Syria, had once been "deep-soiled" (*bathygeios*), from which it is evident that it no longer was so in Philo's time. The discussion in Jeremias, *Parables*, 9f. should be corrected in the light of the remarks of White, "Sower," *passim*, who however grants that the sower behaves "in a way in which any competent Mediterranean farmer of the period would normally behave" (307), and John Drury, "The Sower, the Vineyard, and the Place of Allegory in the Interpretation of Mark's Parables," *JTS* n.s. 24 (1973), 367–379, who does not.

and the existence of Semitisms in Mark's account[34] suggest a somewhat early and probably Palestinian origin for the parable itself.
Does "early" and "Palestinian" imply authenticity? The answer to
this question is uncertain. It is, of course, historically certain that
Jesus' preaching brought a limited response and not impossible
that the parable was given in reference to this fact.[35] Nevertheless,
we have little evidence that Jesus was primarily concerned with
the state of his hearers' hearts[36] rather than the inbreaking Kingdom and its implications for all of human life. Insofar as the parable is primarily concerned with such subjective differences
among men it represents an emphasis that is peripheral, if not
totally foreign, to Jesus' message.

Now, finally, we are ready to examine the details in Mk. and to
inquire about his central concerns. If the interpretation of his intentions in the editing of the context[37] is correct, his central
theme is not parenesis but encouragement. To what extent do the
details of this parable reflect this and other Markan concerns?

The incident begins with "again," which looks back to 2:13 and
3:7ff., where the motif crowd/sea/boat appears; since v.1 is redactional it is probable that Mark intends the same boat he has earlier
(3:9) mentioned as a possible escape from the crowd, the same
boat that reappears in 5:21. Mark's "he began to teach" (v. 1)

---

34. *kai egeneto* (v. 4), omitted by both Matthew and Luke and corrected by
D W *pc* lat; *karpon didonai* (vv. 7, 8), omitted at v. 7 by both Matthew and Luke
and corrected to *karpon poiēsai* by Luke at v. 8; *hen* [*bis? ter?*] with the num-
bers in vv. 8, 20 in various texts, some of which could well have preserved the
original reading against B—a certain Semitism (*cf.* Black, *Aram. Approach*, 90).
The total absence of hypotactic aorist participles here, as in the Markan parables
generally (ibid., 45f.), is also compatible with, though hardly proof of, a Semitic
origin.
35. So, *inter alia*, Wellhausen, *Mk.*, 34; McNeile, *Matt.*, 187; Taylor, *Mk.*, 250f.;
Jeremias, *Parables*, 151; Rawlinson, *Mk.*, 50. Most of these interpreters, of necessity, place it late in Jesus' ministry, not (as in Mk.) early. Léon-Dufour, *Études*,
282f. places it in the middle, after Jesus' teaching had encountered difficulties
but before the break with his opponents was complete.
36. Jülicher, *Gleichn.*, II, 532: the sermon's fate depends on the hearer's heart;
similarly, George Ladd, "The Life-setting of the Parables of the Kingdom,"
JBR 31 (1963), 193–199 (198): "The Kingdom . . . requires a human response to
be effective" and again in "The *Sitz im Leben* of the Parables of Matthew 13: The
Soils," in *Studia Evangelica* II, ed. F. L. Cross (Berlin: Akademie-Verlag, 1964),
203–210 (208f.); George, "Semailles," 167f.; Masson, *Paraboles*, 39.
37. See the opening paragraphs of this section, above.

suggests a new section, as do the redundant phrases in v. 2, which imply that the Sower is the first, or perhaps the most important, of several parabolic passages in Jesus' teaching. Whether Jesus' *sitting* in the boat to teach is simply good sense or rabbinic example[38] is not clear.

Before beginning the parable proper Jesus urges his hearers to "Listen!" This motif, repeated in more elaborate form following the parable (v. 9) and again following the Manifestation of What Is Hidden (v. 23), most naturally suggests, as commonly in the NT,[39] the presence of a mystery,[40] and this would be consistent with Mark's view that a parable is no mere pedagogical device. In any case, the parable describes the fate of four different groups of seeds and furnishes the occasion for the "hardening theory" of vv. 10–12. Jesus then returns to this single parable, saying that if his disciples do not understand this one, they will not grasp the others either. The explanation (vv. 14–20) is, as commonly recognized, parenetic. Quite possibly Mark has both accepted and elaborated this emphasis in his wording, "immediately" (v. 15), "persecution for the sake of the word," (v. 17), and perhaps "the deceitfulness of riches" in the midst of general temptations (v. 19). Good seed, however, in spite of all, hear the Word, accept it, and bring forth fruit in varying degrees.

There is little doubt that the explanation is thus, in its Markan form, Christian parenesis, or that Mark so understood it. Both warning and promise go together. But this alone does not control the import of the whole section for Mark, or he would not have inserted vv. 10–12 into his source.[41] Just as the parable probably

---

38. Cf. Matt. 5:1; 13:1; 24:3; Pes. 26a (on Joḥanan ben Zakkai). Linnemann, *Parables*, 114 sees this feature as indicating that Jesus is understood as a teacher with authority.

39. See the passages listed in note 6 above.

40. Johnson, *Mk.*, 88; its later use as an esoteric formula need not be Mark's meaning. The clearly secondary addition to v. 9, *kai ho syniōn synietō* (D it sy^hmg) imports the Matthean theme of understanding into the Markan text.

41. Haenchen, *Weg*, 170f. holds that vv. 21–25 (which he understands parenetically) were so firmly attached to vv. 14–20 that Mark could not connect vv. 11f. directly to the explanation. But this does not explain why these verses *could* be inserted between the parable and the explanation! Nor does Haenchen really show that vv. 21–25 are parenetic for Mark.

originated in the problematic response to Christian preaching,[42] so Mark is more concerned with the gift of the Kingdom and its manifestation in spite of obstacles and difficulties than with the ethical, moral, and religious life of his readers. If this is correct, the teaching of Jesus, of which the Sower is a key part (v. 13) concerns the mystery of the Kingdom of God, given to some but hidden from others, hidden not because of human obstinacy but in order (eventually) to be revealed (vv. 21f.).

We must, then, distinguish three stages in the growth of this parable:

1. The parable came into existence without the explanation and served in the church as an answer to the problem of the mixed reception given Christian preaching:[43] such reception no more calls into question the full coming of the Kingdom than the loss of some seed creates doubts about the probability of the harvest. (If the parable goes back to Jesus, something like this must also have been its original meaning.)

2. Somewhat later, the details of the parable are allegorized and the explanation appended. It is then used parenetically, to ask the hearers (readers?) "What kind of soil are you?" At this stage the problems which have actually caused some converts to leave the faith are spelled out as dangers to the unsuccessful seed. This parenetic form was presumably the form of Mark's source for chapter 4.

3. Mark himself has reworked the whole, inserting his "hardening theory" between the parable and the explanation and appending a series of statements and parables (vv. 21–35) from various sources to serve a complex purpose, primarily of encouragement for him with ears to hear: the coming of the harvest is sure, for the *mysterion* of the Kingdom has been given.

Which of these three interpretations is most significant at any given time and place will depend largely on whether the individ-

---

42. Loisy, *ES*, I, 757.
43. The term "contrast-parable" is unfortunate. The stress in the parable is the difficulties faced by the seed, not the smallness of the original sowing. (Rightly, Léon-Dufour, *Études*, 274f.)

ual or church using the parable is discouraged, complacent, or fearful.

6. The Lamp and the Bushel (4:21; cf. Matt. 5:15; Lk. 8:16; 11:33)

The literary analysis of this saying in Mark is extremely complex. It is a part of vv. 21–25, a group of sayings that follow the explanation of the Sower (vv. 13–20) and precede the parables of the Seed Growing Secretly (vv. 26–29) and the Mustard Seed (vv. 30–32, Mk., Q). But we do not know how great a unity Mark intended by this arrangement or how many of the sayings in vv. 21–25 he understood as "parables."[1] In addition we do not know whether vv. 21–25 are associated, for Mark, through a mere catchword connection (*modios, metros, metreō*) or by virtue of a true correspondence in content, although the latter seems, on the basis of the use Mark actually makes of the sayings, more probable.

Some things, however, are clear. All the sayings in vv. 21–25 are addressed to the disciples. The double "and he said to them" (vv. 21, 24) indicates, as commonly in this chapter,[2] a rather loose connection. And the fact that these brief sayings are followed by two further parables may mean either that Mark simply left them where he found them and appended the following parables himself[3] or that Mark has inserted these originally independent sayings into his pre-Markan source, which connected v. 26 directly to v. 20.[4] If vv. 21–25 are primarily parenetic, the former view is more probable, since parenesis is obviously central in the explanation of the Sower. If, on the other hand, these verses stress encouragement instead of parenesis, the latter is somewhat more likely,

---

1. Schmid, *Mk.*, 88 is doubtless correct that, since for Mark a parable is any kind of *Rätselwort*, he must have thought of all four sentences (vv. 21, 22, 24, 25) as parables; so also Masson, *Paraboles*, 20. Jeremias, *Parables*, 91 (cf. also 41, n. 69) argues that for Mark the four sayings are "an actual double parable, and not . . . a collection of sayings." In this study vv. 24 and 25 are taken together, while the Lamp and Bushel and the Measure are taken as separate parables.
2. Cf. 4:2, 11, 21, 24: *kai elegen autois*, Markan redaction; 4:9, 26, 30: *kai elegen*, pre-Markan tradition.
3. So Schmid, *Mk.*, 87 and, by implication, Swete, *Mk.*, 77.
4. So Haenchen, *Weg*, 161, n. 2; Linnemann, *Parables*, 180, n. 1.

since Mark's intention in this chapter is not essentially parenetic, as the discussion of the Sower has shown.

The first "parable" in vv. 21–25 is the Lamp and the Bushel (v. 21). Its form in Mk.[5] (unlike Q) is a question, and a rigorous insistence on the difference between *ou* and *mē* in Greek leads to the over-literal translation, "A[6] lamp is not brought[7] to be put under a[6] peck basket or under a[6] couch, is it? Is it not brought to be put on[8] a[6] lampstand?" This leading question is doubtless sharper than the simple statement transmitted by Matthew and Luke, but the answer is clear enough: No, it is not, and Yes, it is.

But what is the reference? The answer to this question is, as so often, related to the question of the saying's origin, as well as its most primitive form.[9] While the furniture (lamp, lampstand, peck

5. For an excellent discussion of the relationship between Mark and the most primitive form of the saying, see Gerhard Schneider, "Das Bildwort von der Lampe. Zur Traditionsgeschichte eines Jesus-Wortes," ZNW 61 (1970), 183–209 (197ff.). He holds that the following are all Markan: a) the question form, b) both *archetai* (cf. v. 22b; the *ēlthon*-sayings of 1:38 and 2:17; and 10:45) and the definite article (= Jesus comes as *the* Light). c) the *hina*-clauses in 4:22, and d) the secondary addition "or under the bed." All but the last point would seem to be well-taken.

6. The definite articles in the Greek should properly be translated as indefinite, since the saying is generalized; on this Semitism, see Black, *Aram. Approach*, 68ff. J. Duncan M. Derrett, *Law in the NT* (London: Darton, Longman & Todd, 1970), 200 suggests rather that "the lamp" = "the Hanukkah lamp," but this would not have been evident to Jesus' hearers or Mark's readers and does not account for the other definite articles in the saying.

7. Literally, " the lamp comes," which is popular speech; cf. Jülicher, Gleichn., II, 81, who cites Bar. 3:33 and Heliodorus viii.12 (both Greek!). Jeremias, "Lampe," in *ABBA*, 100 argues that this, as well as the use of the definite article and the double-question, reflects Palestinian speech-modes, but this is highly uncertain. (Cf. Schneider, "Lampe," 186ff., 197f.) Something like ". . . is brought" must be supplied in translation. The awkwardness of the Greek was early noted and corrected: *haptetai* D it; *kaietai* (W) Φ sa bo[pt].

8. The reading *hypo* for *epi* (so B* ℵ) is very old, but still *lectio corruptior*.

9. Jeremias, "Lampe," in *ABBA*, 99–102 holds that in its original form the saying merely contrasted "lighting" a lamp and "extinguishing" it; on this view, ". . . or under a bed" is a secondary addition, since it weakens the image from "extinguish" to "hide." As Schnackenburg, "Salz der Erde," 183 notes, however, *titheasin* does not fit this interpretation (to extinguish a lamp, one puts something over it; one does not put the lamp under something else), which could only, therefore, fit some even more primitive form. (The significance of the verb is missed by many commentators.) Derrett's study of this parable (*Law*, 189–207) is a charming (if largely irrelevant) attempt to ground the saying in the very practical problems arising for married couples faced with a) the prohibition of sexual intercourse in the presence of a lighted lamp, b) the very severe taboo against sexual relationships during menstruation and the need of a lamp to check the matter, c) the prohibition against extinguishing a lamp on the Sabbath, and d) the general suitability of the Sabbath (a non-work day!) for various forms of festivity. Obviously, the Hanukkah lamp, which must be kept lighted for eight days, poses the problem in a very acute form.

basket, and bed) belong to "the commonest furniture of a Galilean home"[10] this provides little help, because there is nothing geographically or sociologically distinctive about these few items. Quite possibly some popular wisdom-saying has been taken up into this verse,[11] but, since the Q form reduces to something different from Mk., we are no longer able to discern the earliest form(s) or meaning(s).

If the saying originated with Jesus, it could have been used either positively or negatively (or, quite possibly, both). Positively, it would then refer it not so much to the fate of the Word[12] as to Jesus himself and his mission; it might have meant that Jesus did not intend to hide himself (Mk.) but to be a light to all Israel (Matt., Q).[13] Much less probably, the peculiar expression, "the light comes" reflects the "coming" of the Kingdom in the ministry of Jesus,[14] for whatever this interpretation gains by being related to the central motif in Jesus' preaching, the coming of the Kingdom, is more than offset by the fact that it turns the parable into an almost pure allegory.

If the saying was originally used negatively, however, it must have reflected the traditions that Israel, the Law, Jerusalem, righteous men, etc.[15] are the "light" of the world and referred to those among the Jewish leaders who were "hiding" the true meaning of the Law under their particular traditions.[16] This represents at least a plausible form of the controversy between Jesus and his con-

---

10. Swete, *Mk.*, 78. Jülicher, *Gleichn.*, II, 81 is not sure that the *klinē*, a kind of sofa, would self-evidently be part of the furnishings of extremely humble homes.
11. The multiple attestation of both the "salt-" and "light-" sayings does not necessarily guarantee their authenticity; vs. Schnackenburg, "Salz der Erde," 194.
12. Still less to a rudimentary form of the "teaching church." (So Lagrange, *Mc.*, 112–115.)
13. Jeremias, *Parables*, 120f. and "Lampe," in *ABBA*, 102 thinks Jesus refers to his mission, refusing to protect himself from danger; somewhat similarly, Schneider, "Lampe," 208. Even if the contrast is not "light/extinguish" (so Jeremias) but only "give light/hide one's light [i.e., be very cautious]," the interpretation still makes good sense. But it is not easy to find parallels to either this teaching or this problem in the Gospels.
14. Souček, "Salz," 172f., who holds that this is what is meant by *both* Mark and Jesus.
15. See Billerbeck, I, 237; cf. also Schnackenburg, "Salz der Erde," 190f.
16. Dodd, *Parables*, 145; Johnson, *Mk.*, 93; B. T. D. Smith, *Parables*, 171.

temporaries; but the text itself in no way suggests that this was the original reference.

Older commentators often interpreted the saying in the context of the immediately adjoining verses, esp. vv. 13–20: the seed produces harvest, the lamp gives light.[17] Yet the obligation of fruit-bringing can hardly be the original meaning of v. 21, since form-critical analysis shows that the close connection between v. 21 and vv. 13–20 originated not with Jesus but with the pre-Markan tradition or (much more probably) with Mark himself. A very important indicator of the saying's meaning *for Mark*, however, is given by the present context: the "hiddenness" theme, which does not fit after the explanation of the Sower, fits very well with v. 22 (as Jülicher admits) and with Mark's main theological concerns. The suggestion of van Koetsveld, so brusquely rejected by Jülicher, that Christianity is portrayed, in opposition to the mysteries, as the religion of freedom and full public disclosure, contains at least the partial truth that for Mark public disclosure *after the resurrection* is crucial, the obverse of his insistence on hiddenness during the life of Jesus.[18] The "lamp" has become for Mark, not merely any lamp, and not specifically the "light coming into the world," i.e., Jesus himself,[19] but the gospel, the Word being proclaimed in the church of Mark's day.[20] Both the context and the peculiarities of the wording show this motif to be central. In Mk., the lamp is not brought in order that men may see the light (Luke), nor is it brought and put on a stand with the result that it gives light (Matthew); it is brought *in order to be put on a stand*.[21] The public view of the lamp, not its light-giving function, is primary for Mark. So far as this is parenetic at all, it encourages

---

17. Jülicher, *Gleichn.*, II, 86.

18. For the discussion, see ibid., 86f.

19. See Lagrange, *Mc.*, 113; Grundmann, *Mk.*, 96; Schweizer, *Mk.*, 55.

20. Masson, *Paraboles*, 40; Souček, "Salz," 172. Jeremias, in *Parables*, 107, 120 and "Lampe," in *ABBA*, 99–102 argues: Matthew = the disciples; Mark = Jesus' message; Luke (and Jesus) = Jesus himself.

21. Julius Wellhausen, *Einleitung in die drei ersten Evangelien* (Berlin: Georg Reimer, 1905), 22 may be quite right that behind the Greek *hina* in both v. 21 and v. 22 lies the ambiguous Aram. *d*^{e}; so also Dodd, *Parables*, 114, n. 1. In *Mk.*, however, the *hina* must be given its full force.

bold public proclamation. Contextually (especially vv. 24f.) it is an encouragement-saying and implies that the "hiddenness" in Jesus' life and ministry was a deliberate (and temporary) part of the action of the *Deus absconditus* in that ministry.[22] If a polemic purpose is also intended, it can only (like the following verse) be meant to oppose those who hold to a tradition of post-resurrection secret teaching grounded in the "hidden" aspects of Jesus' pre-resurrection ministry.

7. The Manifestation of What Is Hidden (4:22; cf. Matt. 10:26; Lk. 8:17; 12:2f.)

This brief wisdom-saying, so like the proverbial wisdom in which it may have originated,[1] must have had a curious history in the primitive church, as its various forms and multiple attestation show. Käsemann has argued that sayings of this type, especially gnomic sayings which contrast (often by the use of the same word) an earthly action with a heavenly judgment, may have been created out of popular sayings and given an eschatological stamp by early apocalyptic Christian prophets.[2] Such "sentences of holy law," he believes, then became part of the tradition of early Christian communities, often losing their eschatological reference and becoming gnomic utterances in the process. Whether this saying reflects such a development is unclear, but the wording (especially in isolation from the present contexts) shows that it must originally have encouraged prudential action and meant (as in Q) that anything hidden in the past *will be* brought to light in the future—not that it was hidden originally *in order to be* brought to light (Mk.). The Q form is clearly primary, the Markan form secondary.[3]

But does the saying come from Jesus, and if so, what might it

---

22. "Just as it is the *raison d'être* of a lamp to give light, so it is the *raison d'être* of truth to be revealed" (Rawlinson, Mk., 54).

1. Bultmann, *HST*, 95f., 102; Jeremias, *Parables*, 221, n. 66.

2. "Sentences of Holy Law in the NT," *NT Questions of Today* (London: SCM Press, 1969), 66–81. A brief discussion of Mk. 4:22 par. occurs on pp. 99–100 of the same volume.

3. Vs. Jülicher, *Gleichn.*, II, 92.

have meant? Which single context explains its original referent?[4] Some[5] think of an original eschatological reference, in which the "coming to light" is a symbol for the End, but this stress on "hidden secrets" is a rare motif in Jesus' teaching. Further, we must reject the view[6] that the saying represents a grounding in common experience of the demand that faith bring forth fruit; all forms of the saying, as Jülicher notes, refer to the realm of knowledge, not conduct. On the whole, then, we can say little about what the saying might have meant in the teaching of Jesus.

In the pre-Markan tradition, the form[7] of the saying must have been much like what is preserved in Matt. and Lk. from Q, since the repeated uses of *hina* in this section (cf. vv. 12, 21 [*bis*], 22 [*bis*]) represent both Mark's literary modifications and his theological concerns. The possibility that the *hina* comes originally from an ambiguous Aramaic form[8] does not explain what the reference might have been in that earlier form, unless it has been preserved for us by either Matthew or Luke. If the reference has not been preserved there, it has been totally lost to us.

Mark's meaning, however, is not so elusive. The esoteric reference is quite clear: the original hiding was deliberate, and its intention was not preservation but revelation. Jülicher[9] notes,

4. J. M. Bover, "Nada hay encubierto que no se descubra," *Estudios Bíblicos* 13 (1954), 319–323 holds that *both* the Q and the Markan forms are authentic and come from two separate occasions. This is, in view of the close connection between the language and Markan theology, highly unlikely.

5. Davies, *Setting*, 459; Jeremias, *Parables*, 221, n. 66; Engelbert Neuhäusler, "Mit welchem Massstab misst Gott die Menschen?" *Bibel und Leben* 11 (1970), 104–113 (106); Taylor, *Mk.*, 264. Hauck, *Lk.*, 110 suggests the hiddenness of the Kingdom, the hidden dignity of Jesus (both Markan themes!) or something similar. Jacques Dupont, *Gnosis* (Louvain/Paris: E. Nauwelaerts/J. Gabalda, 1949), 196f. thinks Matthew has preserved the original eschatological sense and that Mark has generalized the saying. Lohmeyer, *Mk.*, 85 insists on the connection with the Kingdom, but in the theology of Mark, not Jesus.

6. Jülicher, *Gleichn.*, II, 92.

7. And, probably, its *meaning* as well: the Matt./Lk. forms both fit with the view (Dieter Lührmann, *Die Redaktion der Logienquelle* [Neukirchen: Neukirchener Verlag, 1969], 50f.) that the Q context related to the disciples' preaching (as promise or consolation), not to a contrast between the disciples' understanding and the non-understanding of the crowds.

8. See above, chap. 6, sec. 6, n. 21; Lagrange, *Mc.*, civ. Black, *Aram. Approach*, 58, on the contrary, insists that the meaning "which shall not be revealed" (Matt./Lk., Q?) "commends itself as the simpler and as the necessary and natural one in the context," while Wilkens, "Redaktion," 313, n. 32 rightly notes that the final construction in vv. 21f. is characteristically Markan.

9. *Gleichn.*, II, 92.

although he himself rejects, the view common in his day that the saying (as in Lk. 8) reflects an anti-Gnostic tendency, as if Jesus were here emphasizing the fact that he has no esoteric teaching. Since Jülicher's own interpretation of the saying (faith must bring forth fruit) must be rejected, however, it is fair to ask whether what Jesus could not have meant is not precisely what Mark does. In its present context it refers to the mystery revealed in the parables,[10] to the temporary confiding of the gospel to the disciples for the sake of its public proclamation after the ascension.[11] For although Mark insists that the Kingdom is in many respects a mystery during Jesus' lifetime, a mystery ill-understood even by his disciples, "it will not always be so, and it is not meant to be so."[12] After the Son of Man had risen from the dead (the period in which Mark and all his readers were living), the disciples would understand both Jesus' message and his cross, and they would be powerfully released from the obligation to "tell no one what they had seen" (9:9). The two brief parables in vv. 21f., in other words, have an importance in Mark's theology all out of proportion to their size. No stress on the Messianic secret—a crucial motif in his thought—should be allowed to obscure the fact that Mark sees the church of his own day as not only competent but obliged to proclaim its understanding of the light that came with Jesus Christ.[13]

8. The Measure (4:24f.)

The last two gnomic sayings[1] in vv. 21–25 are introduced by the

---

10. Johnson, *Mk.*, 93.

11. Swete, *Mk.*, 78; Schneider, "Lampe," 196; Gnilka, *Verstockung*, 78; and esp. Wrede, *Messiasgeheimnis*, 70 (ET: 71). For a time only the disciples possess the secret, "but some day—more plainly, *after the resurrection*, they are to lift the veil from it and spread it abroad." (His italics.)

12. Taylor, *Mk.*, 264.

13. "Whatever limitation is intended, it is only temporary" (Siegmann, "Teaching . . . ," 169); so also Jeremias, *Parables*, 221, n. 66; Gnilka, *Verstockung*, 78 and esp. Minette de Tillesse, *Secret*, 281 and *passim*, who further adds (almost certainly correctly) that this full manifestation has already been foreshadowed in the gradual clarification of the Secret in the latter part of Mark, particularly in the great confessions of 14:62 and 15:39.

1. For parallels to v. 24 see Wisd. Sol. 11:15f.; 12:23ff.; 18:4–11; Sir. 16:12, 14; Billerbeck, I, 444–446; Black, *Aram. Approach*, 244, and n. 4 (on these Aramaic

general warning, "Take heed what you hear," which must be taken (given the absence of parenesis in both wording and context) to refer to teaching rather than to conduct; he who has ears is to hear (v. 23), i.e., to listen to what is being authoritatively proclaimed (publicly) in the churches of Mark's day.

This is not, to be sure, the only possible interpretation of the verses. Many commentators[2] connect the sayings in various ways with the Sower, arguing that "your attention to the teaching will be the measure of the profit you will receive from it"[3] or that the results which will follow upon the truth offered depend upon the care and zeal with which one hears and accepts the Word.[4] In spite of the fact that these verses come from different original contexts, they all represent, it is held, a demand for fruit-bearing.[5]

We do not know, of course, what the sayings might have meant in their original context, now lost, since the possible applications are almost limitless.[6] Yet it should be clearly recognized that the two sayings are contradictory in principle: If he who has will be given according to the measure that he has (so both verses), what about him who has not? Will he be given according to the little that he does have (v. 24), or will even this little be taken away (v. 25)? The fact that Mark has not (like Luke)[7] eliminated this dilemma shows that he is using traditional material, on the one hand, and that he does not understand the sayings in terms of a

---

and Hebrew parallels see H. P. Rüger, "Mit welchem Mass ihr messt, wird euch gemessen werden," *ZNW* 60 [1969], 174–182, who shows that the well-known rabbinic saying is used in an eschatological sense in the Targums). On v. 25, cf. Prov. 9:9; (1:5); 4 Ezra 7:25; Billerbeck, I, 660ff.

2. An exception is Dupont, "Chapitre," 804f., who rightly connects all of vv.21–25 with vv. 11f.

3. Swete, *Mk.*, 83; cf. Dodd, *Parables*, 148, n. 2.

4. Schmid, *Mk.*, 101; similarly, Joseph Huby, "Sur un passage du second Évangile, Marc iv, 21–25," *RSR* 1 (1910), 168–174 (172).

5. Jülicher, *Gleichn.*, II, 93.

6. Form-critical analysis suggests that Matt. 7:2 is the most primitive of the various forms of the saying in the Gospels. It is evident, furthermore, on both history-of-religions and form-critical grounds that the original form, esp. of the Measure, implied an exact equivalence; see, in addition to the material in n. 1 above, the Egyptian parallels cited in B. Couroyer, "De la mesure dont vous mesures il vous sera mesuré," *RB* 77 (1970), 366–370, which teach that the *same* measure must be used for both buying and selling, a legalism that Luke (particularly) and Mark have left far behind.

7. Who omits the Measure entirely at this point and rewords v. 25.

general parenetic principle, on the other. What he must intend is a promise and a warning: now that the light has been given its intended place in the open, Christians of Mark's day are to pay solemn heed to that revealed light, in the calm assurance of appropriate, even exorbitant,[8] reward (in this world?) for hearing, and in the certainty of (eschatological) punishment for failure to hear.[9] In one sense, this interpretation is not very much different from the common one. Yet in its stress on the truth then being openly proclaimed rather than the subjective state of the hearers, it supports Mark's general stress on the revelation of the Hidden God and connects vv. 21–25 closely with vv. 11f. (rather than with vv. 14–20): obedient servants, not people of good and thoughtful character, are the objects of the divine approbation.

9. The Mustard Seed (4:30ff.; cf. Matt. 13:31f.)[1]

This brief and familiar parable is, in Mk., the third "seed" parable, the last in a chapter that began with the Sower (4:1–20) and also included the Seed Growing Secretly (4:26–29). Literary details show that Mark is modifying, not creating the basic parable: the opening formula is biblical and rabbinic;[2] the tautological "... or what parable shall we use for it" is a *hapax legomenon*, hardly to be expected if the whole passage were Mark's creation;

---

8. The addition *kai prostethesetai hymin* (omitted by D W *pc* b e) is clearly a (Markan?) corrective to the simple "equivalence" which the saying implies without it; Neuhäusler. "Massstab," 106f. The well-attested further addition *tois akouousin* (ℝ A ⊖ 0107 0133 λ Φ *pm* q sy^p sa bo^pt) should be understood, on internal grounds, as a further addition to restore the balance to the saying which the (Markan?) addition has disturbed.

9. Hauck, *Mk.*, 56f. goes beyond this: the disciples are responsible not only to hear for themselves but also to pass on what they have heard; so also Alex. Pallis, *Notes . . . Mk.*, 15; and *Notes on St. Luke and Acts* (London: Oxford University Press, 1928), 16f., who interprets *akouein* = to be taught.

1. Lk. 13:18f. is apparently based solely on Q; the present work, therefore, does not discuss his interpretation of the Mustard Seed. But the reason Luke omits it at the Markan parallel is evident: his theme in chap. 8 is the responsibility of hearing and doing the will of God, whereas this parable "presupposes no . . . effort on man's part" (Dupont, "Chapitre," 810).

2. See M.-J. Lagrange, "La parabole en dehors de l'évangile," *RB* 6 (1909), 198–212, 342–367 (356); Paul Fiebig, *Altjüdische Gleichnisse und die Gleichnisse Jesu* (Tübingen/Leipzig: J. C. B. Mohr, 1904), 77–80; Billerbeck, II, 7ff. Lagrange, *Mc.*, 118 suggests that the (double) question implies some intimacy between the speaker and his hearers; cf. Is. 40:18.

and a special awkwardness is evident in the relationship between
v. 31 and v. 32: the phrase "when it is sown" makes good sense in
v. 32, but (since the size of the seed is the same both before and
after sowing) it does not in v. 31, which "reads like a rough note
translated without any attempt to remove grammatical difficulties."[3] To avoid these problems Luke apparently ignores Mk. in
favor of Q,[4] Matthew combines Mk. and Q into a smoother
(though not entirely consistent) form, and early scribes rework
the opening formulas in a bewildering variety of ways. It is possible to argue that the Mustard Seed originally belonged somewhere else[5] or that Mark himself first connected it with the other
seed parables[6] or, as seems most probable, that the connection at
least with the Sower was already made in the pre-Markan source
of chapter 4. What is clear is that a proverbial saying[7] about the
smallness of a mustard seed has become part of a general comparison of limited agricultural exactitude.[8] The growth of a tiny
seed into a shrub great enough to support birds and their nests in
its branches is somehow analogous to the Kingdom of God.
Whether the contrast between the beginning and the end or the
inclusion of the birds and nests is the focal point in the story cannot be separated from the particular stage in the tradition one is
talking about.

In Mk., two motifs from the LXX rendering of Dan. 4 are
mingled, the *shade* of the great tree (which provides protection)[9]

---

3. Swete, *Mk.*, 82.
4. See Eberhard Jüngel, *Paulus und Jesus* (Tübingen: J. C. B. Mohr, 1962; 3.
Aufl., 1967), 152f. and, for a proposed reconstruction of the Q form, Harvey K.
McArthur, "The Parable of the Mustard Seed," *CBQ* 33 (1971), 198–210 (200ff.).
5. Loisy, *ES*, I, 768.
6. Jülicher, *Gleichn.*, II, 570.
7. See, besides Matt. 17:20 (= Lk. 17:6, Q?), Ber. 31a; mTohoroth viii.8 and
mNiddah v. 2 (Danby, 728, 750); and C. H. Hunzinger, "*sinapi*," *TDNT*, VII,
287–291.
8. The mature mustard plant is more properly a tall garden herb (Mk.) than a
tree (Matt., Lk., Q), but the seed is not the smallest known. Precision is hardly
to be expected in gnomic sayings, esp. in botanical matters; cf. Kuss, "Sinngehalt,"
645; McArthur, "Mustard Seed," 201, n. 8.
9. Cf. also Judg. 9:15; Is. 51:16; Ezek. 17:23; Bar. 1:12. In the allegory of the
Cedar Tree in Ezek. 31:6, the "branches" provide both nests for the birds and
protection for the animals, the "shadow" protection for the nations.

and its *branches* (which provide a place for nesting birds). Although the readings of LXX, Theodotion, and the Aramaic of Dan. 4:9, 11, 12, 14, 18 (the numbering differs slightly in the Greek) vary in several respects, they seem to agree at least in connecting the animals with the shade and the birds (who alone can fly) with the branches. This would seem to imply that the shade or protection afforded by the mature shrub has not been lost from the imagery, as it has in Q, and that the contrast between the tiny beginning and the great ending (presumably missing in Q) is supposed somehow to stress God's providential care. Since this note of consolation is also prominent in the (Markan?) stress on mustard as the smallest of all seeds, and since consolation is central in the immediately preceding parable of the Seed Growing Secretly,[10] we may feel quite confident that Mark's intended meaning[11] is something like "the Kingdom, like the tiny mustard seed when fully grown, provides protection for all who seek its shelter."

Mark's tradition, however, probably did not stress the contrast between the small beginning and the great ending.[12] In the pre-Markan tradition the parable was probably still understood primarily in terms of the symbol of birds and branches, as a reference to the inclusion of Gentiles in the growing church, as in Q. The growth of the church into a great thing must have recalled the imagery of Dan. 4 to many in the primitive church, especially after the controversies over the terms of Gentile admission (so prominent in the forties and fifties) had died down.[13]

---

10. Swete, *Mk.*, 83: "Any impression of failure derived from the first parable [in Mk. 4] is corrected by the second and the third."

11. The contrast between the small beginning and the great ending is at best implicit in the Q forms of the Leaven and the Mustard Seed, if indeed it is present at all (cf. Lk. 13:18–21 = Matt. 13:31–33). Hence if Mark found the Mustard Seed already paired with the Leaven—which is uncertain—he must have omitted the Leaven not because it was superfluous but because it did not fit his intention.

12. Esp. if the phrase "the least of all seeds"—which Jülicher (*Gleichn.*, II, 580), Dodd (*Parables*, 190, n. 1) and Taylor (*Mk.*, 270) all consider certainly Markan—and the specific form of the concluding biblical allusion are Mark's handiwork.

13. Suhl, *Zitate*, 156 denies that 4:32b has any future reference for Mark, on the grounds that the mission has reached its goal with the possibility of Gentile admission. But the *legitimacy* of the mission and its *successes* in no way imply that it is already complete!

But what, then, might the parable have meant for Jesus? We may exclude at once those allegories, so dear to the early church, in which the seed is simply identified with Jesus (St. Hilary) or the Reign of God (St. Peter Chrystologus)[14] and understood as gradually and inevitably producing a Christianized world. Nothing in Jesus' understanding of the Kingdom suggests such a view. In addition, as Wellhausen noted long ago,[15] a specific reference to the rapid expansion of Christianity is possible only if we deny the authenticity of the parable as a whole. While it is possible that the original purpose was to set aside any doubt that the humble beginnings of the gospel might create about its ultimate fulfillment in the Kingdom,[16] this view meets with the general objection that Jesus does not seem to have been much concerned with the question of men's doubts about the Kingdom[17] and the specific objection that, as Jülicher puts it, "Jesus was a prophet, not a philosopher of history."[18] The progress of the gospel within the ongoing course of human history was at most an ancillary question for Jesus. Similarly, it is possible that Jesus in some sense either intended or foresaw the inclusion of the Gentiles in the Kingdom,[19] but the case is very far from established, and if the allusion to Daniel, which alone suggests the Gentile nations specifically, is a later addition to the original parable[20] this can hardly have been Jesus' intention.

---

14. On these, see Lagrange, Mc., 119.
15. Das Evangelium Matthaei (Berlin: Georg Reimer, 1904), 70.
16. Loisy, ES, I, 771.
17. Jüngel, PJ², 154 points out that Jesus' primary concern was not what he or the Kingdom might need (by way of defense or otherwise) but what his hearers' needs were.
18. Gleichn., II, 581. Similarly, Jüngel, PJ², 154 denies that the parable was originally negative in intention; it reflects, he insists, Jesus' teaching that the future is breaking into the present, offering to his hearers the possibility of entering the beginning of the miraculous End.
19. Dodd, Parables, 191 (who however stresses only the end of the parable—to which Jüngel aptly remarks, "In this case the birds are already building their nests on the seed!" [PJ², 153, n. 3]); Kuss, "Sinngehalt," 645, n. 2; Taylor, Mk., 269f. For the symbolism, birds = Gentiles, see Ezek. 17:23; 31:6; Dan. 4:9, 11, 18; I En. 90: 30, 33, 37; etc. On the whole question see esp. Jeremias, Promise, 46–51.
20. Johnson, Mk., 96; B. T. D. Smith, Parables, 121; Erich Grässer, Das Problem der Parusieverzögerung in den synoptischen Evangelien und in der Apostelge-

It is probable, then, that the original emphasis in the parable was the contrast between the small beginning and the great ending (which the use of a *mustard* seed makes overwhelmingly probable), and that it must have meant that the Kingdom, to be revealed in its full splendor at the Last Day,[21] does not depend upon men and women for its future:[22] from a small band of the relatively insignificant God, by his own act, will make a great Kingdom.[23]

In short, we must probably posit as the original motif what literary analysis shows to be closely related to the Markan emphasis and understand the history of this short parable somewhat as follows:

1. For Jesus, the parable implied primarily a contrast between a small beginning and a great ending and was used either negatively (to defend the presence of the Kingdom in the small beginnings of his own ministry) or positively (to invite his hearers to join in his work and thus to share proleptically in the great End). It is similar at this stage to the parable of the Leaven, with which it may have formed an original pair.

2. The "tree" imagery inevitably suggested various OT passages, among them Dan. 4, which was added to relate the parable to the Gentile mission. This stage is reflected in the pre-Markan tradition and in Q, though the pre-Q tradition (itself composite) may have used the parable without the Danielic reference or intention.

---

schichte (Berlin: Töpelmann, 1957), 62 n. 1; 141f.; Suhl, *Zitate*, 154. As McArthur, "Mustard Seed," 204 points out, if one wished to create a parable about birds nesting in branches, he would hardly start out with a mustard seed! The parable itself, therefore, can only originally have implied a smallness/greatness contrast. Dahl, "Parables," 147 denies the allegorizing allusion to the Gentiles altogether and suggests that passages like Ezek. 31:6; Judg. 9:15; Lam. 4:20; Bar. 1:12; (Ecclus. 14:26 LXX?) show that the representation of a great Kingdom by means of a great tree is traditional.

21. Schmid, *Mk.*, 104.

22. Jülicher, *Gleichn.*, II, 580; Rawlinson, *Mk.*, 58. But Dupont, "Sénevé," 901f. understands Luke (and Q) to teach the "ineluctable necessity" with which the seed becomes a tree, Luke emphasizing particularly the Great Ending.

23. Haenchen, *Weg*, 182. Franz Mussner, "I Q Hodajoth und das Gleichnis vom Senfkorn (Mk 4, 30–32 Par.)," *BibZeit* n.F. 4 (1960), 128ff. shows that something very similar is implied by 1 Q H 6:14b–17 and esp. 1 Q H 8:4–8, although he sees consolation as central to both Qumran and *Jesus*, where we would prefer to emphasize this motif in Qumran and *Mk*.

3. Mark, for whom the Gentile mission is no longer any serious problem, returned to something like the original emphasis, which however he understood as a word of consolation to Christians.

If this analysis is correct, Jesus' intention must have been to illuminate and make available to his hearers a Kingdom that is paradoxically both "already present" and "not yet fulfilled." This is the same Kingdom whether it is seen from its small beginning or its great ending, and it both is and is to come.[24] The activity of God, not the plausibility of the evidence, guarantees that great ending. In perhaps no parable of Jesus is any sharper challenge issued to our modern "scientific" way of conceiving of God's action in history.

10. The Things That Defile (7:1–23; cf. Matt. 15:1–20)[1]

This section, which essentially concludes Jesus' ministry in Galilee, is not, properly speaking, a parable. It is rather a collection of disparate materials, from various sources, into one more or less unified discourse on the general theme of defilement and the Law. How much unity Mark intended is disputed, but the "parable" (so v. 17) in v. 15 is so broadly worded that it must be applied to both what precedes and what follows.[2] Since in its present form the statement is not ambiguous—it explicitly destroys the distinction between clean and unclean foods and would have been

---

24. "It is not the purpose of either parable [the Mustard Seed or the Leaven] . . . to describe a process" (Jeremias, *Parables*, 148). Otto Kuss, "Zur Senfkornparabel," in *Auslegung und Verkündigung*, I (Regensburg: Friedrich Pustet, 1963), 78–84 specifically denies this, insisting that the ancients were not unfamiliar with the notion of "process." Dupont, "Sénevé," 907 understands the symbolism as attempting to express "the decisive significance of the present moment."

1. For a more detailed and somewhat different analysis, see my "The Things That Defile (Mark vii.15) and the Law in Matthew and Mark," *NTS* 15 (1968/69), 75–96 and, for various alternative interpretations of the parable in v. 15, Merkel, "Markus 7,15," 341–350.

2. Mark's hand is evident in the scene in vv. 1f.; in the parenthetical explanation in vv. 3f.; in v. 9 (a doublet of v. 8, connecting two originally independent pericopes); and in vv. 14, 17–18a, 20–23, which are discussed below. (V. 16 is, on textual grounds, a gloss.) Lagrange, *Mc.*, 179–193, Schmid, *Mk.*, 133f., and Merkel, "Markus 7,15" all deny the unity of vv. 1–13 and vv. 14–23, while Schmid and Merkel (somewhat inconsistently) affirm that v. 15 is the key to *both* sections. Minette de Tillesse, *Secret*, 143f. also sees vv. 1–13 as concerned with purification and vv. 14–23 with the distinction between clean and unclean, and underestimates the significance of v. 15 for both sections in Mark's theology.

resented for doing so by all of Jesus' hearers[3]—it is apparent that
the present text reflects some growth and development in transmission. An analysis of the various elements in the pericope is
therefore essential.

In broad outline, the Markan contributions seem to be clear.[4]
The context and position of the incident, plus vv.1f., 3f., 9, and
much of the specific wording are doubtless his. In addition, he has
created v. 14,[5] which serves as an introduction to the saying itself:
Jesus calls the people to himself "again"[6] in order that a little later
(vv. 17–23) he may explain the enigmatic saying privately to the
disciples. Also clearly Markan are vv. 17–18a, which reflect the
common motifs of private teaching in a house and blindness on
the part of the disciples.[7] The final bit of Markan material is
vv. 20–23, the private explanation itself. Presumably it is Mark's
own work, though largely made up of traditional Hellenistic materials.[8] V. 20 is so nearly a doublet of v. 15b that we must also
assume it to be editorial.[9] The vice list is headed by "evil
thoughts," which is not so much a vice as a general category,
elaborated in what follows by six overt acts and six vices, all
characteristically Hellenistic and without any particular cultic or
ecclesiastical reference.[10] In its present context, it may be said

3. Swete, *Mk.*, 142 believes that both Jesus' hearers and the disciples simply misunderstood Jesus, but this is historically credible only if the text was originally
less straightforward than it is now.
4. Marxsen, "Red. Erklärung," 259–263 has pointed out the structural similiarities
between 4:1–20 and 7:14–23; this suggests that the latter section, whatever its
ultimate source, has been edited to correspond with the former. It should also be
noted that 4:10ff. has no counterpart in chap. 7—that particular Markan point has
already been made, and much of the Gospel is merely commentary on it.
5. *Kai elegen autois* is Markan; see above, chap. 5, n. 26.
6. The antecedent is not clear, as the widespread substitution of *panta* for *palin* in
many texts (ℵ A W Θ λ Φ 33 700 sy^{s,p} sa^{pt} bo arm go) shows. But this usage,
most common in controversial contexts, is typically Markan (4:1; 10:1, 24, 32;
11:27).
7. In Mk. the crowds are blind, and the disciples are "also thus" (*houtōs* = *sic*
not *tam*) without understanding (v. 18a; cf. 4:12). In Matt., however, the disciples' blindness is partially mitigated, so that they are "also still" (*akmēn*) without understanding, i.e., as blind as the crowd in one limited respect, although
shortly before (13:51) they are said to have understood everything.
8. Schmid, *Mk.*, 139.
9. In spite of the redundant *ekeino. Casus pendens*, though not unknown in the
Koine, is much more common in Heb. and Aram.; see Black, *Aram. Approach*, 34ff.
10. Unlike contemporary vice lists, both pagan and Jewish, this list deals with
sins against one's neighbor *qua* neighbor, not with sins against God (or the gods),
one's nation, the social order, etc.; Lagrange, *Mc.*, 191.

that the vice list abolishes, in the name of general morality, one essential aspect of the Mosaic understanding of uncleanness. That this is Mark's intention is shown by two details in the text itself: Practically all commentators are now agreed that v. 19b is a Markan editorial comment which can only be translated "(thus) he [Jesus] declared all foods clean."[11] Furthermore, immediately after the vice list and general concluding remark in v. 23, Mark adds the story of the Syrophoenician woman, a concrete example of Jesus' break with the Jewish concept of defilement.[12] For Mark the break with the Law is complete.

In a general way, this is also the attitude toward the Law reflected in the traditional materials used in this section. These materials include the dispute over hand-washing (vv. 5–8), the Corban controversy (vv. 9–13), and (since the original controversy must have had *some* sort of ending) something similar to vv. 18–19a.[13] All of these materials presuppose in varying degrees a radical break from the Law. The hand-washing controversy can only have arisen in such a non-observant milieu, not only because its description of Jewish Palestinian practice is, so far as we can tell, rather ill-informed,[14] or because the charge is directed against the practice of Jesus' disciples rather than Jesus himself, or even because Jesus replies with a quotation from Scripture[15] (all traits that point toward the controversy-discourses of the developing

11. For the possibility that *brōma* might originally have rendered an Aram. term for *excrementum* see Black, *Aram. Approach*, 159. Pallis, *Notes . . . Mk.*, 25 suggests that the Greek word can mean "corruption," "rottenness." Both would involve a different translation, but neither is probable.

12. So Martin Albertz, *Die synoptischen Streitgespräche* (Berlin: Trowitzsch & Sohn, 1921), 37. It is significant that Suhl, who follows Marxsen in seeing Mark as a Jew (*Zitate*, 150f.!) does not treat this story. But that Mark bases his work on the Hellenistic kerygma of his tradition has been demonstrated repeatedly; see, *inter alia*, Siegfried Schulz, "Markus und das AT," *ZThK* 58 (1961), 184–197.

13. Much of the wording of these latter verses is doubtless due to Mark, although the connecting formula, *kai legei autois* (v. 18) probably comes from the pre-Markan source. (See chap. 5, n. 26.)

14. mBerach. viii.2–4 (Danby, 8f.); for discussion, see B. H. Branscomb, *Jesus and the Law of Moses* (New York: R. R. Smith, Inc., 1930), 156–160; C. G. Montefiore, *The Synoptic Gospels* (2 vols., London: Macmillan, 1927), I, 134–144; Billerbeck, I, 695–704.

15. Roughly following the LXX, and "it is just the part where the Greek text deviates from the Hebrew that affords the point of the quotation here" (Nineham, *Mk.*, 195).

church),[16] but also because the Pharisees and scribes show their hypocrisy only by ceremonial washings, which are, after all, in keeping with the spirit if not the letter of the Mosaic Law; this practice, not failure in some other cultic or ethical practice, is the ground of their condemnation.[17]

The Corban controversy, vv. 9–13, is more complex. The important problem here is not so much that the description of Jewish practice regarding oaths in general and Corban in particular is highly problematic.[18] It is rather that Jesus' attitude toward the practice described is rather inconsistent. He rejects the use of one biblical commandment (on oaths) to negate another (on filial responsibilities), which is typically rabbinic, at least in the sense that almost any rabbi of whom we have record would also have condemned the practice described here.[19] But he opposes the practice in terms of a contrast between the Word of God and the tradition of men, which is contrary to everything rabbinic Judaism stood for. Quite probably the kernel of the controversy is very

16. Also typical of the controversy-discourse: the counter-question; cf Mk. 2:25; 10:3; 11:30; 12:16.

17. In the light of these factors it is hard to agree with Bultmann, *HST*, 18 that the controversy arose in Palestine just because that was the scene of early disputes about the Law (or because v. 4 sounds more Semitic than Greek [cf. Black, *Aram. Approach*, 37]). Schmid, *Mk.*, 133 assumes that the original dispute was concerned not with hand-washing, but with the much larger question of the binding nature of traditions of the elders. Conversely, Suhl, *Zitate*, 79ff. holds that the original dispute was a narrow one and defended Christian conduct; only later was it generalized (by the addition of the citation and perhaps the rewording of vv. 3f.) into anti-Jewish polemic.

18. For the Mishnaic regulations, see mNed. viii.1f. (Danby, 274f.) and Billerbeck, I, 711–717. The problems are discussed in Montefiore, *Syn. Gosp.*, I, 147–152; Branscomb, *Jesus*, 165–170; Taylor, *Mk.*, 341; Saul Lieberman, *Greek in Jewish Palestine* (New York: The Jewish Theological Seminary of America, 1942), 129–135; Samuel Belkin, "The Dissolution of Vows and the Problem of Antisocial Oaths in the Gospels and Contemporary Jewish Literature," *JBL* 55 (1936), 227–234. The essential historicity of the description is defended in Lagrange, *Mc.*, 185f. and bNed. iii.2 (sic) is cited as a "close parallel" by Black, *Aram. Approach*, 101. But neither the Mishnah (mNed. iii.2 = Danby, 266) nor the Babylonian Talmud (bNed. 25b–27a) affords close parallels.

19. The materials for the earliest period are very scarce. But by about 100 A.D. it was already a rabbinic rule that a vow detrimental to one's parents was not binding: mNed. ix.1 (Danby, 275). See the discussion in Montefiore, *Syn. Gosp.*, I, 164ff. and Lagrange, *Matt.*, 302f. Belkin, "Dissolution," defends the view that the Pharisees held anti-social oaths, once made, to be binding (unless dissolved by a judge or a court), whereas Jesus (like Philo) held that they were not. None of this suggests a simple identity between the present Markam text and the original dispute.

primitive and reflects a hypocritical practice—certainly not wide-spread, though probably common enough to explain rabbinic disputation over the matter—somewhere in Palestinian Judaism. But the controversy has clearly been shaped and elaborated in the light of the growing split between Judaism and the infant church, so that a practice repugnant to most Jews can be caricatured as common Jewish practice. Well before Mark, then, the tradition on which he drew had begun to break with the Law and with the Jewish scribal interpreters of it. In this milieu the statement of Jesus in v. 15 must have been understood as already pointing toward the radical break with the Law that came only later in the apostolic age.[20]

Finally, what might the parable (v. 15) have meant on the lips of Jesus? In its present unambiguous form, it can hardly be authentic, as I have urged elsewhere.[21] Nevertheless, the lack of rabbinic parallels[22] shows that it must come either from very early times (before the re-Judaizing of Jesus' message reflected in all the

20. Most of what is said here would still apply if, as T. A. Burkill, "The Historical Development of the Story of the Syrophenician Woman (Mk 7:24–31)," *NovTest* 9 (1967), 161–177 (173f.) holds, the controversies behind Mk. 7:1–23 "primarily eventuated within Jewish Christianity itself." But this seems unlikely, since the excessive rigidity reflected (caricatured?) here is improbable in Jewish-Christianity except perhaps as a late and secondary "re-Judaizing," not an early and primary tendency.

21. Carlston, "Things That Defile," 94f.; cf. also Fenton, *Matt.*, 252; Branscomb, *Mk.*, 125ff. Merkel's extremely careful analysis in "Markus 7,15" divides the verse into two parts and understands v. 15a as an authentic "apodiktisches Kampfwort," reflecting a radical break with the Law, and v. 15a as a softening of this view in the early church. This is the best explanation of the problem *if* the wording of v. 15 has remained intact; but it meets the nearly insuperable objection that the explicitness of v. 15a renders the controversies in the primitive church over the keeping of the Law incredible (Carlston, "Things That Defile," 95), an objection that also applies to Merkel's "Jesus und die Pharisäer," *NTS* 14 (1967;68), 194–208, which attempts to show that Jesus openly and explicitly broke with the Pharisaic understanding of the Law and was bitterly opposed to them throughout his ministry. (Many of the passages discussed by Merkel in this article are also analyzed in detail in my essay.)

Merkel himself does not hold that the wording of v. 15a has remained entirely intact. He suggests ("Mk. 7,15," 353f., 359), quite plausibly, that "entering into him" looks like an addition. But this phrase, which (as he notes) connects v. 15a with v. 15b, could also have formed a connecting link from the very beginning, in which case the original statement must have been stronger than v. 15b, weaker than v. 15a, and different from either.

22. Merkel, "Mk. 7,15," 356ff. gives many parallels to the overall concept of inner or spiritual purity (esp. in Hellenistic circles), but these, as he points out, are all quite compatible with a stress on ritual impurity and do not represent the tension v. 15 does.

Gospels), or from a comparatively late period, after the break with Judaism had been practically completed; the former is on all counts more credible. Furthermore, even if Jesus did not deliberately urge the abolition of the Law, his association with sinners reflects a very substantial lack of concern over the details of ritual defilement. There is little doubt that Jesus' God did not demand the separation from sinners that the God of some good men in the first century required.[23]

So in some less specific form the saying is perfectly in keeping with Jesus' basic intention. (Perhaps this original form was more positive in what it urged ["What truly defiles a man comes from within"] than negative in what it opposed ["There is nothing . . ."], but this is speculation.) Passages like Mk. 3:4; Matt. 5:21–47; and the controversy-discourses in Mk. 2–3, however revised in the primitive church, seem to imply a rather fundamental break with the Law as it was understood by Jesus' contemporaries.[24] The difference is watered down in the Matthean church and in Jewish-Christianity as a whole, whereas it is drawn out and fully elaborated in the non-observant Christian communities which lie behind the other Gospels, particularly the Gospel of Mark.

The issue is immensely important and by no means yet resolved. For there are many ways of denying in the modern world the truth urged in this brief and remarkable saying—e.g., by establishing religious techniques for approaching God,[25] by locating all sin in one's upbringing or the social order—in short, by externalizing what is to some irreducible degree an internal problem. Traditionalism, psychologism, and ideology are, in this respect, only different facets of the same fundamental error.

23. Bonnard, *Matt.*, 229 holds that Jesus' concourse with the impure is faithful to the *essence* of the Mosaic law. But theologically Minette de Tillesse is right: "The affirmation by Jesus that the legal distinctions between pure and impure are abolished is a kerygma" (*Secret*, 146).
24. Rudolf Bultmann, "Ist die Apokalyptic die Mutter der christlichen Theologie?" in *Apophoreta. Festschrift für Ernst Haenchen* (Berlin: Töpelmann, 1964), 64–69 (66); Ernst Käsemann, "The Problem of the Historical Jesus," *Essays on NT Themes* (London: SCM Press, 1964), 15–47 (39) [= *Exegetische Versuche und Besinnungen*, I, 207f.]; G. Bornkamm, *Jesus of Nazareth* (New York: Harper & Bros., 1960), 96–143 (96–100).
25. Bornkamm, *Jesus*, 90.

11. Children and Dogs (7:24–30; cf. Matt. 15:21–28)

The brief saying in Mk. 7:27b, "It is not good to take the children's bread and cast it to the dogs," is perhaps best considered part of an apothegm, although the pericope also bears some of the characteristic marks of a miracle-story and some of a controversy-discourse.[1] It is possible, indeed likely, that neither this saying nor the response in v. 28 ("Even the dogs under the table eat of the children's crumbs") originally had anything to do with a healing—or, for that matter, with one another. But they are associated by Mark in a complex literary unit (7:24–9:30) which reflects a clear purpose: immediately after the discussion of the Things That Defile (7:1–23), Mark has placed together several scenes which (except for 8:22–26) all take place on Gentile territory and thus illustrate the acceptability of Gentiles to Jesus; his own positive evaluation of the Gentile mission is supported here by both the woman's actual conduct and Jesus' granting of her request.

Theologically, then, the woman's position is clear: she is a "Greek" (i.e., pagan in religion and possibly Greek-speaking) and a "Syrophoenician" (a political term):[2] she is non-Jewish. But her position geographically is much more obscure. The text reads, literally, "And he went up from there [or: got up from where he was] and went away to the country around Tyre." One possibility is that the participle *anastas* means "stood up," as if Jesus had been seated for the preceding instructions.[3] But 9:30 tells against this understanding, which is most clearly implied in those readings which on textual grounds seem clearly secondary;[4] all other readings connect *ekeithen* with *anastas* and suggest a geographical intention: ". . . went up from there, etc." This itinerary, however, is very vague. This—and the peculiarities of v. 31—suggests that Mark was not fully familiar with the geographical details of the

---

1. See above, chap. 2, sec. 7, n. 1. Cf. the very tentative suggestion in Harrisville, "Woman of Canaan," 284 that the dialogue and the miracle-story were once independent.
2. On the various Greek forms, see Pallis, *Notes . . . Mk.*, 25f.
3. Loisy, *ES*, I, 969, n. 3; Lagrange, *Mc.*, 193.
4. *kai anastas ekeithen* D it; *kai anastas apēlthen* W sy^x.

region.[5] The phrase, "the regions around Tyre [and Sidon?]"[6] is, like the parallel in 10:1, a transitional one of vague reference, occasioned by Mark's own compositional work: he, not his tradition, has created a mission for Jesus in Gentile territory.[7]

In general, the woman illustrates the acceptability to Jesus of non-Jews (whose practice on foods has just been vindicated). The healing-at-a-distance, so unusual for both Mark[8] and Jewish tradition,[9] shows that for Mark Jesus' teaching and deeds are completely consistent. The exact relationships among the various motifs can only be determined by an analysis of the details of the text.

In v. 24, two geographical notices are given. Jesus goes "into the regions of Tyre (and Sidon)," which is not very specific or very important. But he also enters a house,[10] which in Mark is ordinarily a place of private teaching or, as in this case, "privacy." The psychological conjecture that Jesus "desired to reflect upon the scope and course of His ministry"[11] is completely out of place; Mark's point is that although Jesus "wanted no one to know of it," his greatness was such that he could not be hidden.

Both the woman and her daughter are, in v. 26, anonymous, although later tradition, as often, supplied the lack by naming them Justa and Berenice, respectively.[12] The woman asks on her

---

5. Johnson, *Mk.*, 135, 138f.

6. The words are very well-attested: ℵ A B N X Γ II Σ Φ min[pl] f g vg syrr[p hcl] sa bo arm go; on internal grounds, however, there is a slight balance of probability in favor of the view that they represent an assimilation to Matt. 15:21 (Schmid, *Mk.*, 142, vs. Lagrange, *Mc.*, 193).

7. Two facts make this conclusion irresistible: a) the parallels between 3:7f. and the geography of chaps. 1–11, both redactional, and b) the embedding of this story in a section with few and usually vague references; cf. Johnson, *Mk.*, 135f.

8. In *Mk.*, Jesus ordinarily heals by contact (1:31f.; 3:10; 5:41; 6:5, 56) or a word (1:25; 5:8; 9:25); so Taylor, *Mk.*, 348. Matt. 8:5–13 (= Lk. 7:1–10, Q) and Jn. 4:46–54 shows that healings-at-a-distance are known to other strata of the Gospel tradition.

9. There are, however, examples. See Ber. 34b and the discussion in Paul Fiebig, *Jüdische Wundergeschichten des neutestamentlichen Zeitalters* (Tübingen: J. C. B. Mohr, 1911), 19–22.

10. Not *"the* house," since *tēn oikian* (D W Θ Φ 565 *pc*; Or) is probably secondary.

11. Taylor, *Mk.*, 349.

12. Pseudo-Clem. Hom. II.xix and IV.i.

daughter's behalf for healing, and Jesus rebukes her, first by saying, "let the children be fed first" and then again by responding that it is not fitting to throw children's bread to the dogs. The phrase, "Let the children be fed first," which may come from the pre-Markan tradition,[13] is used to soften the rebuke implied in what follows. Apparently Mark is unwilling to portray her request as meeting a flat refusal, even a temporary one—although as literal history it could hardly have offered the woman much comfort; while we and Mark know how the incident was to come out, she did not! Neither the phrase itself nor even the word *prōton* in this sense[14] occurs again, a fairly clear indication that the issue is not of any importance to Mark. Its function in the present context is to prepare for the parable itself, which follows immediately.

The parable proper, v. 27b, has been variously interpreted. Taken over-literally, it could imply in Mk. a gain for the Gentiles at the expense of Israel or suggest that Jesus' power was limited and must not be squandered.[15] In the text, however, what is opposed is the *equating* of Jewish and Gentile privileges,[16] not the substitution of one for the other, which would require *airein tois teknois* or something similar. This is quite clear in the wording of the gnomic saying, which must be a sharp, half-allegorical contrast between Jews ("children") and non-Jews ("little dogs"). Since diminutive formations are very common in the Koine even when no diminutive idea is implied,[17] one should not interpret the term *kynaria* as a gentler term than the severe *kynes* of Matt. 7:6.[18]

13. Jeremias, *Promise*, 29, n. 2.
14. The uses of *prōton* in 3:27; 4:28; 9:11f.; 13:10; (16:9) do not imply that the Gospel must go "first" to the Jews. As McNeile, *Matt.*, 231 rightly notes, the woman could hardly have made any sense out of the word.
15. Haenchen, *Weg*, 274, citing the naive concept of *mana* which lies behind 5:30 as evidence. But such views fit the Hellenistic *theios anēr* more closely than the Markan Jesus.
16. Jülicher, *Gleichn.*, II, 245f.; Loisy, *ES*, I, 974; Schmid, *Mk.*, 143.
17. Cf. Mk. 14:47 and see Blass-Debrunner-Funk, sec. 111; *BAG*, *s.v. kynarion*.
18. So, rightly, Burkill, "Syrophenician Woman," 170–173; Harrisville, "Woman of Canaan," 282f.; Légasse, "Cananéenne," 34f. Lagrange, *Mc.*, 194f. points out that although the Midrash on Psalm 4 calls Gentiles [renegade Jews?] dogs, the oldest texts use the expression for idols; cf. 'Aboda Zara 54b.; Billerbeck, I, 724f.; Montefiore, *Syn. Gosp.*, I, 167f. Ign. *Eph.* vii.1 calls heretics *kynes lyssōntes*; Philo, *Every Good Man Is Free* 90 (Loeb, ix, 62) applies the term "dogs" to certain persecutors of the Jews.

The saying ought not to be understood as irony or banter[19] or as a reflection of Jesus' concern with a problem of his own, viz., that he not arouse further Jewish antagonism by a premature mission among non-Jews.[20] Its harshness must be given full weight in its interpretation.

But how shall it be interpreted? Is it a valid reflection of Jesus' mission and ministry? Some argue that a "Judaizing" Christianity, if it had invented the story, would have imposed conditions (purification, baptism, etc.) on the woman[21] or that the discourse—without the allegorical symbolism—is just the kind of situation we must imagine as constituting the proper setting for Jesus to explain his mission practice.[22] But that these considerations are not conclusive is shown when the following questions are considered: Does the incident square with Jesus' attitude toward a mission to the Gentiles? Is the language appropriate? Is the movement of the story plausible? On balance, all three questions must be answered negatively.

The most important argument in defense of the attitude reflected in this incident is that Jesus, while he largely restricted his activity to Israel (which is certainly true, although statements like Matt. 10:6 and 15:24 surely come not from Jesus but from early Christian controversy),[23] also accepted the OT view that in the last days the Gentiles would share in the Messianic blessings (Is. 2:2–4; 41:21–29; 42:10–17; 45:14ff.; 60:3ff.; Mic. 4:1f.; Zeph. 3:8–10; etc.).[24] But against this it must be said that many, perhaps most, of the interpretations of the OT which we find in the Gospels are post-Resurrection materials which provide little clue to Jesus' own understanding and that in any case the Gospels elsewhere provide little support for the view that Jesus based his action on this motif. In addition, the OT statements are by no means so clear or so all-pervasive as this theory suggests.[25] While a thorough

19. McNeile, *Matt.*, 231; Rawlinson, *Mk.*, 99; Gould, *Mk.*, 136.
20. Branscomb, *Mk.*, 132.
21. Bonnard, *Matt.*, 232f.
22. Loisy, *ES*, I, 977.
23. Vs. Jeremias, *Promise*, 19f., 26–29 and Cranfield, *Mk.*, 246.
24. So Jeremias, *Promise*, esp. 57–62.
25. Haenchen, *Weg*, 272, n. 2.

examination of the evidence is not possible here, it is fair to say that we do not know precisely what Jesus' attitude toward the salvation of the Gentiles was. A fortiori we cannot use this incident to show that Mk. 7:27, Matt. 10:5f., and Rom. 11:11–24 are all basically common Christian conviction,[26] on the one hand, or to establish "an actual development of Jesus' understanding of his mission,"[27] on the other. Jesus' own attitude toward a Gentile mission as such must have been quite unclear to his immediate followers, who otherwise would not have taken such differing attitudes on the matter.

The second question—Is the language appropriate?—must also be answered negatively. The whole point of the elaborate dialogue revolves around the woman's inability to lay any claim on Jesus precisely because she is not Jewish, an attitude Jesus fully supports by contrasting "children" and "dogs." Even if the saying were originally a secular proverb, its use cannot be squared with Jesus' attitude toward the poor, women, non-Jews, or any of the other things the woman represents. The terms are simply too harsh.[28] Further, they run counter to the general tendency of Jesus' teaching and ministry, which is precisely to abolish such distinctions.

Finally, the story itself contains implausibilities as an authentic incident in the life of Jesus. The Phoenician woman's answers are instant and clever—not of course impossible but also not self-evidently historical—and the clear implication of the dialogue is that her wit is at least as important as her faith[29] in gaining her a

---

26. So, roughly, Schmid, *Mk.*, 142; Jeremias, *Promise*, 71.

27. Johnson, *Mk.*, 137 suggests this possibility. A much more extreme—and less acceptable—form of the same view is Taylor's: "In a sense, He is speaking to Himself as well as to the woman. Her reply shows that she is quick to perceive this" (*Mk.*, 350); similarly, Cadoux, *Parables*, 150f.; Benjamin W. Bacon, *The Beginnings of Gospel Story* (New Haven: Yale University Press, 1909), 90: ". . . an enlargement of His own point of view. . . ."

28. Jesus rejects her, says Loisy, in terms which "would have made every Pharisaic heart rejoice" (*ES*, I, 971). Lagrange, who accepts the authenticity of the whole conversation, insists (properly) that the remark goes beyond even Jewish Christianity toward a "Pharisaic" spirit (*Mc.*, 196). Cadoux, *Parables*, 49 denies this.

29. Klostermann, *Mk.*[5], 72; vs. Minette de Tillesse, *Secret*, 88, who argues that Jesus was convinced by "the woman's irresistible faith," and Jeremias, *Parables*, 118, n. 4, who sees her faith in "her recognition . . . that Jesus was the giver of the Bread of Life," a very artificial note.

hearing.[30] The healing takes place at a distance, a legendary trait with few parallels elsewhere in the Gospel tradition. And the conversation, understood in the terms in which it purportedly originally took place, implies that Jesus, knowing what he was eventually going to do, simply played a somewhat unfair game with an honest suppliant. What if she had taken his initial response as his final answer?

Yet the "more or less Judaistic tendency"[31] of the whole incident stamps it as clearly pre-Markan.[32] At some point in the tangled history revealed here a miracle-story became attached to a dialogue which afforded it a special point and eventually completely overshadowed it.[33] The saying itself and the emphasis on the fact that the woman was non-Jewish suggest that it served for some time to justify the Gentile mission, and quite probably the incident was composed in those circumstances. Mark also doubtless accepted this point.[34]

Another factor is also of importance, explicit only in Matthew (v. 28) but probably implied to some extent in the Markan stress on the woman's persistence: she is an example of faith in the face of initial discouragement, and so encourages Mark's Christian readers not to weaken in faith when their own hopes and prayers at first are not realized.[35] The Reformation homiletic tradition merely elaborates this basic motif, Calvin by pointing out that Jesus' response serves to inflame the woman's ardor, not to extin-

---

30. Vs. Johnson, *Mk.*, 136 and Schmid, *Mk.*, 143. The Matthean form of the woman's reply is, to be sure, a logical improvement of the Markan wording (Schmid, *Matt.*, 241), but in neither Gospel should her wit obscure the fact that she is willing to number herself with the "dogs." (So, rightly, Harrisville, "Woman of Canaan," 284.)

31. Jülicher, *Gleichn.*, II, 258.

32. Burkill, "Syrophenician Woman," 177 suggests that Mark got all of 7:25–30 from the tradition except (vv. 24, 31, and) possibly the saying in v. 27a.

33. Légasse, "Cananéenne," 22.

34. The very awkward phrase in v. 25 *hēs eichen to thygatrion autēs (pneuma akatharton)* is perhaps a Semitism; so Black, *Aram. Approach*, 75. But the narrative as a whole is Markan language, so this tells us little about the ultimate origin of the pericope.

35. Haenchen, *Weg*, 275. Harrisville, "Woman of Canaan," 284ff. points out that the ground of the woman's faith is simply the word of the Lord, "even when that word did not appear to be a word for her but for someone else" (286).

guish her faith, and Luther by encouraging his hearers to emulate the woman's ability to see the yes beyond the no of God.[36]

12. The Savorless Salt (9:50; cf. Matt. 5:13; Lk. 14:34f.)

The basic parable is the simple saying in v. 50: "But if the salt has lost its salinity, with what will you season it?" which follows several sayings on Gehenna (vv. 42–48) and (with v. 49) forms the conclusion of vv. 33–50. The text of v. 49, the connections (if any) between v. 50 and the immediately preceding verses, and the interpretation of the parable in the various levels of tradition are all disputed.

The best solution to the textual problem in v. 49 seems to be that the original reading was "for everyone will be salted with fire" and that this reading was then expanded, doubtless under the influence of Lev. 2:13, to read "... and every sacrifice will be salted with salt."[1] If the longer reading were original, the "fire" of v. 49a could not be eschatological, unless by some complex imagery, now incomprehensible, the salting of the sacrifice were also thought of as eschatological. Since the shorter form of v. 49 is almost certainly the better (and probably original) reading, however, this argument does not tell us whether or not the "fire" is eschatological. We are thus reduced to the context and exact wording of the shorter form.

It is often held that the allusion in v. 49 must be to the Gehenna of fire, as in v. 48, an interpretation which is supported not only by the context but also by the "everyone" in v. 49, which seems to go well beyond the mere thought of widespread suffering in the

---

36. See Calvin on Matt. 15:32; Luther, *Fastenpostille* (1525) in WA xvii/2, 200–204: "... *das tieffe heymliche Ja unter und uber dem .Neyn mit festen Glauben auff Gotts wort fassen und hallten ...*" (203).

1. The shorter reading, *pas gar pyri halisthēsetai*, is supported by ℏ (W) λ *al* (k) sy[s] sa bo[pt]. The readings *pas gar* (+*en* C) *pyri halisthēsetai* (*analōthēsetai* Θ) *kai pasa thysia hali* (−*hali* Ψ 579 *pc* vg[codd]) *halisthēsetai* (*analōthēsetai* Ψ) are supported by C ℵ A Θ Ψ Φ *pm* lat sy[p] bo[pt] and look very much like conflations of the shorter and the Western readings, *pasa gar thysia halisthēsetai* (D *pc* it). Jülicher, *Gleichn.*, II, 76f. holds to the longer reading on the grounds that the other two are merely fragments of a longer original, but most commentators rightly reject this view: cf. Swete, *Mk.*, 200; Lagrange, *Mc.*, 253; Cranfield, *Mk.*, 315; Johnson, *Mk.*, 167; Aland, 250. For discussion of these and various conjectural readings, see Taylor, *Mk.*, and Pallis, *Notes . . . Mk.*, 34.

direction of a general Judgment. This interpretation is also consistent with the centrality of eschatology in the teaching of Jesus, if the saying originated there, and clearly suggested by Mark's use of *gar* to introduce v. 49, which would seem to confirm the association of vv. 48 and 49, at least in Mark's mind. Finally, it may be noted that the symbolism of fire and eschatological judgment is extremely widespread and that a few sayings of uncertain antiquity in early Christianity closely associate "fire" and Jesus' coming and teaching.[2] Hence many commentators insist that v. 49, like v. 48, must have a specifically eschatological reference.[3]

Others, however, note that in the parenetic tradition the symbolism must have gone beyond this narrow meaning, particularly as persecution became more common in the church, and the saying understood of suffering, sacrifice, persecution, "trial" in general.[4] It must be pointed out, however, that in either interpretation, vv. 48 and 49 are not readily compatible: the fire of v. 48 punishes; the fire of v. 49 purifies.

It is thus best to assume that even for Mark (and, a fortiori, for the pre-Markan tradition) the connection between vv. 48 and 49 is not very explicit and rests on catchwords (fire, v. 48; salted with fire,[5] v. 49; salt, v. 50) rather than inner coherence. We must therefore either theologize the whole passage to suit our individual tastes[6] or admit that we do not know exactly what the reference

2. In addition to the fairly common view that the addition of ". . . and fire" to John's promise of the coming baptism with the Holy Spirit (Matt. 3:11 = Lk. 3:16, Q) is a Christianizing of his message of uncertain reference, note Sayings 10, 16, and 82 from the Gospel of Thomas. The first two of these sayings are related (and probably secondary) to Lk. 12:49. But the exact interpretation of all three is unclear, as is their origin.
3. Loisy, *ES*, II, 83f.; Haenchen, *Weg*, 332; Gould, *Mk.*, 181; Hauck, *Mk.*, 117. Friedrich Lang, "*pyr, ktl.*," *TDNT*, VI, 944 wishes to retain the eschatological reference but to understand it in the light of Jesus' ministry, not the Parousia.
4. Jülicher, *Gleichn.*, II, 77; Wellhausen, *Mk.*, 82; Klostermann, *Mk.*[3], 97; Schmid, *Mk.*, 183; Rawlinson, *Mk.*, 131; Troadec, *Mc.*, 174; Taylor, *Mk.* 413; Johnson, *Mk.*, 167; *BAG, s.v. halidsō*; Lagrange, *Mc.*, 253, who notes that he formerly held the other view but abandoned it because it breaks the connection between vv. 49 and 50.
5. Pliny, *Nat. hist.* xlv. 98 had already connected salt and fire; *Salis natura per se ignes est et inimica ignibus* ("the nature of salt is both of itself fiery and hostile to fires").
6. Euthymius Zigabenus suggests that fire and salt refer to "the fire of faith in God or love of neighbor" (Migne, *PG* cxxix.824). Cadoux, *Parables*, 211f. interprets "fire" as "the pain of conflict."

is, or just how the connection between "fire" and "salt" arose in the first place; in this case "the fire of 49 has nothing to do with that of 48."[7] Then *gar* simply introduces the gnomic saying without binding it too closely with what precedes.

If this is true, it is useless to look to the immediate context for the interpretation of v. 50, which is made up of the gnomic saying plus an introductory phrase ("Salt is good") and two (related) parenetic conclusions ("Have salt in yourselves, and be at peace with one another"). The specific reference is uncertain; either it intends the rather impure salt from the Dead Sea (and elsewhere), which by a process of leaching could lose its salinity and leave only an impure residue[8] or it states a deliberate paradox: salt does not lose its salinity and a good disciple does not lose his character.[9] The former interpretation is more appropriate if the salt represents some quality which may be or has been lost, the latter if the quality envisaged is to be encouraged. In either case[10] it is patient (in the pre-Markan tradition) of an almost unlimited number of applications, both positive and negative.

The history-of-religions parallels do not provide much help in determining the reference,[11] although Jewish hearers (and read-

---

7. Taylor, *Mk.*, 413.

8. So Jülicher, *Gleichn.*, II, 68; Schmid, *Mk.*, 183; Lohmeyer, *Mk.*, 98; Jeremias, *Parables*, 169; and (as a possibility) Johnson, *Mk.*, 167. For salt obtained by leaching, see Pliny, *Nat. hist.* xxxi.73–105.

9. So Johnson, *Mk.*, 167; cf. Hauck in *TDNT*, I, 229; Billerbeck, I, 236. The often-cited rabbinic parallel, "When salt becomes unsavory, wherewith shall it be salted?" (Behoroth 8b) immediately follows the question, "Can a mule give birth?" (The answer implied to the salt-riddle is thus, "With the afterbirth of a mule!") The saying about the salt, consequently, which "has all the look of a proverbial phrase" (Abrahams, *Studies*, II, 183), is used to show the absurdity of the notion that salt can lose its savor.

10. A third possibility also exists: the reference might be to salt used in ovens to enhance their burning. These slabs eventually change their chemical composition and must be discarded. For this, see Ludwig Köhler, "Salz, das dumm wird," *ZDPV* 59 (1936), 133f., rev. in *Kleine Lichter* (Zürich: Zwingli-Verlag, 1945), 73–76; Cullmann, "Salz," 194; Jeremias, *Parables*, 168, n. 80. If this rare custom is the original reference—which seems extremely unlikely—the meaning is essentially identical with the first interpretation.

11. Dodd, *Parables*, 142 and Jeremias, *Parables*, 169 hold that the saying was originally directed against Israel; Davies, *Setting*, 250, 457 suggests the Qumran sect.

ers) might perhaps think of "salt" in terms of wisdom or fidelity to the Covenant and Greek hearers might think it implied friendship or hospitality.[12]

The only keys to the meaning in Mark are the two phrases.at the end of v. 50, in which the use of the second person (instead of the third, as in Matt./Lk.=Q) shows a parenetic concern. Yet it is probably not greatly different from Matthew, who uses the general statement in support of his own introductory phrase, "You are the salt of the earth." The double imperative ("Have salt... and be at peace...") suggests that Mark is urging his readers to be or do something that is not automatic. Love, self-forgetfulness, religious seriousness, readiness for sacrifice (cf. 9:43–48), service —some such virtues are perhaps in Mark's mind, especially if he still intends a close connection with the paradoxical statement in the first part of the verse: he who loses these is totally useless.[13] Another possibility is that, since salt is a seasoning and preserving agent, the reference is to a peaceful life, brought about by love,[14] the exercise of wisdom or common sense,[15] or even *"l'affabilité*

---

12. As early as Aristotle (*Nic. Eth.* VIII.4 1156[b]) salt is a symbol of friendship among the Greeks; he cites the proverb, "People cannot truly know one another until they have eaten salt together." Philo suggests that salt symbolizes the total permanence of something because it prevents corruption (*De Spec. Leg.* I.289; cf. *Quaest. in Gen.* IV.52 [Loeb, VII, 266 and Suppl. I, 330]). Two rabbinic sayings may be relevant here: Sopherim 15.8, "The world cannot endure without salt [and the Torah is like salt]" (cited, Billerbeck, I, 235 and II, 23), and the Jerusalem proverb cited in Keth. 66b, "the salt of money is diminution" (*ḥeser*; some texts read *ḥesed*, benevolence), which implies that money is improved or given added value when used for charity (see Billerbeck I, 235f. and the notes in the Soncino ed.). Wolfgang Nauck, in his important study, "Salt as a Metaphor in Instructions for Discipleship," *StudTh* 6 (1952), 165–178 argues for the equation, salt = wisdom, on three grounds: a) the Jewish parallels suggest this; b) the basic and most common meaning of *mōrainesthai* is "to be foolish, silly, stupid," while the notion of "insipidity" is much less common; and c) the Aram. *s^erî* (or *s^erā'*) and the Heb. *tāpēl* both mean "insipid," "unsavory," and (though less commonly) "foolish" and thus may lie behind the Gr. *mōrainesthai*; so also Black, *Aram. Approach*, 123f. Nauck's conclusion is essentially accepted by Jacques Dupont, *Les Béatitudes* (3 vols., Louvain: E. Nauwelaerts, I², 1958; II, 1969; III, 1973), I², 82–93 (89f.).
13. Hauck, *Mk.*, 117; Schmid, *Mk.*, 184. But Schmid goes well beyond the text when he suggests that something objective, possibly the teaching of Jesus (cf. 4:25) is the primary reference (ibid.). Similarly, Cranfield, *Mk.*, 316; Branscomb, *Mk.*, 175; Lohmeyer, *Mk.*, 197.
14. Hauck, *Mk.*, 117.
15. Taylor, *Mk.*, 415; Jeremias, *Parables*, 217, n. 43; Haenchen, *Weg*, 332; and

dans les relations."[16] Perhaps Mark knew no more clearly than we do exactly how peaceful relationships are brought about. But he knew, as did Matthew (5:9) and Paul (1 Thes. 5:13), of the necessity for them and perhaps of men and women who had helped create them; for such people, and such relationships, salt seemed to him an appropriate metaphor. An objective observer, noting the level of virtue in the church and in the modern world, would probably conclude that the proper course for the modern preacher is to urge *all* the virtues discovered by the commentators. *Ce n'est pas de l'exégèse—mais c'est la vie!*

13. The Wicked Husbandmen (12:1–12; cf. Matt. 21:33–46; Lk. 20:9–18)

In Mk. this parable forms part of the long controversy-discourse extending from 11:27 through 12:37. It follows the dispute in the Temple with the high priests, scribes, and elders (11:27) about Jesus' authority and carries on Jesus' general response to the question of the Sanhedrin; in a sense it is part of the claim to be the Son sent by God.[1] Both this context and the scriptural summation show that the Markan conception is not so much ecclesiastical (as in Matthew) as christological.[2] And v. 12 seems to imply that the Jewish leaders understood the parable as a whole as christological. Apparently the Messianic "secret" is beginning to be disclosed; Jesus' true nature is soon to be publicly proclaimed (14:61f.) and openly confessed (15:39).[3] Thus Judaism, by its rejection of the Son, stands condemned.

---

esp. Nauck, "Salt," *passim*: an active and practical rather than an intellectual wisdom.

16. Lagrange, *Mc.*, 254; cf. Dodd, *Parables*, 140. Rawlinson, *Mk.*, 131 suggests "true Christian charity and readiness for sacrifice"; Troadec, *Mc.*, 175 thinks of salt as a symbol *"de ce qui fait le charme des relations sociales,"* perhaps *"un certain sens de l'humour. . . ."* The Meyer-Weiss commentary, in the eighth ed. (I/2: *Die Evangelien des Markus und Lukas* [Göttingen: Vandenhoeck & Ruprecht, 1892], 170, n.*) rejects as purely arbitrary the following from the older commentaries: the salt refers to reason (de Wette), discretion (Ewald), wisdom (Meyer), faith (Klostermann), inner purification (Bleek), self-denial (Nösgen), the preaching of repentance (Volkmar), and the Word of God (Keil).

1. Lagrange, *Luc*, 507.
2. Trilling, *Christusverkündigung*, 170.
3. Minette de Tillesse, *Secret*, 218f.

The same twofold reference is evident by the unfriendly questions about paying tribute to Caesar (12:13–17), the resurrection of the dead (12:18–27), the first commandment (12:28–34), and the Son of David (12:35–37), in the course of which Jesus silences his opponents (12:34b), although the crowd listens willingly (12:37b). Judaism's failure *vis-à-vis* Jesus in these controversies is thus, for Mark, a continuation of the *Unheilslinie* of Jewish history, as Jesus' victory is a christological affirmation.

The parable opens with a Markan introduction (v. 1a), which connects the parable proper with the surrounding narrative; Jesus speaks "in parables," i.e., as in 3:23 and 4:2, in words which (for outsiders) condemn rather than illumine. The parable itself takes much of its imagery and language not from life but from a text of Scripture, viz., Is. 5:2 (LXX), from which it may originally have been created.[4] A man plants a vineyard, cares for it, and then, as the custom was in Palestine,[5] leases it to tenants and goes away— not necessarily very far away or for a very long time.[6] After a few years, when the vineyard begins to produce,[7] he sends servants to collect payment: first, a single servant, who is beaten; then another servant, who is violently mistreated;[8] then another, who is killed;

4. For Israel as God's vineyard (usually in a context of Judgment), cf. Ps. 80[79]:8f.; Jer. 2:21; 12:10; Ezek. 15:1, 6; 19:10; Hos. 10:1. Jeremias, *Parables*, 70f. attempts to eliminate the primacy of the reference to the vineyard on the grounds that it is missing from Lk. and Thomas; Léon-Dufour, *Études*, 316f. argues only that the Isaiah reference is a pre-synoptic addition to the original parable, without attempting to locate an earlier form elsewhere. But since the citation rests on the LXX of Is. 5:2, we cannot tell whether the reference to Isaiah is secondary, as Léon-Dufour thinks, or whether the parable itself was created or reworded in Hellenistic circles in the early church.
5. The tenants ordinarily paid expenses and returned from one-quarter to one-half of the crop. For details, see Hengel, "Weingärtnern," 11–16, 19–25; Derrett, *Law*, 292–295.
6. *Apedēmēsen* in itself implies no more than "go away," although Hengel "Weingärtnern," 21f. sees a "widespread usage" which requires the translation "he took a trip abroad"; similarly, Derrett, *Law*, 290f.; Klauck, "Weinberg," 122; *per contra*, Léon-Dufour, *Études*, 318.
7. Vines produce in Palestine after three years (Lagrange, *Mc.*, 306). If the rule in Lev. 19:23, 25 applies (which is not certain), harvest-payments could be expected to begin in the fifth year—the first year in which a vineyard would ordinarily be profitable, in any case (Derrett, *Law*, 290).
8. The spelling and sense of *ekephalaiōsan* are uncertain. For such conjectures as *ekolaphisan, ephalakrōsan, eksephaulisan*, see Jülicher, *Gleichn.*, II, 389 and, for instructive brief notes, M-M, *Vocab.*, 342; BAG, *s.v.* "*kephalioō*"; Taylor, *Mk.*, 474; Pallis, *Notes . . . Mk.*, 41f. The reading inserting *lithobolēsantes* before

then many more, some of whom are beaten and some killed.[9] Finally the owner sends his only and well-loved son (v. 6) in hopes
that he will be respected, but he too is killed[10] and thrown out of
the vineyard, suffering even the indignity of being refused a de-
cent burial. At this point the parable proper breaks off and Jesus
asks a question: "What will the master of the vineyard do?" "He
will come," Jesus answers, "and destroy [*apolesei* cannot mean
anything less] the tenants and give the vineyard to others"—a
reply that implies a judgment within history, not beyond it, since
otherwise the vineyard could hardly be *given*[11] to others. It has
been argued that the unanswered question is (on the basis of
Lk. 17:9) more probable, that the answer must be an addition to
the parable.[12] But the question is so general that it must have been
connected with its answer from the first, and the motif of v. 9b has
parallels not in the teaching of Jesus but in the primitive church;[13]
either the question and answer formed the original ending of the
parable or the ending has been lost.

For vv. 10f. are, by almost universal consent, a secondary addition to the parable, quite possibly added by Mark himself.[14] These

---

ekephalaiosan is rather well-attested (C ℛ A Γ Φ φ 157 892 *pm*) but clearly
secondary; it shows that the scribes understood *kephalaioō* to imply violence but
did not know its precise significance. That Matthew and Luke have modified
Mk., not the other way around, is, on textual grounds, indisputable.
9. The secondary nature of v. 5b has long been noted; see Klostermann, *Mk.*[5],
121; Taylor, *Mk.*, 475; Haenchen, *Weg*, 399. It probably comes from Mark himself.
10. That "Come, let us kill him," an exact quotation from Gen. 37:18, 20 LXX,
reflects a Joseph-typology (so, tentatively, Klauck, "Weinberg," 124f.) is, in
view of the absence of the motif in early Christianity, improbable. It is quite
possible, however, that the phrase, *pros heautous eipan*, rests on a Semitic ethical
dative; see Hengel, "Weingärtnern," 7 [8], n. 31, item *l*. Theologically it is important to note that the son is instantly recognized by the tenants; the crime is no
tragic error; Bonnard, *Matt.*, 316.
11. Pallis, *Notes . . . Mk.*, 42 would be correct that *kakdōsei* (". . . and lease")
should be read instead of *kai dosei*—if agriculture rather than allegory were deter-
minative of the language. On the other hand, if the "vineyard" were simply
allegorically "the Kingdom," it could only have been given (not leased) in the
first place. The truth seems to be that a parable with allegorical elements has
been influenced by allegory in its present wording.
12. Dodd, *Parables*, 126f.; Taylor, *Mk.*, 476.
13. Matt. 22:13 is clearly Matthean; Matt. 8:11 (= Lk. 13,28f., Q) is (vs.
Taylor, *Mk.*, 476) no true parallel.
14. Kümmel, "Weingärtnern," 121; Jülicher, *Gleichn.*, II, 405; Klostermann,
Mk.[5], 122f.; Dodd, *Parables*, 128; Schmid, *Mk.*, 218–222; Jeremias, *Parables*, 73f.;
Léon-Dufour, *Études*, 315f. (cf. 326: "Jesus was not in the habit of citing

verses disturb the context (the wrath of Jesus' opponents springs
from vv. 1–9, not vv. 10f.); they change the emphasis from the
killing to the vindication of the son; they reflect early Christian
usage of the "stone" motif—and they fit, as Mk. 2:21f., 27f.;
11:23ff. show, Mark's own redactional technique. It is surely
Mark, not Jesus, who asks if they have *not even* read the Scripture
which foretold the action they were soon to take (14:46) and its
aftermath. This peculiar phrasing suggests that "the passage was
one in common use,"[15] along with other "stone" prophecies.[16]
V. 12 is, as the rambling logic of the verbs shows, a Markan transitional verse, concluding the passage and providing a brief pause
in the narrative.

In few other Markan passages is interpretation so intimately
connected with the question of authenticity, and in treating it we
must avoid two extremes. On the one hand, we must not assume
that the existence of semi-allegorical traits in itself establishes
inauthenticity; since the imagery is derivative, coming from a
biblical text rather than from life, its details are inevitably influenced by the precise wording of that text and some awkwardness
is therefore to be expected. On the other hand, we must be certain
that any reconstruction of some more primitive form is motivated
by the concrete details of the text itself, "not by the preconceived
opinion that it must be possible to set forth an earlier form of the

---

Scriptural texts literally—esp. not in Greek"). Lagrange, *Mc.*, 310 assigns only
v. 11 to the post-resurrection community; Taylor, *Mk.*, 476f. concludes that early
Christian usage "is based upon the memory that . . . [Jesus] used Psa. cxviii.22f.
in a devastating attack upon the Jewish hierarchy"; similarly, Hauck, *Mk.*, 142.
15. Swete, *Mk.*, 255.
16. The text is from the LXX of Ps. 117 [118]:22f., used also in Acts 4:11
and in 1 Pet. 2:4–8 (in combination with Is. 28:16 [cf. also 1 Q S viii.7f.] and
8:14f.). In addition to these passages about the "cornerstone" ("capstone"?—
see the bibliography cited by Derrett in "The Stone that the Builders Rejected,"
Studia Evangelica IV [Berlin: Akademie-Verlag, 1968], 181, n. 1), note 1 Cor.
3:11; Eph. 2:20; Rom. 9:33; and the well-known "Peter" passages. "Stone"
prophecies also occur in Barn. 6:2ff.; Justin, *Dial.* 34:2; 36:1. For the possible
use of the theme in early Christian hymnody, see Edward Gordon Selwyn, *The
First Epistle of St. Peter* (London: Macmillan & Co., Ltd., 1961), 273–277. A
good discussion of the entire motif may be found in Cadbury's essay in F. J.
Foakes-Jackson and Kirsopp Lake, *The Beginnings of Christianity. Part I: The
Acts of the Apostles* (5 vols., London: Macmillan & Co., Ltd., 1922–1939), V,
373f.

parable which will be freer of allegorical elements."[17] In the light of these considerations, is the parable authentic?

Some defenders of authenticity are content with urging only that there is nothing in the parable which is fundamentally inconsistent with Jesus' teaching[18] or that the story itself is quite natural and has been modified only in very modest ways, such as perhaps by adding the citation in v. 11.[19] Others go further, eliminating at least v. 5b and vv. 10f.[20] or even somewhat more of the text.[21] Dodd and Jeremias go further still, suggesting that the original parable can be reconstructed only by modifying Mark in the light of the shorter (and possibly more primitive, though not original) form found in Lk. (and now in Thomas)[22] and that the improbability of the action in the reconstructed parable becomes understandable in the light of the chaotic conditions in politically troubled first-century Palestine.[23] It is also further commonly argued that the parable must be authentic since it (unlike vv. 10f.) makes no reference to the resurrection, which we should expect in a post-resurrection creation of the primitive church[24]—although

17. Kümmel, "Weingärtnern," 125.
18. Lohmeyer, *Mk.*, 249; Cranfield, *Mk.*, 367ff.
19. Lagrange, *Mc.*, 311f.; Rawlinson, *Mk.*, 162ff.
20. Schmid, *Mk.*, 218–222; Hengel, "Weingärtnern," 33, 36 sees 5b, 10f., and the "expanded" Isaiah-citation in v. 1 as Markan accretions but is very cautious on the overall question of authenticity. Léon-Dufour, *Études*, 332–335 thinks the major additions to the original parable are the detailed description of the vine (taken from Is. 5) and the concluding scriptural quotation, although he finds several minor additions in the text as well.
21. B. T. D. Smith, *Parables*, 22f., 59, 222ff. proposes the elimination of 5b–8 and 9b. Branscomb, *Mk.*, 209ff. inclines toward the view that Jesus used the basic figure of Israel as God's vineyard and that the parable has been greatly elaborated.
22. B. M. F. Van Iersel, *"Der Sohn" in den synoptischen Jesus-worten* (Leiden: E. J. Brill, 1961), 132–141 seeks on more objective (linguistic and critical) grounds to reconstruct the most primitive form by a careful verse-by-verse comparison of all three Synoptics; similarly, Léon-Dufour, *Études*, 316–327. But the basic assumption behind all such efforts is that *both* Matthew and Luke had some (presumably oral) source in addition to what they read in *Mk.*, and this assumption, unlikely in itself, is plausible only in cases where details of the texts are otherwise inexplicable. In addition, what might have motivated them to act as this theory requires?
23. Dodd, *Parables*, 124–132; Jeremias, *Parables*, 74ff.; cf. Cadoux, *Parables*, 40ff.
24. The argument was first proposed, so far as I know, by F. C. Burkitt in the *Transactions of the Third International Congress for the History of Religion* (2 vols., Oxford: Oxford University Press, 1908), II, 321–328. But the resurrection-predictions we have in the Gospels, which probably do originate in the primitive church, are given to the disciples, not to Jesus' opponents; see Léon-Dufour, *Études*, 316.

just what *function* the Risen Son would have had in the parable is never explained.

On the other hand, a great many interpreters, on various grounds, argue that on balance the parable cannot be assigned to Jesus,[25] primarily—though by no means exclusively—because of the difficulties of the action. Even at the start, a minor problem exists: a man who plants his own vineyard is not a lord capable of taking distant voyages[26] (although it would be a very foolish land-lord who during the early non-bearing years could not find *something* else to occupy his time!). Again, technically he would probably have obtained an accounting or the proceeds of a sale rather than "some of the fruit" (v. 2).[27] But the real problem lies in his extraordinary slowness to act: instead of calling the police, which (as v. 9 insists) he is fully capable of doing whenever he wishes, he repeatedly (and perhaps over a long period of time)[28] sends servants even after knowing of the ill-treatment they had received.[29] Then, even though he knows that his hired hands are capable of violence (even of murder, if v. 5a is not an elaboration of the original parable), he sends his (only and well-loved) son, in the *hope* that he will be respected.[30] Finally, when the disaster is complete, he murders the original tenants (!) and hires others without (as Matthew apparently noted) taking any precautions to insure that the same thing will not happen all over again. It

25. Loisy, *ES*, II, 306–319; Bultmann, *HST*, 177, 205; Klostermann, *Mk.*[5], 120–123; Jülicher, *Gleichn.*, II, 406; Bonnard, *Matt.*, 314f.; Montefiore, *Syn. Gosp.*, I, 273ff.; Haenchen, *Weg*, 399–403; and esp. Kümmel, "Weingärtnern," *passim*.
26. Loisy, *ES*, II, 306.
27. Hengel, "Weingärtnern," 14f, esp. 15, n. 55 notes that a vineyard may be used for growing many different items and defends the expression as an exact representation of the payment required: it might include (besides money) grapes, wine, grain, etc. or even (Derrett, *Law*, 295) a proportion of the vege-tables and other crops planted between the rows of the vines.
28. Derrett, *Law*, 296–303 explains the delay as really portraying growing dis-satisfaction on the part of the landowner over the first four or five years.
29. Derrett's view (*Law*, 297) that the ill-treatment may have been fully justified, or that the beaten servant was sent back "to explain the situation, and to show that the tenants were not to be trifled with" is a purely gratuitous importation into the text.
30. Derrett, *Law*, 302f. argues that action could be taken only after a formal protest had been made and that slaves could not make such a protest. But the texts he cites hardly establish the wisdom or necessity of sending one's *son* as one's representative, or of sending him without adequate police support.

hardly goes beyond the evidence to say bluntly that the owner of the vineyard "acts throughout like an absolute idiot!"[31] It is hard to hold that such peculiar conduct on the human level can be explained by any natural exegesis.[32]

Nor is the action of the tenants any more credible. A law did exist, to be sure, according to which unclaimed land might be claimed by the tenants *if* a man died without heirs and the vineyard was essentially both distant and abandoned.[33] But none of these conditions are met in the parable. In no civilized country, certainly not in the Roman Empire, was it ever possible *legally* for tenants to acquire "intestate" land through the simple expedient of guaranteeing intestacy through murder! In addition, this view requires us to believe that the tenants have mistakenly assumed the landowner himself to be dead.[34] In keeping all of the fruit for themselves, then, and in murdering the son in order to obtain the inheritance, the tenants act with a kind of illogic which no appeal to the chaotic conditions of first-century Palestine[35] can render credible.[36]

31. Hirsch, *Frühgeschichte*, I, 129.
32. Dodd, *Parables*, 127, n. 1 and Cranfield, *Mk.*, 66 refer to Brutus' use of cavalry to collect a debt (Cicero, *Letters to Atticus*, V.21; VI.1 [Loeb, I, 406–410, 420]) as a parallel showing the feasibility of the details. But the parallel is a very faulty one, since in our parable the owner, with a *just* cause, refuses for an incredible period of time to act like Brutus, who (in Cicero's view, as least) acted quite *unjustly*. With equivalent power and a better case, the landowner still refuses to act as Brutus did.
33. Ernst Bammel, "Das Gleichnis von den bösen Winzern (Mk 12, 1–9) and das jüdische Erbrecht," *Revue Internationale des Droits de l'Antiquité*, 3e Série 6 (1959), 11–17 (14f.). See also Billerbeck, I, 871ff.; Jeremias, *Parables*, 75f.; Hengel, "Weingärtnern," *passim*; and, for the Jewish law of "adverse possession," Derrett, *Law*, 300f.
34. Jeremias, *Parables*, 75f. and Van Iersel, "Sohn," 131f. hold that the tenants made this assumption; Bammel, "Winzern," 16, n. 25 denies this. The theory, though unsupported by the text, at least recognizes that the owner *acts* as if he no longer possessed life or sense!
35. Dodd, *Parables*, 125f. and esp. Hengel, "Weingärtnern," 23ff. It is, of course, conceivable that only the murder itself, not the motivation expressed, belonged to the original parable; Hengel, 35[36], n. 114 insists flatly that the "heir-motif" is "certainly" secondary, though there is no literary evidence for this. (Thomas includes it, but in an obviously secondary form.) Derrett, *Law*, 306 accepts the heir-motif, assuming that the son had acquired title to (part of) the land and thus become his father's official representative; similarly, Bammel, "Winzern," *passim*. But in that case his death would transfer the land, not to the tenants, but back to the father.
36. The ingenuity shown by Derrett (*Law*, 286–312 and *passim*) in defending

Yet every one of these items becomes entirely clear and reasonable if the story is understood as constructed backward from the lesson it is intended to point up. The prolonged refusal of the owner to come in judgment becomes a sign of his patience,[37] of the "blessed idiocy" of grace. The sending of the servants, whether in two groups or a series or any other way, becomes the sending of the prophets to call God's people back to their responsibilities. The "only" and "beloved" son is Jesus, God's last (not latest) envoy in the long series. The central crime of the tenants, and the one for which alone[38] they are really punished, is the murder, not of all the owner's messengers, but of God's Son. And so on.

The allegory, to be sure, is neither total nor pure: The vineyard is, as Is. 5 shows, Israel;[39] yet later in the story it is taken from the tenants (who have now become Israel) and given to others.[40] God (= the owner) could hardly be said to have gone away, even in the limited sense of the suspension of prophecy and the temporary abandonment of his people[41] or, for that matter, to "come" in judgment, a function which early Christianity associated not with God but with Jesus as the Son of Man. Nor are the details— the hedge, the winepress, the tower, etc.—given any allegorical significance in the text.[42] The meaning of the murder of the son is

---

all the actions of the parable poses one additional problem which he seems not to have noticed: *defensible* conduct would have put Jesus' hearers on the side of the tenants—and thus robbed the parable of any point!

37. Hengel, "Weingärtnern," 27f. specifically denies this; he understands the owner as motivated by pragmatic necessities instead. The original hearers, he insists, would have recognized the limits on his power and freedom to act, as well as the fact that the husbandmen of the period, feeling themselves exploited by the rich, could be very hostile and dangerous. But this can at best be defended, as Hengel himself notes (28, n. 91), for the pre-Markan, "pre-allegorical" form of the parable, in which the motif of the killing of the prophets was not yet present. If all this is true, however, the murder of the son becomes crucial in explaining the parable; see next note.

38. Not "primarily" (vs. Hengel, "Weingärtnern," 31; Van Iersel, "*Sohn*," 128), since their previous misconduct has brought neither warning nor retribution.

39. On this text among the rabbis, see esp. Hengel, "Weingärtnern," 16–19.

40. This inconsistency is sometimes used to minimize or eliminate the vineyard as central to the parable (which hardly makes sense) or to show that the vineyard = the Kingdom or something similar; see Klauck, "Weinberg," 137f.

41. Vs. Swete, *Mk.*, 251.

42. This did not prevent the Fathers from finding such significance there; see, e.g., Origen in Migne, *PG* xiii.1488.

clear, but its motivation (the obtaining of the inheritance)[43] is palpably supplied by the storyteller's necessity of explaining the climactic event of the parable and has no allegorical meaning beyond itself. The inconsistencies in the story show clearly that it arose as a parable with allegorizing traits, not as a pure allegory— but this says nothing conclusive about the ultimate *origin* of the parable. What is important is the fact that again and again details which require tortuous explanation as historical reality fit almost without remainder into the life and experience of the primitive church.

The argument does not stop here, however. The story, if authentic, could only contrast some of the Jews (the hierarchy?) with others, since "Jesus cannot have thought of a simple exchange: formerly the Jews, henceforth another people."[44] Yet any attempt to relate this parable to a particular segment of Judaism remains unconvincing, since, in addition to the fact that the prophets always addressed the nation, not just a few of its leaders, the expression "high priests and scribes and elders" (11:27) is Markan redaction, not historical reminiscence, and any limited application in the thought of Jesus is pure conjecture.

Further, it is hard to understand the Christology implied here as historical: Mark and his readers naturally understood the "son" in a messianic sense,[45] although the mere expression "beloved" need not imply this;[46] but it is difficult to imagine that the hearers

---

43. Van Iersel, "Sohn," 143ff. argues that the inheritance has no allegorical meaning and must therefore belong to the earliest form of the parable; this in turn shows that the "son" (and "heir") is original, not a later accretion; and the origin of the whole is in the teaching of Jesus. But since the acquisition of the "inheritance" by murder is historically implausible, the development must have been just the reverse: a) the Son (Jesus) is killed; b) he is recognized in Christian tradition as the "heir"; and c) a parable is created by the community in which Is. 5 is used to reflect these two convictions.

44. Jülicher, *Gleichn.*, II, 404; Lagrange, *Luc*, 507f. denies this. Van Iersel, "Sohn," 144 denies the centrality of *either* the vineyard or the son in the original parable, and thus can identify the husbandmen with the leaders of Israel. Klauck, "Weinberg," 135 suggests a conflict with the Pharisees.

45. Thus Mark himself could easily (and unconsciouly) have added the note that the son was *agapētos*; see Van Iersel, "Sohn," 137f. Cf. the heavenly voice at 1:11 and 9:7.

46. It has no Messianic implication in Gen. 22:2, 12, 16; Jer. 6:26; Amos 8:10; Zech. 12:10, where "only" (Heb. *yāḥîd*) is rendered "beloved" (Gr. *agapētos*)

of Jesus would have done so, since the designation "son of God" was probably unknown to them[47] and thus they could not have understood the son's *heilsgeschichtlich* significance in the story. Yet, since the murder of the son is the climax of the parable, this is the ground of their own condemnation. Finally, it must be noted that even if some understanding of the "son" could be attributed to Jesus (and understood by his opponents),[48] the story still implies Jesus' foresight into his own death,[49] and this, not any conflict between Jesus' vocation or teaching and the privileges enjoyed by the hierarchy, provides the focal point of the story. The death of the son and heir[50] motivates the destruction of the tenants and the transfer of their rights to others.

It is, then, highly unlikely that this parable is to be ascribed to Jesus. It is equally clear, however, that it does not come from the pen of Mark himself. The text contains a disproportionate number of Semitisms, on the one hand, and comparatively few distinctively

in the LXX; in Judg. 11:34 the LXX is divided between *monogenēs . . . agapētē* and *monogenēs* alone (Cod. B). F. C. Burkitt, "Notes and Studies: *agapētos*," *JTS* 20 (1919), 339–344 suggests that *agapētos* implies "only," "unique" both here and elsewhere in the NT, and C. H. Turner, "*ho hyios mou ho agapētos*," ibid., 27 (1926), 113–129 even insists that "Only Son" is the proper translation of *agapētos hyios*.

47. It was formerly argued that we have no single instance of the Messianic use of the title "Son of God" in Judaism during early Christian or early Tannaitic times, from which it may be deduced either that its use must be unhistorical (so Kümmel, "Weingärtnern," 129f.) or, more cautiously, that it could not have been understood messianically, as the story requires (so Jeremias, *Parables*, 73; Schmid, *Mk.*, 221f.). It is harder to be so certain today, however, since unpublished material from Cave 4 at Qumran uses both "Son of Man" and "Son of God" as titles; but experts are not agreed on whether the terms are to be understood as *messianic* or *royal* titles. (I am indebted to Prof. James Sanders of Union Seminary in New York for bringing the Qumran material to my attention.)

48. Van Iersel, "Sohn," 127, n. 1 holds that Jesus' hearers would have understood the allusion because the parable reflected the current situation, which is debatable, and because they were already determined to kill Jesus (3:6), which is Markan theology!

49. Jülicher, *Gleichn.*, II, 406 inclines toward inauthenticity but admits that, in the light of Mk. 14:21–24, we cannot flatly deny that Jesus felt himself to be a son, not merely a servant, and that he eventually foresaw his own death with certainty. But both items are highly problematic. Hengel, "Weingärtnern," 37f. defends merely a general awareness of coming disaster and an indirect Christology.

50. "This is the heir" is Christian theology; Jesus' opponents would never have said (or even thought) such a thing; Jülicher, *Gleichn.*, II, 406. Is it accidental that the son is *sent*? (Cf. Rom. 8:3; Gal. 4:4; and see Bultmann, *John*, 50, n. 2.) Attempts to remove the son altogether from the original form of the parable (so, *inter alia*, Klauck, "Weinberg," 125) fail in part because this is the natural climax to the story.

Markan terms, on the other.[51] The parable proper (vv. 1–9) reflects almost no distinctive Markan interest; on the contrary, it contains, in the present framework, a double tension: between the Messianic secret and this open proclamation of Jesus' sonship[52] on the one hand and between the *private* nature of the other passion predictions and the public (and polemic) implications of both the parable and the vindication-theme in vv. 10f. on the other.[53] We cannot say with any certainty, however, just where the precise point of entry into the tradition was. The "son" seems to be a normal, not an adopted, son and heir, which might point toward a Hellenistic rather than a Jewish-Christian milieu—the slight Septuagintal influence would point in the same direction—but the Semitic coloring to the language indicates a different possibility. The reconstruction of a more primitive form, on which there is no general agreement whatever, would bring a certain difficulty along with it: the more primitive such a proposed form is, the *less* usable it becomes in primitive Christian controversy (and thus the less likely to have survived at all). We must therefore either postulate a form quite different from what we have and ascribe it to Jesus (a view rejected here) or accept it as an elaborately artificial construct used within the community (probably not in actual controversy) to express opposition to those responsible for the death of Jesus (here understood to be not Jews and Romans in collusion but simply Jews).[54]

Within the church, then, where it almost certainly arose, the parable could be understood in at least three different (though related) ways:

1. It could mean that God will turn from the Jews who killed

---

51. For the linguistic details, see Kümmel, "Weingärtnern," 125, nn. 20, 21; Black, *Aram. Approach,* 41, 70, 251 (*bis*), 253 (*bis*).

52. Schmid, *Mk.,* 222. But Mark perhaps uses the story specifically as a *partial* unveiling of the Secret at the end of Jesus' ministry.

53. Haenchen, *Weg,* 400.

54. It would be startling evidence of "early Catholicism" in Mk. if, with Origen (Migne, *PG,* xiii.1489; cf. Swete, *Mk.,* 255), as well as Troadec, *Mc.,* 206, we were to understand the *allois* to whom the vineyard was given as the apostles (and their successors). But Mark is doubtless thinking of the church as a whole, not its leaders.

his Son and heir (cf. Gal. 4:1; Heb. 1:2) to others who are more worthy of being God's vineyard, i.e., to those who believe the gospel. The action is, of course, *past* from the point of view of those who first told the parable. In this earliest interpretation and use the parable is seen as a judgment on the Jews and a vindication of Jesus. A high (if indirect) Christology is thus implied from the beginning of the tradition (although, in our view, the tradition is not particularly early). A still earlier understanding might see in the parable a judgment on Jewish leaders only, which would not be likely after a very early date.[55] But there is something artificial about this interpretation, since the parable presupposes the mistreatment of God's servants, which in the OT is the act of the whole people, not merely of a few leaders; in addition, the contrast between the leaders and the (favorably disposed) people is a *Markan* motif which is differently motivated. Nothing in the parable suggests that the husbandmen represent a limited group of people—except of course the obvious fact that "others" exist to whom the vineyard may be given.

2. The parable could also imply that Jesus foresaw God's turning from the Jews to the Gentiles. It would then be used primarily after the origin of the Gentile mission by those who, unlike Paul, had lost all real hope of Jewish conversion. In the light of the motif reflected in 1:1 (with 15:10f. and 39); 2:20; 3:6; and 11:15–18, this is almost certainly Mark's intention, so far as the context is polemic. Positively, its aim is also christological: Jesus vanquishes his opponents in argument and even in death; God has made him (not one of the numerous other prophets who suffered the same fate but) the chief Cornerstone.

3. Finally, the parable could be understood to reflect a regular

---

55. Cf. Matt. 23:37f. (= Lk. 13:34f., Q); Mk. 15:11–15; and esp. Matt. 23:4, 13, 29ff. (= Lk. 11:46, 52, 47f., Q), which Siegfried Schulz, "Die neue Frage nach dem historischen Jesus," *Neues Testament und Geschichte . . . Oscar Cullmann zum 70. Geburtstag* (Zürich/Tübingen: Theologischer Verlag, J. C. B. Mohr, 1972), 33–42 (35, n. 4) considers a part of the oldest Q-material. On this view, "the parable is intended solely as a judgment proclamation directed toward the Jewish leaders and toward them alone" (Schmid, *Mk.*, 220; so also Hauck, *Mk.*, 142).

principle in the divine economy: just as God has turned from the Jews to the Gentiles, so he will always turn from those who do not produce "fruit" to those who do. This seems to be Matthew's meaning, unknown to Mark and probably unthinkable for most Christians ever since.

At some point, not necessarily early in the transmission and possibly as late as Mark himself, a scriptural proof is added; Ps. 118 [117]:22f. is cited to show that God foresaw his using in the future the very people whom he had rejected in the past. The largely negative stress in the parable itself is here transmuted into a positive emphasis on the vindication of the Son and God's work through him in the world. This complete form of the parable is probably the most directly applicable to the modern church and relevant to the modern world.[56]

14. The Fig Tree as Herald of Summer (13:28f.; cf. Matt. 24:32f.; Lk. 21:29ff.)

This brief parabolic saying occurs toward the end of the Markan apocalypse (chapter 13) and cannot be interpreted without reference to the literary construction of the chapter as a whole.[1] It is also widely, though by no means universally, held that behind this chapter lies a writing, either Jewish or Jewish-Christian in origin, which Mark has taken over and adapted,[2] a

---

56. Some moderns will doubtless find a psychologizing understanding more congenial. They might well ponder the luckless efforts in the same direction evidenced by Saying 65 of Thomas: "a good man"; "perhaps they did not recognize him"; "perhaps they will respect my son"; etc. See Haenchen, Weg, 403, n. 14; Klauck, "Weinberg," 135f. and esp. Schrage, Verhältnis, 137–145.

1. Two works of particular importance on the structure of Mk. 13, both based largely on a redaction-critical method and viewpoint, should be mentioned here: Jan Lambrecht, Die Redaktion der Markus-Apokalypse (Rome: Pontifical Biblical Institute, 1967), and Rudolf Pesch, Naherwartungen. Tradition und Redaktion in Mk 13 (Düsseldorf: Patmos-Verlag, 1968).

2. This theory is fully discussed (and rejected) by G. R. Beasley-Murray in "The Rise and Fall of the Little Apocalypse Theory," ExpT 64 (1952), 346–349 and Jesus and the Future (London/New York: Macmillan, St. Martin's Press, 1954), as well as his A Commentary on Mark 13 (London/New York: Macmillan/ St. Martin's Press, 1957), esp. 15–18.

Other opinions have varied widely: a) It is generally accepted (in some instances with substantial reservations) by Bultmann, HST, 122; Rawlinson, Mk., 180ff.; Branscomb, Mk., 231ff.; Taylor, Mk., 498f.; and Günther Harder, "'Das

theory that cannot be discussed in detail in this study, although obviously it has implications for many of the disputed questions in this chapter. What is of crucial importance, especially for those who deny the theory as a whole, is the recognition that pre-Markan apocalyptic material has been woven into a context in which most of it did not originally fit.[3]

The latter part of the discourse (vv. 28–37) consists of a parable (the Fig Tree, vv. 28f.), three sayings (vv. 30ff.), and a parable (the Waiting Servants, 33–36), concluding with a solemn "And what I say to you, I say to all: Watch!" which brings the discourse to a close. The materials are united not only by themes but also by catchwords, clear evidence of Markan redactional activity.

It is evident on even a cursory reading that this section, like the chapter as a whole, is composite: In vv. 24f., the cosmic phenomena are "signs" that "he" is at the door and vv. 26f. portray the coming itself (not the premonitory signs of it), while "these

---

eschatologische Geschichtsbild der sogenannten Kleinen Apokalypse Markus 13," *Theologia Viatorum* 4 (1952), 71–107 (74).

b) It is specifically rejected not only by Beasley-Murray in the works cited above but also by Cranfield in his articles on "St. Mark 13," *ScotJTh* 6 (1953), 189–196, 287–303, and ibid., 7 (1954), 284–303 as well as in his *Mk.*, 387–391; by Kümmel, *Promise*, 98; Grässer, *Parusieverzögerung*, 153; Lohmeyer, *Mk.*, 285, as well as by those who hold to various other theories of the pre-Markan traditional material.

c) Of such differing theories perhaps the most important is that of Lars Hartman, *Prophecy Interpreted* (Lund: Gleerup, 1966). Hartman holds that the basis of chap. 13 is a "parenetic eschatological midrash" (245) on Daniel ([2:31–45]; 7:7–27; 8:9–26; 9:24–27; and 11:21–12:4[13]); that this midrash probably came originally from Jesus himself; and that the midrash was expanded in several (reconstructable) stages before its final inclusion in chap. 13.

d) Jan Lambrecht, in his several studies of the problem, has shifted his grounds from open rejection (so *Redaktion*, 258) to a qualified acceptance of something like Hartman's parenetic eschatological midrash ("Die 'Midrasch-Quelle' von Mk 13," *Biblica* 49 [1968], 254–270).

In general, closest to the views set forth here is Pesch, *Naherwartungen*, in which the theory is vigorously defended (see esp. 207–223).

3. Hans Conzelmann, "Geschichte und Eschaton nach Mc 13," *ZNW* 50 (1959), 210–221 finds the Markan "apocalyptic" atypical in two respects: a) its eschatological expectation has been Christianized, i.e., related to a historical figure of the immediate past, and b) it distinguishes a historical period of testing and woe, on the one hand, from a supernatural End, on the other (a distinction greatly elaborated by Lk.). But Conzelmann puts Mark somewhat too quickly into a simple pre-Lukan context, as if his primary concern were also the delayed Parousia. Pesch has more correctly argued that Mark's problem is apocalyptic enthusiasts in his community and that he wishes to hold to a *Naherwartung* while opposing apocalyptic calculation; *Naherwartungen*, 239.

things" in v. 29 makes sense only as a reference not to the coming but to signs; v. 30 offers assurance of the coming within a generation, whereas v. 32 says that even Jesus does not know when the coming will be; and v. 31 is used here as assurance of the truth of v. 30, even though its wording is so general that it must originally have referred to Jesus' teaching as a whole. It is consequently impossible to know from the present context either when any of these sayings arose or what relationship (if any) they might originally have had with one another. Only Mark's intention will be reflected in their present position and use.

The saying in v. 28 is introduced by words that, literally translated, mean, "So from the fig tree learn the *parable,*" i.e., the lesson implied[4] in what happens annually in the growth of the fig tree. Needless to say, no particular fig tree, certainly not the tree in 11:13, is intended; the phenomenon is admirably illustrated by the fig tree because in Palestine most other trees are evergreen.[5] The fig tree is common, and its bursting into leaf[6] is a well-known sign[7] that one season (winter) is ending and the other (summer)[8] is about to begin. All men know the simple agricultural phenomenon described here and draw the proper conclusions from it.

"So also," Jesus goes on to say (v. 29), "when you see these things taking place, you know that he (it?) is near, even at the gates." In this verse, surely reworded and perhaps even created by

---

4. Existentially, not intellectually: "The 'parable' of the fig-tree (13:28) is more an exhortation than an instruction" (J. M. Robinson, *Problem of History,* 76).
5. It is therefore not true that "any tree would have served as an illustration" (McNeile, *Matt.,* 354); note too that the fig tree puts out its leaves first, even before the vines (Pallis, *Notes . . . Mk.,* 44).
6. Editors and commentators are divided between ἐκφύῃ (put forth [leaves]) and ἐκφυῇ (sprout), but the sense is approximately the same in both cases. See BAG, *s.v. ekphyō.*
7. Song of Sol. 2:11ff. In addition, the dry fig tree is a sign of desolation, Judgment, etc. (Is. 34:4; Jer. 8:13; Hos. 2:12; Joel 1:7, 12; Hab. 3:17; Hag. 2:19), the budding fig tree a sign of God's blessing (Joel 2:22; Zech. 3:10).
8. Palestinians commonly reckoned two seasons to the year. Note that the term *theros* here means summer, not harvest (which comes long after the sprouting of the branches); "harvest" would be appropriate if the saying were a simple allegory of the Judgment (cf. Matt. 13:38, 39; Rev. 14:15), which it is not—a point missed by many commentators. Dupont, "Figuier," 542 is right that in Semitic thought "summer" is the "season of fruit"—cf. 2 Sam. 16:1f.; Is. 28:4; Jer. 8:20; 40:10, 12; 48:32; Amos 8:1f.; Mic. 7:1–but of these texts only Is. 28:4 and possibly Mic. 7:1 are really relevant for the very *beginning* of summer.

Mark to connect the parable with what precedes, the analogy is clear enough. But the reference in "these things" (*tauta*) is not, and commentators are sharply divided. Lagrange[9] thinks the words refer solely to the destruction of the Temple, but since Jerusalem has not even been mentioned since v. 5 (!), this can hardly be its meaning in Mk.[10] Taylor suggests that the original reference was to some definite event, probably the fall of Jerusalem, but that in its present context it refers to everything mentioned in vv. 5–27.[11] For its reference in some other context we are restricted to pure conjecture, while *for Mark* we can say with assurance only that in v. 29 he did not intend those events (in vv. 5–27) that were more than premonitory "signs." (In v. 30 he must have intended a somewhat wider reference.)

The "lesson" (parable) of the fig tree, then, is: Just as all men "know" by the sprouting of fig leaves that summer is near, so the disciples "should know" from the "signs" that he is near. Most translators correctly see the "know" of v. 28 as general knowledge, the "know" of v. 29 as an imperative, and this fits well with the mood of exhortation toward which the text is beginning to turn. The hortatory emphasis in v. 29—as in the overall intention of Mark in this chapter—is clear. The disciples do not know automatically, with the same complete assurance all men have about the beginning of summer; they must note the signs well and discern their significance.[12]

The natural reading of v. 28f. is that "he," i.e., the Son of Man (cf. v. 26f.), is near, though of course only in the Markan context, since the saying may originally have had nothing to do with v. 26: Only a person could properly be said to be "at the gates."[13] And

9. *Mc.*, 348.
10. Schmid, *Mk.*, 247.
11. *Mk.*, 521—although it is hard to see how this could be known if, as seems likely, 13:1–4 is the Markan, not the historical, context.
12. Of course the central point of the parable has to do with the Kingdom or the coming of the Son of Man, not with human disposition; see Dupont, "Figuier," 532, n. 13; Lambrecht, *Redaktion*, 200.
13. McNeile, *Matt.*, 354; Beasley-Murray, *Mark 13*, 97; Lambrecht, *Redaktion*, 199.

since for Mark the person of the Son of Man is of central concern, the words "at the gates" would well be a Markan addition,[14] strengthening the original word of consolation and elaborating the thought of "nearness." It is plausible, then—though by no means certain—to postulate an original saying (without "at the gates") of impersonal reference, perhaps "the End is near" or even something deliberately vague, which would be "in better accord with the mysterious vagueness of an apocalypse."[15]

The following three verses (vv. 30–32) reinforce, elaborate, and explain what has been implied in the parable of the fig tree. Since v. 31 is so broadly worded as to suggest the teaching of Jesus in general (not merely the teaching of chapter 13),[16] and since v. 30 assumes on Jesus' part a knowledge which v. 32 denies him, it is evident that these verses come originally from diverse contexts. In Mk., however, they form a rough unity. V. 30 begins with a solemn "Truly I tell you" (cf. the introductory words in 9:1, to which this verse is clearly related) and was possibly consciously created by the evangelist himself on the analogy of 9:1.[17] The final fulfillment of all the portents described, Jesus says, is near, within one generation—i.e., within about 30[18] or 40[19] years, although these figures should not be too precisely understood. Attempts to read these words some other way are legion,[20] but the plain mean-

14. So, inter alia, Dupont, "Figuier," 538f. and Pesch, Naherwartungen, 180, who note Mark's predilection for doubled formulas.

15. Swete, Mk., 295.

16. Vs. Lambrecht, Redaktion, 212; Pesch, Naherwartungen, 189f. Of course v. 31 in its present context serves to confirm esp. what precedes and, to a lesser extent, to unite v. 30 and v. 32.

17. Johnson, Mk., 218; Pesch, Naherwartungen, 184–187; Bultmann, HST, 123, 125, who also suggests the possibility that v. 30 (with different wording) formed the original ending of the incorporated Jewish apocalypse. Obviously, the reverse is also possible; see the bibliog. in Lambrecht, Redaktion, 203, n.1.

A more probable view, however, is that both verses come from early Christian prophecy; so Siegfried Schulz, Die Stunde der Botschaft (Hamburg/Zürich: Furche-Verlag/Zwingli Verlag, 1967; 2. durchges. Aufl., 1970), 97f.

18. Herodotus, Hist. II. 142 (Loeb, I, 448: 3 generations = 100 years); Heracleitus in Plut., De Defectu Oraculorum 415E (Loeb, Moralia V, 382).

19. So the OT reckoning: cf. Gen. 7:1; Ex. 1:6; Deut. 1:35; Judg. 2:10.

20. Modern interpreters suggest a reference to the fall of Jerusalem (Gould, Mk., 253; A. Feuillet, "Le discours de Jésus sur la ruine du Temple d'après Marc xiii et Luc xxi, 5–36," RB 55 [1948], 481–502; 56 [1949], 61–92 [82f.]; Jerusalem Bible) or to the Jewish people (Schniewind, Matt.[10], 246); Cranfield, Mk., 409 and ScotJTh 7 (1954), 290f. lists several other possibilities. The ancient church

ing of the statement is almost certainly correct, not only for Mark but also for his tradition. On any scheme, Mark must have reckoned with the nearness, though not necessarily the imminence, of the Parousia.[21]

This prediction is then solemnly grounded in the overall authority of Jesus' teaching (v. 31) and strengthened and further interpreted[22] by the insistence (v. 32) that the exact time is known to God alone. The effect of this verse is quite different from the primary christological concerns of many modern interpreters; it insists only that what man cannot know (vs. the false prophets) God does know. And what he knows he will, in his own proper time, certainly do. The rhetorical triad, "no one . . . , not even the angels . . . , nor the Son" is clearly the foil to "but only the Father," whatever the form of the pre-Markan saying might have been.[23] Obviously if Mark's theology were dominated by an imminent expectation of the Parousia he would not have insisted so strongly on this particular point, which is polemic in intention. In other words, v. 32 is at once a confirmation of the *Naherwartung* and a correction of the apocalyptic and enthusiastic understanding of it,[24] which means that Mark has really fashioned traditional materials of various kinds into an *anti*-apocalyptic discourse, in which expectation and consolation are combined.

---

understood the words to imply the passing away of the Christian church, of humanity itself, of the world, etc.; cf. Loisy, *ES*, II, 436; Lagrange, *Mc.*, 348; McNeile, *Matt.*, 354; and the devastating criticism in Jülicher, *Gleichn.*, II, 7f.

21. Charles B. Cousar, "Eschatology and Mark's *Theologia Crucis*. A Critical Analysis of Mark 13," *Interp.* 24 (1970), 321–335 (325f.) rightly points out that Mark has toned down both 9:1 and 13:30 by the context in which he places them. (Otherwise the false prophets would be right!) See next note.

22. Harder, "Geschichtsbild," 95 rightly argues that v. 32 is "undoubtedly a correction" of v. 30. It thus seems most improbable that v. 30 is a Markan construct (vs. Lambrecht, *Redaktion*, 208–211 and esp. Pesch, *Naherwartungen*, 184–187) and equally improbable that v. 30 should be taken—with or without 9:1—as the key to Mark's eschatology.
As a pre-Markan prophetic saying, of course, v. 30 could only have read "all things," not "all these things."

23. Bultmann, *HST*, 123 suggests that Mark has used a Jewish or Jewish-Christian saying which spoke only of human (and angelic?) ignorance. Pesch, *Naherwartungen*, 192ff. prefers (although he does not insist on) the possiblity that Mark created the whole rhetorical conclusion. Lambrecht, *Redaktion*, 235, 239, n. 2 notes that the saying fits so well into the context that we must assume it was written for it, although he is open to a pre-Markan, even authentic, origin for the saying's content (238, n. 3).

24. Pesch, *Naherwartungen*, 190; so also Cousar, "*Theologia Crucis*," *passim*.

The parable itself can hardly be located with any certainty in the history of the tradition. Some interpreters are content only with asserting its genuineness.[25] Others suggest that it must somehow have been related originally to Jesus' teaching about the coming of the Kingdom (not the signs of the End), possibly early in his ministry.[26] Still others defend an original reference to the Parousia.[27] Jülicher argues for authenticity on the dubious grounds that sayings like 9:1 and 14:25, which point in the same direction, cannot have been created in the early church.[28] But "discerning the Signs" of the "nearness of the Ineffable" is Jülicher's theology, not Jesus',[29] so the argument is inconclusive. On the other hand, Jesus, who consistently rejected the giving of signs, would probably have seen the definite predictions of chapter 13 as infringing upon the prerogatives of God.[30] Certainly Jesus could have called for discernment on the part of his disciples, but what kinds of things, properly discerned, would show the nearness (coming?) of the End we hardly know. And Markan redactional activity is so extensive that even the original form, as well as the context, of the parable is irrecoverable.

If it is authentic, the parable must have originated in a discussion (dispute?) about whether or not the events of Jesus' ministry reflected the inbreaking of the Kingdom, not which signs in the future would foreshadow the Parousia. With only slight rewording it would quickly be found useful as a Parousia-parable addressed to believers. Obviously, this "reinterpretation" could be the original Sitz as well, especially since any different wording rests to some degree on speculation.[31] A small, but by no means conclusive

25. "Doubtless a genuine utterance of Jesus" (McNeile, Matt., 354).
26. Kümmel, Promise, 20ff.; B. T. D. Smith, Parables, 89ff.; Taylor, Mk., 520; Dodd, Parables, 137, n. 1; Jeremias, Parables, 119f.; Dupont, "Figuier," 536–546.
27. Feuillet, "Ruine," 83; Beasley-Murray, Mark 13, 95f.: "The parable authenticates the fundamental viewpoint presumed in the Discourse"(!).
28. Gleichn., II, 8f.
29. It is, however, quite close to Luke's. Jülicher (ibid., 11) thinks that Luke has "appropriately buttressed" the correct meaning by adding the phrase aph' heautōn in v. 30 and by inserting v. 28 (peculiar to Luke).
30. Johnson, Mk., 219. Cf. Dupont, "Figuier," 543. Beasley-Murray, Mark 13, 95f. expressly denies this.
31. Lambrecht, Redaktion, 201f. notes how thoroughly vv. 28f. reflect, in context

indication that the parable arose in a Parousia-context is the fact
that the "sign" mentioned here (even in the parable proper, without the application in v. 29, which could be secondary) is purely
future, whereas in the teaching of Jesus (cf. Matt. 12:28=Lk.
11:20, Q; Lk. 12:54ff.; Matt. 12:39=Lk. 11:29, Q) the "signs" are
present.[32]

Of this parable, then, we can say with some assurance only that
it arose in a Palestinian milieu—the agriculture is really comprehensible only there—and that it is used by Mark to strengthen
and console his readers. That he chose to embed this parable in a
chapter of marked apocalyptic outlook shows how seriously he
took persecution and suffering as not beyond the knowledge and
grace of God. The true *telos* of the Christian is not cosmic desolation but hope.

15. The Waiting Servants (13:34-37; cf. Lk. 12:35-38)

This brief parable, which might equally be titled the parable of
The Absent Householder,[1] is, especially in v. 35f., partially allegorical. It would be a mistake, however, to argue from either the
allegorical elements or the occasional roughness of the Greek that
Mark has not attempted to fit the parable into a rather carefully
worked-out framework. And its function is quite clear.

Vv. 33–37 conclude the great eschatological discourse of chapter 13. If the analysis in the preceding chapter is correct, vv. 28–32
have stressed both the nearness and the unknowability of the End-
time, its firm place in the knowledge and plan of God. Vv. 33–37,

---

and wording, Markan interests and warns against reconstructing a pre-Markan
parable (with the same or a different point). Dupont's rejoinder (Figuier," 540f.)
that the parable fits "perfectly" (?) within the context of Jesus message and that
Mark gives little evidence of having created parables is correct; but this does not
exclude the possibility that the parable arose in the pre-Markan tradition and
meant just what Mark understands it to mean.
32. Cf. Beasley-Murray, *Mark 13*, 95.

1. So Taylor, *Mk.*, 523; Jülicher, *Gleichn.*, II, 161: "Vom spät heimkehrenden
Hausherrn"; Dupont, "La Parabole du Maître qui rentre dans la nuit (Mc 13,
34–36)," *Mélanges bibliques en hommage au R. P. Béda Rigaux* (Gembloux:
J. Duculot, 1970), 89–116; Jeremias, *Parables*, 53ff., stressing what be believes
to have been the core of the original parable: "The Parable of the Doorkeeper."
Harder, "Geschichtsbild," 95 thinks of the merging of two parables, one *Vom
nächtlichen Wachen* and one *Von der Bereitschaft der Knechte*, with the commission to the Doorkeeper as a secondary (Markan) addition.

overwhelmingly though perhaps not entirely Markan, are so ar-
ranged and worded as to make the parenetic implications of the
coming End clear to Mark's readers. V. 33, which like v. 37 is
entirely Markan, takes up again the theme of taking heed (*blepete*,
vv. 5, 9, 23), which is *"la morale du discours."*[2] Coupled with the
exhortation is the (synonymous) "watch" (*agrypneite*; cf. also
grēgoreite[3] in vv. 35, 37), which again expresses Mark's fundamental concern.[4] The exhortation is based in v. 33, as in vv. 35f.,
on the unknown hour of the coming of the End. In v. 34 a simple
parable is introduced by a simple *hōs* (cf. rabbinic *lᵉ*) best translated as "your situation is similar to one like this: . . . ." It speaks
of a man[5] who takes a journey and leaves obligations behind. In
the parable proper (v. 34), the stress is on the responsibility of
all; the doorkeeper's job of "watching" must also be implied for
all or the parable itself breaks down. Since parabolic applications
are notoriously secondary, it is quite possible that the parable
originally ended here[6] and also possible that all reference to any
servants other than the doorkeeper is secondary.[7] But since the
function of a doorkeeper is to "watch," even this theoretical reconstruction is essentially parenetic, while a fortiori the parable in its
present form can never have had any other purpose.[8] Parenesis,

2. Lagrange, *Mc.*, 351. As Cousar, *"Theologia Crucis,"* 322 points out, except
for 13:21f. *all* the words of warning in this chapter (vv. 5, 9, 23, 33, 35, 37)
are redactional. Nor is this surprising, since chap. 13 is something like a farewell-
discourse, and farewell-discourses commonly reflect the central concerns of the
redactor; cf. F. Neirynck, "Le discours anti-apocalyptique de Mc., xiii," *ETL* 65
(1969), 154–164 (158).
3. Six times in Mk., 3 here (13:34, 35, 37) and 3 in Gethsemane (14:34, 37, 38),
a scene which shows other linguistic parallels to these verses, where also "watching" is portrayed as a primary obligation of the disciple.
4. A third imperative, *kai proseuchesthe*, is added by ℵ A C L Wᵇ X Γ Δ Π (E)
Φ Θ *pl* lat syˢ·ᵖ sa [bo] arm; the text without it is supported by B D *pc* a c k.
The argument that Lk. 21:36 seems to presuppose prayer in his Markan source
is canceled out by Luke's special interest in prayer and by the fact that no good
reason can be given for Matthew's failure to use it in 24:42 and 25:13. On
balance, the addition seems to be a secondary assimilation to 14:38; so Jülicher,
Gleichn., II, 167; Beasley-Murray, *Mark 13*, 111; Grässer, *Parusieverzögerung*, 85,
n. 1; Dupont, "Maître," 94, n. 2; vs. Lambrecht, *Redaktion*, 242f.
5. Both the asyndeton and the use of *anthrōpos* (= *tis*) are Semitisms.
6. Bultmann, *HST*, 174; Pesch, *Naherwartungen*, 197; Dupont, Maître," 106.
7. Bultmann, *HST*, 174; Dupont, "Maître," 105ff.; Jeremias, *Parables*, 53ff.
8. It therefore makes little difference whether the delayed Parousia was responsible for the origin of the parable (Nineham, *Mk.*, 361f.) or only for its present
form. For a "doorkeeper" parable at the beginning of the tradition, see Jeremias,

not eschatology, seems to lie behind all forms.

In what follows (vv. 35f.) the application emphasizes the basic point. Now all are to watch, although they do so not to fulfill the responsibilities assigned to them (cf. v. 34)[9] but because they do not know the hour of the master's coming.[10] The master might return, the text suggests, in any of the four night watches—a combination of specificity and uncertainty that seems to reflect Markan opposition to enthusiasts who believe themselves able to calculate more closely than this an End they consider imminent. This coming might, according to v. 36, be sudden (i.e., without warning); it might also find unwary disciples "sleeping," a common metaphor that cannot be stressed for all the servants (only for the watchman), since obviously one can stay awake only for very limited periods, although he could remain watchful throughout his (Christian) life. In v. 37 Mark generalizes what is directed to the disciples in vv. 33, 35 and makes it plain that this instruction is not, even primarily, for the Apostolate, but simply for all Christians.[11] Since the time of the master's coming is completely unknown to man and not preceded by any unambiguous sign they must be constantly "watching." Since Christians are fully empowered to

---

Parables, 53ff.; Grässer, *Parusieverzögerung*[2], 86ff.; and esp. Dupont, "Maître," 107–116. On the other hand, Harder, "Geschichtsbild," 96 thinks the Doorkeeper was added to the fusion of two parables (see note 1 at the beginning of this chapter), while Pesch, *Naherwartungen*, 198f. leans toward the possibility that the original non-allegorical parable included neither "authority" nor the Doorkeeper, but only the assignment of work to each servant.

9. The formula *exousian didonai* (cf. 6:7; 11:28) may reflect the authority transmitted by Jesus, the master, to the disciples, his servants. If so, the phrase is an allegorical trait which "hardly speaks for authenticity" (Pesch, *Naherwartungen*, 198).

10. There is something attractive about the form-critical conjecture that the parable has gone through three stages: a) an original parable about a Doorkeeper, b) an elaboration which includes other servants, each with his own work, and c) a shift in emphasis to the *unknowability* of the time of the master's return (this last certainly Markan). But in any case two fixed points in the interpretation seem to be: a) an original parenetic emphasis, and b) the importance of *unknowability* in the Markan redaction. The rest is speculation.

11. Dupont, "Maître," 107; so also Beasley-Murray, *Mark 13*, 114f.; Cranfield, *Mk.*, 412; Lambrecht, *Redaktion*, 248; vs. Swete, *Mk.*, 298; Lohmeyer, *Mk.*, 284f.; and Harder, "Geschichtsbild," 96, who speaks of the *"besondere Aufgabe"* of the four disciples. The view that the parable was originally a warning to the leaders of the people, esp. the scribes (Jeremias, *Parables*, 55, 166) though not impossible, rests on an over-interpretation of the responsibility-motif in Mk. 13:34b (so, rightly, Dupont, "Maître," 115) and an under-estimation of Mark's redactional work.

do their daily work, assigned by the master before he left (v. 34), the present is no brief, pointless, meaningless interlude before an imminent End. Again the combination of parenesis and polemic shines through.[12]

Where is the origin of these materials to be sought? Hardly in the teaching of Jesus, with which little of the material fits.[13] The parable proper—the only thing in these verses that does not seem to be surely Markan—is more likely to be a variant form of the parable of the Talents/Pounds[14] or something like "a homiletical echo of several parables."[15] Perhaps the simplest explanation is that it is an interweaving (Markan in form) of materials, some of them very primitive, common to many kinds of early Christian theology. The coming of Christ is a common theme in the liturgy (1 Cor. 16:22; Mk. 14:25; 1 Cor. 11:26) and missionary preaching

---

12. See Pesch, *Naherwartungen*, 199.

13. Jülicher, *Gleichn.*, II, 171. Dodd's attempt (*Parables*, 165ff.) to understand the basic parable as originally a reference to the crisis of Jesus' own ministry and the "immediately impending attack upon Him and His followers" I find unconvincing. (Jeremias, *Parables*, 55 argues similarly, suggesting an original address to the disciples, the crowds, or the scribes: he prefers [166] the last.) The same must be said of Dupont's extremely careful study of the parable ("Maitre," 115 and *passim*), which also imports into the text an emphasis on Jesus' mission during his lifetime. The complex literary phenomena have led both Lagrange (*Mc.*, 351) and Fiebig (*Gleichnisreden Jesu*, 164) to understand the parable as resting on (presumably authentic) oral tradition, whereas Beasley-Murray, *Mark 13* insists on an original reference to the Parousia (rather than the Kingdom) but remains noncommittal as to whether vv. 34ff. are an original parable or a Markan construct based on authentic themes.

14. Haenchen, *Weg*, 453 thinks the section was composed by Mark on this basis. A plausible—though hardly demonstrable—explanation is that an original parable about a doorkeeper has been *generalized* by the use of materials from the parable of the Talents; so Schmid, *Mk.*, 249f.; Jeremias, *Parables*, 53ff.; cf. Grässer, *Parusieverzögerung*, 86ff.; Nineham, *Mk.*, 361f.; Schweizer, *Mk.*, 160f. Even this explanation, however, does not establish the authenticity of the (presumed) original parable, since the eschatology behind *any* presumed form of the parable implies that the master is *absent*, not (as in the teaching of Jesus) in some sense *present*.

15. Taylor, *Mk.*, 524; similarly, Rawlinson, *Mk.*, 193; Cranfield, *ScotJTh* 7 (1954), 296. Lambrecht, *Redaktion*, 240–256 and "Logia-Quellen," 350, 354 thinks Mark created the parable from four others present in his source: the Waiting Servants (Lk. 12:35–38); the Thief in the Night (Lk. 12:39f. = Matt. 24:43f.); the Faithful Servant (Lk. 12:42–46 = Matt. 24:45–51); and the Pounds or Talents (Lk. 19:12–27 = [?] Matt. 25:14–30). But it is most unlikely that Mark's sources included any form of Q, as Lambrecht holds, so this, like much else in his valuable book, becomes artificial and unconvincing.

Dupont, "Maître," 95 finds a genuine parable behind these verses but admits that the section "gives the impression of being the result of a collection of elements rather imperfectly adapted."

(1 Thes. 1:10; cf. Heb. 6:2) of very early Christianity. Scattered throughout various traditions we find parenesis based on his coming (Phil. 3:20f.; 1 Thes. 4:13–18; Tit. 2:12f.; Heb. 10:37; Jn. 14:1–3; Rev. 22:20), often described as at night or like a thief (Matt. 24:43=Lk. 12:39, Q; 1 Thes. 5:2, 4; 2 Pet. 3:10; Rev. 3:3; 16:15) or suddenly (Lk. 18:8), at an unexpected hour (Matt. 24:44=Lk. 12:40, Q; Lk. 21:34; Rev. 3:3). The theme of Jesus' leaving, as on a journey, assigning various tasks to servants, is also primitive (Matt. 24:45–51=Lk. 12:42–46, Q; Matt. 25:14–30= [?]Lk. 19:12–27, Q?). And an eschatological setting for parenesis, sometimes contrasting wakefulness and sleep, sometimes drunkenness and sobriety, most often simply urging "watchfulness" is equally common: Rom. 13:11f.; 1 Thes. 5:2–6; 3:13; Matt. 25:1–13; Lk. 21:36; Eph. 6:18; Rev. 3:2; 16:15. Obviously, not all of this material—none of it in *written* form—was known to Mark. But it is so widespread, in so many layers of the tradition, that it is best to presume that Mark himself has used these common themes to fashion an ending to the last instructions given by Jesus to his disciples.

In this light the Markan message is unmistakable. Nothing in these verses emphasizes the immediacy of the Parousia.[16] But the coming of the End, although its time is unknown to man, is known to God and thus certain, and it is precisely this paradoxical "known but unknown" answer to the questions of v. 4, not the imminence of the Parousia, that forms the basis of the parenesis: the Christian is to live in this world like a servant who, knowing the certainty of his master's coming, but not the hour, watches for him.[17] It is particularly important to note that this lesson is taught

16. Both the Markan revisions of his sources throughout this chapter and the special language of these concluding verses make it impossible to believe that Mark expected an imminent Parousia in Galilee; vs. Willi Marxsen, *Der Evangelist Markus* (Göttingen: Vandenhoeck & Ruprecht, 1956; 2. durchges. Aufl., 1959), 53–59 (ET: 83–92) and Suhl, *Zitate*, 20ff., 156 and *passim*. Both scholars hold e.g., that Mk. 13:10 is already fulfilled (as an explicit prediction) for Mark, a view that is probably impossible if, with Conzelmann, "Geschichte und Eschaton," 219, the verse is understood as redactional, not as an isolated logion.
17. Pesch, *Naherwartungen*, 196 rightly notes that the admonitions to wakefulness make fully evident the anti-apocalyptic nature of Mark's eschatological expectation.

by Jesus before his death; in Mark's view "watchfulness" is not the creation of theologians dealing with the unexpected continuance of human history. It is part of Jesus' own history (the stage is now set for Gethsemane and the Passion) and of his will for his disciples.[18] We perhaps understand the historical origin of the materials of these verses somewhat differently from the way Mark understood them. But to say this and no more is to avoid the theological issue he so clearly and cogently raises. Discipleship without suffering, moralism without theology, theology without eschatology—these are things he would not even have understood, much less countenanced.

16. The Seed Growing Secretly (4:26–29)

This little parable does not really belong in a study of the parables of the Triple Tradition, since neither Matthew nor Luke uses it. We append it here, however, to make the examination of Mark's parables complete. Whether it is more appropriately entitled the parable of the Patient Husbandman[1] or the parable of the Confident Sower[2] depends on the interpretation of the central emphasis.

Theologically, the failure of both Matthew and Luke to include the parable is easily explained. Luke cannot use it because its stress on the sower's inactivity runs counter to his own intention in 8:19ff. (which in the Lukan context immediately follows and provides the keynote of the whole section), namely, to describe those as Jesus' brethren who hear *and do* the Word of God. Matthew, on the other hand, does not use it because the parable of the Tares, which he substitutes for it,[3] expresses his own concept

---

18. In a general way, Mark's emphasis is more on a negative warning against sleeping, Luke's on a positive promise for the wakeful; so Dupont, "Maître," 99.

1. B. T. D. Smith, *Parables*, 129ff.; Jeremias, *Parables*, 151.

2. Karl Weiss, *Voll Zuversicht! Zur Parabel Jesu vom zuversichtlichen Sämann* (Münster i.W.: Aschendorff, 1922), 22 and *passim;* so also his "Mk 4,26 bis 29— dennoch die Parabel vom zuversichtlichen Sämann!" *BibZeit* 18 (1929), 45–67.

3. Cf. Charles W. F. Smith, *The Jesus of the Parables* (Philadelphia: Westminster Press, 1948), 86ff. The occurrence in both Gospels (in the same order) of *katheudō, blasta(n)ō, sitos,* and *therismos* as well as *prōton* and *karpos* (which are casual and not in order) shows that Matthew had read Mark's parable, probably that he was reading it as he wrote the Tares.

of the Church as a *corpus mixtum*; this is a different concern[4] and since the farmer of the Markan parable sows and does nothing more until harvest, it reflects an entirely different view of reality as well.[5] While it is possible that the Markan text used by both Matthew and Luke did not include it,[6] such a possibility is very much less likely than deliberate omission on the part of the other two evangelists.

The parable is introduced with the (Markan) introductory formula, "The Kingdom of God is like this, as (if [*hōs*+subj.]) a man . . . ," a formula which occurs only here, but which does not differ essentially from similar formulas in other passages.[7] The unusual wording creates grammatical difficulties, as the varied textual tradition shows,[8] but clearly the writer intends to compare two situations, not to compare the Kingdom with a man.[9] "It is with the Kingdom," Jesus says, "as if a man should sow seed . . . and sleep . . . and rise night after night, day after day. . . ."[10] However popular the interpretation may be, nothing in the text sug-

---

4. On this motif in Matthew's theology, see Bornkamm-Barth-Held, *Tradition, passim* and C. W. F. Smith, "The Mixed State of the Church in Matthew's Gospel," *JBL* 82 (1963), 149–168. That Matthew rejected Mk. 4:26–29 because he does not share Mark's interest in portraying the growing understanding of the disciples (so Wilkens, "Redaktion," 314–319) rests on a misinterpretation of Matthew and possibly also of Mark.

5. Haenchen, *Weg*, 184.

6. Hirsch, *Frühgeschichte*, I, 29f.; Baltensweiler, "Saat," 69; Günther Harder, "Das Gleichnis von der selbstwachsenden Saat. Mark. 4, 26–29," *Theologia Viatorum* 1948/49, 51–70 (70).

7. The parable of the Mustard Seed, which immediately follows (vv. 30ff.) uses a less unusual formula ("With what shall we compare the Kingdom of God?"); but both parables speak expressly of the Kingdom, and it is possible that Mark thought of them as a pair.

8. *hōsper anth.* Θ Φ 565 *pc*; *hōs ean anth.* (C)ℜ 0107 0133 *pm* lat Gel; *hōs anth. hotan* W λ e; *hōs anthrōpos* ℜ D.

9. Rightly, Dupont, "Semence," 376; Jeremias, *Parables*, 101ff.; vs. Franz Mussner, "Gleichnisauslegung und Heilsgeschichte. Dargetan am Gleichnis von der selbstwachsenden Saat (Mk 4, 26–29)," *TThZ* 64 (1955), 257–266 (264). Lagrange, *Mc.*, 115 suggests that if the *ean* is expressed, the Kingdom of God is compared to a situation, but with *hōs* alone, to a man; but shortly afterward (117) he notes more correctly that "one must compare the two situations in their totality." The following subjunctives show that the writer understands an *ean* (*an*) throughout.

10. Since in Semitic thought the day begins at sundown, the "night" is mentioned first.

gests that the sower is Christ himself;[11] he is any sower. The striking thing about the rest of the parable is that the farmer, once
having sown the seed, is not mentioned again until the harvest (if
then); once he has sown the seed he "continues in his tranquil
life,"[12] i.e., he does the very things he did before sowing.[13] By this
time Mark has forgotten the conditional way the sentences began;
he now turns from aorist to present subjunctives, describing not
the single act of sowing but the ongoing activities of the life of the
seed. This odd grammatical phenomenon has the effect of stressing the difference between the single initiatory act of the farmer
and his subsequent relative passivity.[14] It also suggests, like most
such awkward introductions, that he did not create the parable.

Several other minor phenomena in the succeeding verses reinforce the emphasis on the inactivity of the farmer. The middle
form of the verb *mēkynesthai*, a *hapax legomenon* in the NT, "emphasizes the activity of growth internal to the plant."[15] The sower's sleeping and rising night and day are, so to speak, repeated
acts of non-participation: he exerts no influence on the maturing
of the seed.[16] Similarly, "he knows not *how* [not *that*!] it grows"
implies that what he does not know he can hardly cause.[17]

<hr>

11. So, rightly, Jülicher, *Gleichn.*, II, 545; Taylor, *Mk.*, 266f.; vs. Mussner,
"Gleichnisauslegung," 264 and *passim* and K. Weiss, *Voll Zuversicht!*, 18 and
passim, as well as his "Mk 4,26 bis 29."
12. Lagrange, *Mc.*, 115; Dupont, "Semence," 377. Pallis, *Notes . . . Mk.*, 15f.
cites many parallels for the idea that "things will take their own satisfactory
course whilst a man sleeps." Note, e.g., Philo, *De Opif. Mundi* 167 (Loeb I,
132): the earth bears "without the skill of the husbandman" (*dicha geōrgikēs
epistēmēs*).
13. Jülicher, *Gleichn.*, II, 540. Fuchs, *Frage*, 392ff. elaborates this to show that
"the Kingdom of God frees you for yourself!"—which requires him (392, n. 4)
to minimize the importance of v. 29. Dupont, "Semence," 382f. understands the
parable to refer to the inactivity of *God* before the harvest, an interpretation
which seems to rest at least partially on the (quasi-allegorical) assumption that
the farmer = God (because God reaps in v. 29). Harder, "Saat," by insisting
that the Sower and the Harvester are the same (= God), really allegorizes the
parable. Better, Eduard Lohse, "Die Gottesherrschaft in den Gleichnissen Jesu,"
EvTheol 18 (1958), 145–157 (148): "The farmer remains the subject even in
the last sentence, without any allegorical allusion to God somehow shining
through."
14. Jeremias, *Parables*, 151; Schweizer, *Mk.*, 56f.
15. Swete, *Mk.*, 80.
16. Schmid, *Mk.*, 102; Jeremias, *Parables*, 151, n. 91.
17. Jülicher, *Gleichn.*, II, 540. Incidentally, this phrase, which has no parallels
in Mk. (13:32 refers to a quite different kind of non-knowing), shows that the

Finally, the word *automatē*, strengthened in force by its position at the beginning of the sentence, makes the centrality of this point clear. (One hardly knows what to make of the elaborate attempts of Anglo-Saxon exegetes in particular[18] to import into the saying some openness to human activity, which the parable has in so many ways so deliberately excluded.) The latter part of v. 28 goes on to portray the stage-by-stage maturation of the seed —surely not with any *temporal* intent (see below)—each step in the process guaranteed by what the farmer himself cannot even understand. Finally, in v. 29, the whole is summed up in an allusion to Joel 3[4]:13, in which the harvest is described as "at hand."[19] From sowing to harvest is a sure and certain step.

V. 29 raises a critical interpretive question: Is it or is it not consonant with the rest of the parable? Jülicher[20] insists that it is not, that vv. 26–28 concentrate on the development of the Kingdom of God, while v. 29 allegorizes the parable and is more concerned with the consummation of the Kingdom, "its precondition and the certainty of its coming"; the eschatological Judge of v. 29, he holds, is inappropriate and shows that Mark has either created or (more probably) reworked v. 29 to express his own views of the Kingdom.[21] Yet this interpretation seems somewhat forced, espe-

---

Sower cannot be identified with Christ. (Vs. K. Weiss, *Voll Zuversicht!*, 21–31 and *passim*.) Harder, "Saat," 60 follows Weiss (ibid., 12ff.) in translating *ouk oiden* as "he does not trouble himself . . . ," but this is linguistically unlikely and seems to rest on the allegorical identification of the Sower with Christ. Mussner, "Gleichnisauslegung," who also accepts this identification, does not treat the phrase.

18. Taylor, *Mk.*, 267; Gould, *Mk.*, 81; Cadoux, *Parables*, 162: "There can be no reasonable doubt as to the main point of the parable. It is the co-operation [!] of man with the mysterious powers of nature."

19. In Joel, as in Rev. 14:14ff., the stress is on the wrath of God, not (as here) on his promise. For the harvest, see also Jer. 27[50]:16.

20. *Gleichn.*, II, 545; similarly, Wellhausen, *Mk.*[2], 34, who thinks of v. 29 as an addition to the original parable. (Vs. this, see Harder, "Saat," 52f.) On quite different grounds, Cave, *Parables*, 385 holds that v. 29 was added, perhaps "to provide a kind of fulfillment of prophecy." Kümmel, *Promise*, 128, n. 82 insists that the elimination of all or part of v. 29 really rests on a root-and-branch elimination of allegory, i.e., on the assumption that Jesus never spoke in metaphors. Harder, "Saat," 54, on the other hand, understands Wellhausen's motive to be rather the elimination of the transcendental Judge (v. 29) from what he perceives as an immanent process (vv. 26–28).

21. Suhl, *Zitate*, 155f. grants that v. 29 may once have been a word of consolation *vis-à-vis* the delayed Parousia. But he thinks that Mark reinterprets the verse: The goal of "church history" has arrived! The Parousia is imminent!

cially if the stress has been correctly placed above on the divine
activity in contrast with human passivity; in this case the solemn
biblical assurance that the Sower (perhaps here only: =Christ)[22]
will thrust forth the sickle and reap is the fitting consummation of
the central point. Naturally, v. 29 need not have been part of the
original parable—especially if the parable goes back to Jesus—
since the addition of biblical allusions is a clear mark of the developing tradition.[23] But nothing in v. 29 seems to represent a really
fundamental shift in emphasis.

In any case, there is little to be said for the view that vv. 26ff.
speak of the *development* of the Kingdom. Much more probably
they (and especially v. 28b) are merely a dramatic description of
God's continuing influence in this life (not in the next, where
there can be no question of growth):[24] step by step, inexorably,
God fulfills his promise. In this, as in other misnamed "parables of
growth," we shall have little difficulty with the agricultural phenomena if we keep in mind that Mark writes after some time has
already passed; he cannot have objected to expressions which suggested the passage of time. But this does not mean that he—still
less, Jesus—thought of the Kingdom as developing on earth.

The parable as a whole has been subject to an incredible variety
of interpretations, many of them mixing the views of Jesus and
Mark together into one harmonized whole.[25] Some are certainly
wrong, for either Jesus or the Markan tradition or Mark himself.
The extremely popular view in which the Sower (Christ) plants
the seed (the Word) in the earth (the human heart, the church),
etc.[26] tells us much about the history of Christendom but little

22. In an indirect sense, the parable as a whole is christological, since for Jesus
and the early church the Kingdom's power and presence come in Jesus' historical
ministry; so, rightly, W. G. Kümmel, "Noch einmal: Das Gleichnis von der
selbstwachsenden Saat," in Paul Hoffmann et al., *Orientierung an Jesus [Fest-
schrift für Josef. Schmid]* (Freiburg/Basel/Vienna: Herder, 1973), 220–237 (234).
But this is far from allegory.
23. Jeremias, *Parables*, 31f., who however accepts the authenticity of the reference in this case.
24. Jülicher, *Gleichn.*, II, 546, noting that this implies a present, not merely a
future, Kingdom.
25. A fairly full listing of the various views, with critical comments, may be
found in Harder, "Saat," 53–60.
26. Harder, "Saat," 51 is well aware of the artificiality of this view. Yet because

about the parable itself. Also to be flatly rejected are those interpretations, especially common in the nineteenth century, which understand the parable as teaching a gradual evolution of the Kingdom in society, on earth.[27] And finally, we must reject as well-intentioned but wrong-headed all moralizing or parenetic interpretations according to which the field is somehow the human heart and the goal of the parable the inculcation of a certain kind of conduct, "because the Seed Growing Secretly is a picture of the Kingdom of God, not of its individual members."[28]

Two other views have somewhat more to commend them. According to one interpretation, the parable springs out of Jesus' immediate situation, implying that "the Kingdom is already present before the eyes of men."[29] This is not impossible—but the more clearly it is spelled out, the less likely it becomes. Negatively, for example, it could have been directed against Pharisaic or Zealot attempts to "bring" the Kingdom by repentance, keeping the Law, force, or any other human activity.[30] But there is no parallel to such an anti-Pharisaic parable in Jesus' authentic teaching, while open opposition to Zealots is not only unattested but incredible; had Jesus been an outspoken opponent of the Zealots, his

---

he really shares the same allegorical starting place he comes in the end (68) to prefer the allegorical interpretation to one which stresses the *automatē*.

27. B. Weiss, *Das Markusevangelium und seine synoptischen Parallelen* (Berlin: Wilhelm Hertz, 1872), 159; Wellhausen, *Mk.*², 35; Jülicher, *Gleichn.*, II, 538–546, who stresses the *certainty* of the further development of the coming Kingdom. For further examples, see George Eldon Ladd, *Jesus and the Kingdom. The Eschatology of Biblical Realism* (New York/Evanston/London: Harper & Row, 1964), 185, n. 42. Similar views were shared by "most exegetes at the beginning of this century" (Lohse, "Gottesherrschaft," 151). Even K. Weiss, who stresses the *internal* rather than the *external* development of the Kingdom (*Voll Zuversicht!*, 33f.) could suggest in 1922 that "On this almost all exegetes are in agreement today. . . ."

28. Schmid, *Mk.*, 103.

29. Taylor, *Mk.*, 265–268 (266); so also Cadoux, *Parables*, 162ff.; Dodd, *Parables*, 176–180.

30. So many commentators. See, *inter alia*, Rawlinson, *Mk.*, 56 (hesitantly); Dahl, "Parables," 149f.; Grundmann, *Mk.*, 99; Hauck, *Mk.*, 58; Jeremias, *Parables*, 152; and Lagrange, *Mc.*, 118, who finds the parable esp. appropriate to Galileans. Schweizer, *Mk.*, 57 suggests, in addition to Zealots and Pharisees, "apocalyptists" (who might seek by *calculation* to bring it about), which would fit into the Markan context, perhaps, but is not really fitting, since an apocalyptic emphasis on calculation does not imply "forcing" the Kingdom.

208 THE PARABLES OF THE TRIPLE TRADITION

followers would have been differently constituted (Mk. 3:8f.) and he might very well have died of old age.[31] In addition, this view does not adequately recognize the positive side of the coin: God acts; man does not.[32] Furthermore, the "immediate presence of the Kingdom" is a one-sided understanding of the peculiarly paradoxical ("already/not yet") nature of the Kingdom's presence in Jesus' teaching.[33] In any case, for Mark, this view is clearly erroneous.

There remains, then, only[34] an eschatological interpretation in which the stress is on the future and God's action in bringing it about. Typical of the older form of this view is Loisy,[35] who correctly stresses human passivity and the divine initiative, as well as the certainty of the consummation. It is highly questionable, however, that Loisy is right in emphasizing the *immediacy* of the inbreaking Kingdom,[36] which is an extraneous element here. More precisely, the parable would seem to teach the certainty of God's action. So far as it has a parenetic point it can only be a negative one: "All anxiety is superfluous. . . ."[37] Not when the sower has

31. This is not in any way to suggest that Jesus shared the Zealot outlook; no teacher with tax-collectors among his close friends could have been reckoned anything but an enemy by the Zealots.
32. Harder, "Saat," 56f., 60f would eliminate any stress on the human implications by starting from the insight that the Sower and the Reaper are identical. But, if one must argue allegorically, so are the Sower and the *Sleeper* identical!
33. A much more satisfactory form of this view is that of Dahl, "Parables," 149f., according to which the parable teaches neither the presence nor the certainty of the Kingdom as such, but the intimate connection between the Kingdom *and the ministry of Jesus;* so also Jeremias, *Parables,* 152 and others among those mentioned in note 30 above. This motif is certainly authentic; it is not, however, unambiguously present in this parable.
 Related to this is the interpretation of K. Weiss, *Voll Zuversicht!* and "Mk 4,26 bis 29," who holds that Jesus understands himself as the Sower and the success of his work as certain. But (even aside from this allegorical equation, Jesus = the Sower) this misinterprets *Jesus,* in whose authentic teaching "success" plays no significant role.
34. The curious view of Baltensweiler, "Saat," 71f. that the (unbelieving!) farmer forgets about the seed and fails to trust in God, but God works anyway (!) is founded, as Dupont rightly notes, *"sur une mauvaise lecture du texte"* ("Semence," 374, n. 18).
35. *ES,* I, 764f.
36. So also Suhl, *Zitate,* 156, who holds that *for Mark* the time is ripe, God's Judgment at hand. At the same time, we must also avoid speaking of "the duration of time" in this connection (vs. Lagrange, *Mc.,* 117), esp. for Jesus.
37. Lagrange, *Mc.,* 117; cf. K. Weiss, "Mk 4,26 bis 29," 63f. Fuchs, *Frage,* 393 grants that the parable is primarily consolation but goes on to existentialize the point still further: Since the sower can rely on the earth to do its work, the time between sowing and harvest is a time of unlimited freedom; God's time

accomplished certain tasks but when the hour has come, the Kingdom arrives—with complete certainty. It needs no human aid; it
comes in spite of human opposition.[38]

Whether this parable goes back to Jesus or not is hard to say,
since the original context has been lost. It might have been
intended, for example, as a reply to those who see no evidence in
Jesus' ministry of the dawning Kingdom; in this case Jesus is either
pointing to the "unexpected presence of the supernatural Kingdom"[39] or assuring his hearers that God will act in his own time.[40]
Far less probably, it might originally have been a reply to the
disciples' question, "But what will happen to the Kingdom after
your death?"[41] although this interpretation rests on a purely speculative question as well as on the authenticity of the passion-predictions. And the view that the parable expresses Jesus' full confidence in what he has begun[42] requires not only the simple identification of Jesus and the sower but also the consistent interpretation of everything between sowing and harvest as mere symbols of
confidence. None of this, on balance, is particularly persuasive.

It is quite clear, however, that the parable arose somewhere
before Mark. Its basis and form are apparently Aramaic.[43] It occurs
in a notoriously composite chapter (chapter 4), seems to reflect a
"seam" in its awkward introduction, and begins with the formula
kai elegen, which is not used by Mark (except at 4:9, 30, where it

---

creates time for us (393f.), *alles hat seine Zeit* (339—a phrase reminiscent of
Goethe's "*Mein Acker ist die Zeit*" [cited, Wellhausen, *Mk.*[2], 35]). But Fuchs
himself admits that this notion is at best implicit in the text (339), and Kümmel,
"Saat," 228f. objects that the question of the Kingdom of God has here been
replaced by the question of human existence.

38. So, in various ways, Jülicher, *Gleichn.*, II, 546; Hauck, *Mk.*, 58; Masson,
Paraboles, 43f.; Kümmel, *Promise*, 128f. and "Saat," 232; Schmid, *Mk.*, 103;
Lohse, "Gottesherrschaft," 147f.; Schweizer, *Mk.*, 57; Jeremias, *Parables*, 151f.;
Gnilka, *Verstockung*, 75.

39. Ladd, *Jesus*, 188.

40. Dupont, "Semence," *passim*; note that Dupont also believes Jesus wished
to turn his hearers' attention from the future to the present (386), which is
hardly evident in the parable, although it finds support elsewhere in the teaching
of Jesus.

41. Mussner, "Gleichnisauslegung," 265f.

42. K. Weiss, *Voll Zuversicht!* and "Mk 4,26 bis 29."

43. Black, *Aram. Approach*[2], 121f.

seems to come from his source); his formula is ordinarily *kai elegen autois* (cf. 2:27; 4:21, 24; 6:10; 7:9; 8:21; 9:1). In addition the situation requiring such assurances as this parable offers is certainly pre-Markan. Finally—if our other judgments in this study have been approximately correct—practically all of the Markan parables seem to be pre-Markan in origin. In this context, its force is primarily consolatory.

Similarly in the present Gospel. Like the rest of chapter 4 it assures Mark's readers that God is still in control. It is an exhortation to patient passivity in the face of God's ineluctable promise to bring to final fruition what he began in the ministry of Jesus.[44]

For some this lesson will seem to be much too harsh, much too unwilling to take freedom and responsibility seriously. But Mark is not, except indirectly, a theologian of human freedom. His concern is with the grace of the hidden but ever-active God—something more ultimately liberating than all the tracts on human freedom ever penned. *Soli Deo gloria!*

44. For Dupont, "Chapitre," 802f. all of vv. 10–25 is understood by Mark as a brief parenthesis addressed not to the crowds but to the small group of disciples. Similarly, and perhaps more precisely, Gnilka, *Verstockung*, 78 relates 4:26–29 with 4:10ff. by noting that for Mark the assurance and consolation of the parable are part of what was given to the disciples.

SELECT
BIBLIOGRAPHY
AND
INDEXES

SELECT BIBLIOGRAPHY

In the interest of conserving space, and because most of the technical material cited in this work is well-known to those readers who will want it, this bibliography omits a) source material, b) concordances, grammars, dictionaries, lexicons, and dictionary or lexicon articles, as well as c) commentaries on individual Synoptic Gospels. Publishing details on all items cited are given at the first mention in the body of the work.

Abrahams, I. *Studies in Pharisaism and the Gospels.* First Series, Cambridge: The University Press, 1917. Second series, 1924.

Albertz, Martin. *Die synoptischen Streitgespräche.* Berlin: Trowitzsch & Sohn, 1921.

Ambrozic, A. M. "Mark's Concept of the Parable." *CBQ* 29 (1967), 220–227.

Aune, D. E. "The Problem of the Messianic Secret." *NovTest* 11 (1969), 1–31.

Bacon, Benjamin W. *The Beginnings of Gospel Story.* New Haven: Yale University Press, 1909.

————. *Studies in Matthew.* London: Constable & Co., Ltd., 1930.

Baird, J. Arthur. "A Pragmatic Approach to Parable Exegesis: Some New Evidence on Mk 4:11, 33–34." *JBL* 76 (1947), 201–207.

Baltensweiler, H. "Das Gleichnis von der selbstwachsenden Saat (Markus 4, 26–29) und die theologische Konzeption des Markusevangelisten." *Oikonomia. Heilsgeschichte als Thema der Theologie. Mélanges O. Cullmann.* Hamburg-Bergstadt: Herbert Reich Evang. Verlag, 1967.

Bammel, Ernst. "Das Gleichnis von den bösen Winzern (Mk 12, 1–9) und das jüdische Erbrecht." *Revue Internationale des Droits de l'Antiquité.* 3e série 6 (1959), 11–17.

Bartsch, Hans-Werner. "Das Thomas-Evangelium und die synoptischen Evangelien." *NTS* 6 (1959/60), 249–261.

Beasley-Murray, G. R. *A Commentary on Mark 13.* London/New York: Macmillan & Co., Ltd./St. Martin's Press, 1957.

———. *Jesus and the Future. An Examination of the Criticism of the Eschatological Discourse, Mark 13 with Special Reference to the Little Apocalypse Theory.* London/New York: Macmillan & Co., Ltd./St. Martin's Press, 1954.

———. "The Rise and Fall of the Little Apocalypse Theory." *ExpT* 64 (1952), 346–349.

Belkin, Samuel. "The Dissolution of Vows and the Problem of Anti-social Oaths in the Gospels and Contemporary Jewish Literature." *JBL* 55 (1936), 227–234.

Berger, Klaus. "Hartherzigkeit und Gottes Gesetz: Die Vorgeschichte des antijüdischen Vorwurfs in Mc 10 5." *ZNW* 61 (1970), 1–47 (48).

Black, Matthew. *An Aramaic Approach to the Gospels and Acts.* 3d ed. Oxford: The Clarendon Press, 1967.

Black, Matthew. See also Moule, C. F. D.

Boobyer, G. H. "The Redaction of Mark iv. 1–34." *NTS* 8 (1961/62), 59–70.

———. "The Secrecy Motif in St. Mark's Gospel." *NTS* 6 (1959–60), 225–235.

Bornkamm, Günther, Barth, Gerhard, and Held, Heinz-Joachim. *Tradition and Interpretation in Matthew.* Translated by Percy Scott. Philadelphia: Westminster Press, 1963.

Bover, J. M. "Nada hay encubierto que no se descubra." *Estudios Biblicos* 13 (1954), 319–323.

Branscomb, B. Harvie. *Jesus and the Law of Moses.* New York: R. R. Smith, Inc., 1930.

Braumann, Georg. "Jesu Erbarmen nach Matthäus." *ThZ* 19 (1963), 305–317.

———. "Das Mittel der Zeit: Erwägungen zur Theologie der Lukasevangeliums." *ZNW* 54 (1963), 117–145.

Braun, Herbert. *Qumran und das Neue Testament.* 2 vols. Tübingen: J. C. B. Mohr (Paul Siebeck), 1966.

———. *Spätjüdisch-häretischer und frühchristlicher Radikalismus: Jesus von Nazareth und die essenische Qumransekte.* 2 vols. Tübingen: J. C. B. Mohr (Paul Siebeck), 1957. (Beiträge zur historischen Theologie, 24)

Brown, John Pairman. "An Early Revision of the Gospel of Mark." *JBL* 78 (1959), 214–227.

Brown, Raymond E. "Parable and Allegory Reconsidered." *NovTest* 5 (1962), 36–45.

Brownlee, W. H. "Messianic Motifs of Qumran and the NT." *NTS* 3 (1956/57), 12–30, 195–210.

Bultmann, Rudolf. *The History of the Synoptic Tradition.* Translated by John Marsh. Oxford: Basil Blackwell, 1963.

———. "Ist die Apokalyptik die Mutter der christlichen Theologie? Eine Auseinandersetzung mit Ernst Käsemann." *Apophoreta. Festschrift für Ernst Haenchen . . . 1964.* Berlin: Alfred Töpelmann, 1964. Pp. 64–69. (BZNW, 30)

———. *Theology of the New Testament.* Translated by Kendrick Grobel. 2 vols. New York: Charles Scribner's Sons, 1951, 1955.

Burkill, T. A. "Anti-Semitism in Mark's Gospel." *NovTest* 3 (1959), 34–53.

———. "The Hidden Son of Man in St. Mark's Gospel." *ZNW* 52 (1961), 189–213.

———. "The Historical Development of the Story of the Syrophenician Woman (Mk 7:24–31)." *NovTest* 9 (1967), 161–177.

———. *Mysterious Revelation. An Examination of the Philosophy of St. Mark's Gospel.* Ithaca: Cornell University Press, 1963.

———. "St. Mark's Philosophy of History." *NTS* 3 (1956/57), 142–148.

Burkitt, F. C. "Notes and Studies: *agapētos.*" *JTS* 20 (1919), 339–344.

———. "The Parable of the Wicked Husbandmen." *Transactions of the Third International Congress of the History of Religions.* 2 vols. Oxford: Oxford University Press, 1908. II, 321–328.

Cadbury, Henry J. *The Style and Literary Method of Luke.* Cambridge: Harvard University Press, 1920. (Harvard Theological Studies, 6)

Cadoux, A. T. *The Parables of Jesus. Their Art and Use.* London: James Clarke & Co., Ltd., 1931.

Carlston, Charles E. "The Things That Defile (Mark vii.15) and the Law in Matthew and Mark." *NTS* 15 (1968/69), 75–96.

Carlston, Charles E. and Norlin, Dennis. "Once More—Statistics and Q." *HTR* 64 (1971), 59–78.

Cave, C. H. "The Parables and the Scriptures." *NTS* 11 (1964/65), 374–387.

Cerfaux, Lucien. "La connaissance des secrets du royaume d'après Matt xiii.11 et parallèles." *NTS* (1955/56), 238–249.

———. "Fructifier en supportant (l'épreuve), à propos de Luc, viii, 15." *RB* 64 (1957), 481–491.

Cerfaux, Lucien. See also Garitte, G.

Colpe, Carsten. "Der Spruch von der Lästerung des Geistes." *Der Ruf Jesu und die Antwort der Gemeinde. Exegetische Untersuchungen Joachim Jeremias zum 70. Geburtstag gewidmet. . . .* Göttingen: Vandenhoeck & Ruprecht, 1970. Pp. 63–79.

Conzelmann, Hans. "Geschichte und Eschaton nach Mc 13." *ZNW* 50 (1959), 210–221.

———. "Geschichte, Geschichtsbild, und Geschichtsdarstellung bei Lukas." *ThLit* 85 (1960), 341–350.

———. "Zur Lukasanalyse." *ZThK* 49 (1952), 16–33.

———. *The Theology of St. Luke.* Translated by Geoffrey Buswell. London: Faber & Faber, 1960.

Couroyer, B. "De la mesure dont vous mesures il vous sera mesuré." *RB* 77 (1970), 366–370.

Cousar, Charles B. "Eschatology and Mark's *Theologia Crucis.* A Critical Analysis of Mark 13." *Interp* 24 (1970), 321–335.

Coutts, John. "The Authority of Jesus and of the Twelve in St. Mark's Gospel." *JTS* n.s. 8 (1957), 111–118.

Cranfield, C. E. B. "St. Mark 4.1–34." *ScotJTh* 4 (1951), 398–414; 5 (1952), 49–66.

———. "St. Mark 13." *ScotJTh* 6 (1953), 189–196, 287–303; 7 (1954), 284–303.

Cremer, Franz Gerhard. *Die Fastenansage Jesu. Mk 2,20 und Parallelen in der Sicht der patristischen u. Scholastischen Exegese.* Bonn: Peter Hanstein Verlag, 1965. (Bonner Biblische Beiträge, 23).

———. " 'Die Söhne des Brautgemachs,' (Mc 2 19 parr.) in der griechischen und lateinischen Schrifterklärung." *BibZeit* n.F. 11 (1967), 246–253.

Cross, F. L., ed. *Studia Evangelica.* Vol. II. Papers presented to the Second International Congress on New Testament Studies held at Christ Church, Oxford, 1961. Part I: The New Testament Scriptures. Berlin: Akademie-Verlag, 1964. (TU, 87)

Crossan, John Dominic. *In Parables.* New York: Harper & Row, 1973.

———. "The Parable of the Wicked Husbandmen." *JBL* 90 (1971), 451–465.

Cullmann, Oscar. "Das Gleichnis vom Salz. Zur frühesten Kommentierung eines Herrenworts durch die Evangelisten." *Vorträge und Aufsätze. 1925–1962.* Hrsg. von Karlfried Fröhlich. Tübingen/Zürich: J. C. B. Mohr (Paul Siebeck)/Zwingli Verlag, 1966. Pp. 192–201. (Fr. orig. in *RHPR* 37 [1957], 36–43.)

———. "Das Thomasevangelium und die Frage nach dem Alter der in ihm enthaltenen Tradition." *ThLit* 85 (1960), 321–334. (Rev. in *Vorträge,* 566–588. Engl. in *Interp* 16 [1962], 418–438)

———. *Vorträge und Aufsätze. 1925–1962.* Hrsg. von Karlfried Fröhlich. Tübingen/Zürich: J. C. B. Mohr (Paul Siebeck)/Zwingli Verlag, 1966.

(Cullmann, Oscar.) *Neotestamentica et Patristica. Eine Freundesgabe, Herrn Professor Dr. Oscar Cullmann zu seinem 60. Geburtstag überreicht.* Leiden: E. J. Brill, 1962. (Suppl. to NovTest, 6)

Dahl, Nils. "The Parables of Growth." *StudTh* 5 (1951), 132–166.

Davies, W. D. " 'Knowledge' in the Dead Sea Scrolls and Matthew 11:25–30." *HTR* 46 (1953), 113–139.

————. *The Setting of the Sermon on the Mount.* Cambridge: Cambridge University Press, 1963, repr., 1966.

Deden, D. "Le 'Mystère' paulinien." *ETL* 13 (1936), 405–442.

de la Potterie, Ignace (et al.), *De Jésus aux Evangiles. Tradition et Rédaction dans les Évangiles synoptiques.* Donum Natalicium Iosepho Coppens Septuagesimum Annum Complenti. Gembloux/Paris: J. Duculot/P. Lethielleux, 1967. (BETL, 25/2)

Delorme, J. "Aspects doctrinaux du second Évangile. Études récentes de la rédaction de Marc." I. de la Potterie et al., *De Jésus aux Évangiles.* Gembloux/Paris: J. Duculot/P. Lethielleux, 1967. Pp. 74–99. (BETL, 25/2)

Derrett, J. Duncan M. *Law in the New Testament.* London: Darton, Longman & Todd, 1970.

————. "The Stone that the Builders Rejected." *Studia Evangelica IV.* Papers presented to the Third International Congress on New Testament Studies held at Christ Church, Oxford, 1965. Part I: The New Testament Scriptures. Berlin: Akademie-Verlag, 1968. Pp. 180–186. (TU, 102)

Dibelius, Martin. *From Tradition to Gospel.* Translated . . . in collaboration with the author by Bertram Lee Woolf. New York: Charles Scribner's Sons, n.d.

Didier, M. et al. *L'Évangile selon Matthieu. Rédaction et Théologie.* Gembloux: J. Duculot, 1972. (BETL, 29/2)

Dietzfelbinger, Christian. "Das Gleichnis vom ausgestreuten Samen." *Der Ruf Jesu und die Antwort der Gemeinde. Exegetische Untersuchungen Joachim Jeremias zum 70. Geburtstag gewidmet. . . .* Hrsg. von Eduard Lohse. Göttingen: Vandenhoeck & Ruprecht, 1970. Pp. 80–93.

Dillon, Richard J. "Towards a Tradition-history of the Parables of the True Israel (Mt 21:33–22:14)." *Biblica* 47 (1966), 1–42.

Dodd, Charles Harold. *The Parables of the Kingdom.* London: James Nisbet & Co., Ltd., 1935, repr. many times.

Drury, John. "The Sower, the Vineyard, and the Place of Allegory in the Interpretation of Mark's Parables." *JTS* n.s. 24 (1973), 367–374.

Dupont, Jacques. *Les Béatitudes.* Louvain: E. Nauwelaerts, 1954.

Nouv. éd.: I. *Le problème littéraire. Les deux versions du Sermon sur la montagne et des Béatitudes.* 1958. II. *La bonne nouvelle.* Paris: J. Gabalda et Cie, 1969. III. *Les évangélistes,* 1973.

———. "Le chapitre des paraboles." *NRT* 89 (1967), 800–820.

———. *Gnosis. La connaissance religieuse dans les épîtres de Saint Paul.* Louvain/Paris: E. Nauwelaerts/J. Gabalda, 1949. (Universitas Catholica Lovaniensis. Dissertationes ad gradum magistri in Facultate Theologica Consequendum Conscriptae, Series II, Tomus 40)

———. "La parabole du Figuier qui bourgeonne (Marc xiii, 28–29 et par.)." *RB* 75 (1968), 526–548.

———. "La parabole du Maître qui rentre dans le nuit (Mc 13, 34–36)." *Mélanges Bibliques en hommage au R. P. Béda Rigaux.* Gembloux: J. Duculot, 1970. Pp. 89–116.

———. "La parabole de la semence qui pousse toute seule (Mc 4 26–29)." *RSR* 55 (1967), 367–392.

———. "La parabole du semeur dans la version du Luc." *Apophoreta. Festschrift für Ernst Haenchen.* Berlin: Alfred Töpelmann, 1964. Pp. 97–108. (BZNW, 30)

———. "Les paraboles du sénevé et du levain." *NRT* 89 (1967), 897–913.

———. "Le point de vue de Matthieu dans le chapitre des paraboles." In M. Didier et al., *L'Évangile de Matthieu.* Gembloux: J. Duculot, 1972. Pp. 221–259. (BETL, 29/2)

———. "Repentir et conversion d'après les Actes des Apôtres." *Sciences ecclésiastiques* 12 (1960), 137–173.

———. "Vin vieux, vin nouveau (Luc v,39)." *CBQ* 25 (1963), 286–304.

Dupont-Sommer, A. "Note archéologique sur le proverbe évangélique: Mettre la lampe sous le boisseau." *Mélanges Syriens offerts a . . . René Dussaud . . .* 2 vols. Paris: Paul Geuthner, 1939. II, 789–794. (BAH, 30)

Easton, Burton Scott. "The Beezebul Sections." *JBL* 32 (1913), 57–73.

Ebeling, Hans Jürgen. "Die Fastenfrage (Mk 2,18–22)." *Theol. Stud. u. Krit.* 108, n.F. III (1937/38), 387–396.

Eckert, Willehad Paul .*Antijudaismus im Neuen Nestament? Exegetische und systematische Beiträge.* Hrsg. von Willehad Paul Eckert et al. Munich: Chr. Kaiser Verlag, 1967. (Abhandlungen zum christlich-jüdischen Dialog, 2)

Edlund, Conny. *Das Auge der Einfalt. Eine Untersuchung zu Matth. 6, 22–23 und Luk. 11, 34–35.* Copenhagen: Ejnar Munksgaard, 1952. (ASNU, 19)

Ellis, E. Earle. "Present and Future Eschatology in Luke." *NTS* 12 (1965/66), 27–41.

Feldman, A. *The Parables and Similes of the Rabbis*. Cambridge: Cambridge University Press, 1924.

Feuillet, A. "La controverse sur le jeune (Mc 2, 18–20; Mt 9, 14–15; Lc 5, 33–35)." *NRT* 90 (1968), 113–136, 252–277.

———. "Le discours de Jesus sur la ruine du Temple d'après Marc xiii et Luc xxi, 5–36." *RB* 55 (1948), 481–502; 56 (1949), 61–92.

Fiebig, Paul. *Altjüdische Gleichnisse und die Gleichnisse Jesu*. Tübingen/Leipzig: J. C. B. Mohr, 1904.

———. *Die Gleichnisreden Jesu im Lichte der rabbinischen Gleichnisse des ntlichen Zeitalters. Ein Beitrag zum Streit um die "Christusmythe" und eine Widerlegung der Gleichnistheorie Jülichers*. Tübingen: J. C. B. Mohr, 1912.

———. *Jüdische Wundergeschichten des neutestamentlichen Zeitalters unter besonderer Berücksichtigung ihres Verhältnisses zum Neuen Testament bearbeitet*. Tübingen: J. C. B. Mohr, 1911.

Fitzer, Gottfried. "Die Sünde wider den Heiligen Geist." *ThZ* 13 (1957), 161–182.

Flender, Helmut. *St. Luke: Theologian of Redemptive History*. Translated by Prof. and Mrs. R. H. Fuller. Philadelphia: Fortress Press, 1967.

Flückiger, Felix. "Die Redaktion der Zukunftsrede in Mark 13." *ThZ* 26 (1970), 395–409.

Fuchs, Ernst. *Zur Frage nach dem historischen Jesus*. Tübingen: J. C. B. Mohr (Paul Siebeck), 1960. (Gesammelte Aufsätze, II)

Garitte, Gérard and Cerfaux, Lucien. "Les paraboles du royaume dans l'évangile de Thomas." *Le Museon* 70 (1957), 307–327.

George, Augustin. "Le sens de la parabole des semailles (Mc iv, 3–9 et parallèles)." *Sacra Pagina. Miscellanea Biblica Congressus Internationalis Catholici de Re Biblica*. Edited by J. Coppens et al. 2 vols. Paris: J. Gabalda, 1959. II, 163–169. (BETL, 12–13)

Gerhardsson, B. "The Parable of the Sower and Its Interpretation." *NTS* 14 (1967/68), 165–193.

———. "The Seven Parables in Matthew xiii." *NTS* 19 (1972/73), 16–37.

Gnilka, Joachim. "'Bräutigam'—spätjüdisches Messias-prädikat?" *TThZ* 69 (1960), 298–301.

———. *Die Verstockung Israels: Isaias 6, 9–10 in der Theologie der Synoptiker*. Munich: Kösel-Verlag, 1961. (Studien zum Alten und Neuen Testament, 3)

――――. "Das Verstockungsproblem nach Matthäus 13, 13–15." In Willehad Paul Eckert et al., *Antijudaismus im NT?* (Munich: Chr. Kaiser Verlag, 1967. Pp. 119–128. (Abhandlungen zum christlich-jüdischen Dialog, 2)

Goulder, M. D. "Characteristics of the Parables in the Several Gospels." *JTS* n.s. 19 (1968), 51–69.

Grässer, Erich. "Jesus in Nazareth (Mark vi. 1–6a): Notes on the Redaction and Theology of St. Mark." *NTS* 16 (1969/70), 1–23.

――――. *Das Problem der Parusieverzögerung in den synoptischen Evangelien und in der Apostelgeschichte.* Berlin: Alfred Töpelmann, 1957. 2. ber. u. erw. Aufl., 1960. (BZNW, 22)

Haenchen, Ernst. *Der Weg Jesu. Eine Erklärung des Markus-Evangeliums und der kanonischen Parallelen.* Berlin: Alfred Töpelmann, 1966. (Haenchen, Ernst. *Apophoreta. Festschrift für Ernst Haenchen.* Berlin: Alfred Töpelmann, 1964. [BZNW, 30])

Hahn, Ferdinand. "Die Bildworte vom neuen Flicken und vom jungen Wein (Mk 2:21f. parr)." *EvTheol* 31 (1971), 357–375.

Harder, Günther. "Das eschatologische Geschichtsbild der sogenannten Kleinen Apokalypse Markus 13." *Theologia Viatorum* 4 (1952), 71–107.

――――. "Das Gleichnis von der selbstwachenden Saat. Mark. 4, 26–29." *Theologia Viatorum* (1948/49), 51–70.

Harnack, Adolf. *The Sayings of Jesus.* Translated by J. R. Wilkinson. New York: G. P. Putnam's Sons, 1908. (Crown Theological Library, 23)

Harrisville, Roy A. "The Woman of Canaan. A Chapter in the History of Exegesis." *Interp* 20 (1966), 274–287.

Hartman, Lars. *Prophecy Interpreted. The Formation of Some Jewish Apocalyptic Texts and of the Eschatological Discourse Mark 13 par.* Translated by Neil Tomkinson with . . . Jean Gray. Lund: Gleerup, 1966. (Coniectanea Biblica. NT Series, 1)

Haufe, Günter. "Erwägungen zum Ursprung der sogenannten Parabeltheorie Mk 4, 11–12." *EvTheol* 32 (1972), 413–421.

Hawkins, John C. *Horae Synopticae. Contributions to the Study of the Synoptic Problem.* 2d ed., rev. & suppl. London: Oxford University Press, 1909, repr., 1968.

Hengel, Martin. "Das Gleichnis von den Weingärtnern Mc 12 1–12 im Lichte der Zenonpapyri und der rabbinischen Gleichnisse." *ZNW* 59 (1968), 1–39.

Hirsch, Emanuel. *Frühgeschichte des Evangeliums.* Tübingen: J. C. B. Mohr. I. *Das Werden des Markusevangeliums.* 2. verm. Ausgabe,

1951. II. *Die Vorlagen des Lukas und das Sondergut des Matthäus*, 1941.

Hoffmann, Paul, ed. *Orientierung an Jesus. Zur Theologie der Synoptiker. Für Josef Schmid.* Hrsg. von Paul Hoffman in Zusammenarbeit mit Norbert Brox und Wilhelm Pesch. Freiburg/Basel/Vienna: Herder, 1973.

Huby, Joseph. "Sur un passage du second Évangile, Marc iv, 21–25." *RSR* 1 (1910), 168–174.

Hummel, Reinhard. *Die Auseinandersetzung zwischen Kirche und Judentum im Matthäusevangelium.* 2. durchges. u. verm. Aufl. Munich: Chr. Kaiser Verlag, 1963. (Beiträge zur evangelischen Theologie, 33)

——. "Unbekannte Gleichnisse Jesu aus dem Thomas-Evangelium." *Judentum-Urchristentum-Kirche. Festschrift für Joachim Jeremias.* 2. Aufl., hrsg. von Walther Eltester. Berlin: Alfred Töpelmann, 1960. Pp. 209–220. (BZNW, 26)

Jeremias, Joachim. *ABBA. Studien zur neutestamentlichen Theologie und Zeitgeschichte.* Göttingen: Vandenhoeck & Ruprecht, 1966.

——. "Die Lampe unter dem Scheffel." *ZNW* 39 (1940), 237–240. (=ABBA, 99–102)

——. *Jesus' Promise to the Nations.* Translated by S. H. Hooke. Naperville, Ill.: Alec R. Allenson, Inc., 1958. (SBT, 24)

——. *New Testament Theology.* Part One: The Proclamation of Jesus. Translated by John S. Bowden. London: SCM Press, 1971.

——. "Palästinakundliches zum Gleichnis vom Säemann (Mc iv: 3–8 par.)." *NTS* 13 (1966/67), 48–53.

——. *The Parables of Jesus.* Rev. ed. Translated by S. H. Hooke from the German, 6th ed., 1962. New York: Charles Scribner's Sons, 1963.

——. "Perikopen-Umstellungen bei Lukas?" *NTS* 4 (1957/58), 115–118. (=ABBA, 93–97)

——. "Zöllner und Sünder." *ZNW* 30 (1931), 292–300.

Jeremias, Joachim. See also Lohse, E.

Johnson, Sherman. "The Biblical Quotations in Matthew." *HTR* 36 (1943), 135–153.

Jülicher, Adolf. *Die Gleichnisreden Jesu.* Tübingen: J. C. B. Mohr (Paul Siebeck). I. 1888; 2. Aufl., 1899 (=1910.) II. 1899 (=1910).

Jüngel, Eberhard. *Paulus und Jesus: Eine Untersuchung zur Präzisierung der Frage nach dem Ursprung der Christologie.* Tübingen: J. C. B. Mohr (Paul Siebeck), 1962. 3. Aufl., 1967.

222 SELECT BIBLIOGRAPHY

Käsemann, Ernst. *Exegetische Versuche und Besinnungen.* 2 vols. Göttingen: Vandenhoeck & Ruprecht, I⁴, 1965; II³, 1968. Translated by W. J. Montague. London: SCM Press, I, 1964; II, 1969.

Kee, Alistair. "The Old Coat and the New Wine. A Parable of Repentance." *NovTest* 12 (1970), 13–21.

――――. "The Question about Fasting." NovTest 11 (1969), 161–173.

Kilpatrick, G. D. *The Origins of the Gospel according to St. Matthew.* Oxford: The Clarendon Press, 1946.

Kingsbury, Jack Dean. *The Parables of Jesus in Matthew 13: A Study in Redaction-Criticism.* Richmond: John Knox Press, 1969.

Klauck, Hans-Josef. "Das Gleichnis vom Mord im Weinberg (Mk 12, 1–12; Mt 21, 33–46; Lk 20, 9–19)." *Bibel und Leben* 11 (1970), 118–145.

Klein, Günter. *Die zwölf Apostel: Ursprung und Gehalt einer Idee.* Göttingen: Vandenhoeck & Ruprecht, 1961. (FRLANT, 77)

Knox, Wilfred Lawrence. "Jewish Liturgical Exorcism." *HTR* 31 (1938), 191–203.

Köhler, Ludwig. "Salz, das dumm wird." *Zeitschrift der Deutschen Palästina-Vereins* 59 (1936), 133f. Rev. and printed in *Kleine Lichter: fünfzig Bibelstellen erklärt.* Zürich: Zwingli-Verlag, 1945. Pp. 73–76.

Kruse, Heinz. "Die 'Dialektische Negation' als semitisches Idiom." *VT* 4 (1954), 385–400.

Kuby, Alfred. "Zur Konzeption des Markus-Evangeliums." *ZNW* 49 (1958), 52–64.

Kümmel, Werner G. "Das Gleichnis von den bösen Weingärtnern (Mk 12:1–9)." *Aux Sources de la Tradition Chrétienne. Mélanges offerts à M. Goguel.* Neuchâtel/Paris: Delachaux & Niestlé, 1950. Pp. 120–131. (=Heilsgeschehen und Geschichte, 207–217.)

――――. *Heilsgeschehen und Geschichte. Gesammelte Aufsätze 1933–1964.* Hrsg. von Erich Grässer et al. Marburg: N. G. Elwert Verlag, 1965. (Marburger Theologische Studien, 3)

――――. "Noch einmal: Das Gleichnis von der selbstwachsenden Saat." Paul Hoffmann et al., *Orientierung an Jesus.* Freiburg/Basel/Vienna: Herder, 1973. Pp. 220–237.

――――. *Promise and Fulfilment. The Eschatological Message of Jesus.* Translated by Dorothea M. Barton. 2d Engl. ed. London: SCM Press, 1961. (SBT, 23)

Kuhn, Heinz-Wolfgang. *Ältere Sammlungen im Markusevangelium.* Göttingen: Vandenhoeck & Ruprecht, 1971. (Studien zur Umwelt des NTs, 8)

Kuss, Otto. *Auslegung und Verkündigung. I. Aufsätze zur Exegese des Neuen Testamentes.* Regensburg: Friedrich Pustet, 1963.

————. "Zur Senfkornparabel." *Theologie und Glaube* 41 (1951), 40–46. (=*Auslegung und Verkündigung*, I, 78–84.)

————. "Zum Sinngehalt des Doppelgleichnisses vom Senfkorn und Sauerteig." *Biblica* 40 (1959), 641–653. (=*Auslegung und Verkündigung*, I, 85–97.)

Ladd, George Eldon. *Jesus and the Kingdom. The Eschatology of Biblical Realism.* New York/Evanston/London: Harper & Row, 1964.

————. "The Life-setting of the parables of the Kingdom." *JBR* 31 (1963),193–199.

————. "The *Sitz im Leben* of the Parables of Matthew 13: the Soils." In *Studia Evangelica*, II. Edited by F. L. Cross. Berlin: Akademie-Verlag, 1964. Pp. 203–210. (TU, 87)

Lagrange, Marie-Joseph. "La parabole en dehors de l'évangile." *RB* 6 (1909), 198–212, 342–367.

Lambrecht, Jan. "Die Logia-Quellen von Markus 13." *Biblica* 47 (1966), 321–360.

————. "Die 'Midrasch-Quelle' von Mk 13." *Biblica* 49 (1968), 254–270.

————. "The Parousia Discourse. Composition and Content in Mt. xxiv–xxv." M. Didier et al., *L'Évangile selon Matthieu.* Gembloux: J. Duculot, 1972. Pp. 309–342. (BETL, 29/2)

————. *Die Redaktion der Markus-Apokalypse. Literarische Analyse und Strukturuntersuchung.* Rome: Pontifical Biblical Institute, 1967. (Analecta Biblica, 28)

————. "La structure de Mc., xiii." I. de la Potterie et al., *De Jésus aux Évangiles.* Gembloux/Paris: J. Duculot/P. Lethielleux, 1967. Pp. 141–164. (BETL, 25/2)

Lampe, G. W. H. "The Lucan Portrait of Christ." *NTS* 2 (1955/56), 160–175.

Légasse, S. "Le Discours eschatologique de Marc 13 d'après trois ouvrages récents." *Bulletin de Littérature Ecclésiastique* 71 (1970), 241–261.

————. "L'épisode de la Cananéenne d'après Mt. 15, 21–28." *Bulletin de Littérature Ecclésiastique* 73 (1972), 21–40.

————. "L' 'homme fort' de Luc xi 21–22." *NovTest* 5 (1962), 5–9.

Léon-Dufour, Xavier. *Études d'Évangile.* Paris: Éditions du Seuil, 1965.

Lewy, Heinrich. "Zum Dämonenglauben." *ARW* 28 (1930), 241–252.

Lieberman, Saul. *Greek in Jewish Palestine. Studies in the Life and Manners of Jewish Palestine in the II-IV Centuries* C.E. New York: The Jewish Theological Seminary of America, 1942.

Linnemann, Eta. "Das Gleichnis von den bösen Weingärtnern." *ZSystTh* 18 (1941), 243–249.

———. *Parables of Jesus: Introduction and Exposition.* Translated by John Sturdy from the 3d ed. (1964). London: SPCK, 1966.

———. "Der Sinn der Gleichnisse Jesu." *ZSystTh* 15 (1938), 319–346.

Lövestam, Evald. *Spiritus Blasphemia. Eine Studie zu Mk 3,28f. par Mt 12, 31f, Lk 12, 10.* Lund: Gleerup, 1968. (Scripta Minora, 1966–67:1)

Lohse, Eduard. "Die Gottesherrschaft in den Gleichnissen Jesu." *EvTheol* 18 (1958), 145–157.

———. "Lukas als Theologe der Heilsgeschichte." *EvTheol* 14 (1954), 256–275.

Lohse, Eduard, ed. *Der Ruf Jesu und die Antwort der Gemeinde. Exegetische Untersuchungen Joachim Jeremias zum 70. Geburtstag gewidmet.* . . . Hrsg. von Eduard Lohse gemeinsam mit Christoph Burchard und Berndt Schaller. Göttingen: Vandenhoeck & Ruprecht, 1970.

Loisy, Alfred Firmin. *Les Évangiles synoptiques.* 2 vols. Ceffonds: Chez l'auteur, 1907–08.

Lührmann, Dieter. *Die Redaktion der Logienquelle.* Neukirchen: Neukirchener Verlag, 1969. (WMANT, 33)

Luz, Ulrich. "Das Geheimnismotiv und die markinische Christologie." *ZNW* 56 (1965), 9–29.

McArthur, Harvey K. "The Gospel according to Thomas." Harvey K. McArthur, ed., *New Testament Sidelights (Festschrift Alexander Converse Purdy).* Hartford: Hartford Seminary Foundation, 1960. Pp. 43–77.

———. "The Parable of the Mustard Seed." *CBQ* 33 (1971), 198–210.

Manson, T. W. *The Sayings of Jesus as Recorded in the Gospels according to St. Matthew and St. Luke.* London: SCM Press, 1949, repr., 1957.

Marxsen, Willi. *Mark the Evangelist. Studies on the Redaction History of the Gospel.* Translated by J. Boyce et al. Nashville: Abingdon Press, 1969.

———. "Redaktionsgeschichtliche Erklärung der sogenannten Parabeltheorie des Markus." *ZThK* 52 (1955), 255–271. (=*Der Exeget als Theologe.* Gütersloh: Gütersloher Verlagshaus [Gerd Mohn], 1968. Pp. 13–28)

Masson, Charles. *Les Paraboles de Marc IV avec une introduction à l'explication des Évangiles.* Neuchâtel/Paris: Delachaux & Niestlé, 1945. (Cahiers théologiques de l'actualité Protestante, 11)

Maurer, Christian. "Das Messiasgeheimnis des Markusevangeliums."
NTS 14 (1967/68), 515–526.

Merkel, Helmut. "Jesus und die Pharisäer." NTS 14 (1967/68), 194–
208.

———. "Markus 7, 15. Das Jesuswort über die innere Verunreinigung."
ZRG 20 (1968), 340–363.

Meye, R. P. "Mark 4:10: 'Those about Him with the Twelve.'" In
Studia Evangelica, II. Edited by F. L. Cross. Berlin: Akademie-
Verlag, 1964. Pp. 211–218. (TU, 87)

Michiels, R. "La conception lucanienne de la conversion." ETL 41
(1965), 42–78.

Minette de Tillesse, G. Le secret messianique dans l'évangile de Marc.
Paris: Éditions du Cerf, 1968.

Montefiore, C. G. The Synoptic Gospels. Edited with an Introduction
and a Commentary. 2d ed. 2 vols. London: Macmillan, 1927.

Montefiore, H. W. "A Comparison of the Parables of the Gospel According to Thomas and of the Synoptic Gospels." NTS 7 (1960/61),
220–248.

Morgenthaler, Robert. "Formgeschichte und Gleichnisauslegung." ThZ
6 (1950), 1–17.

Moule, C. F. D. "Mark 4:1–20 Yet Once More." In Neotestamentica et
Semitica. Studies in Honour of Matthew Black. Edited by E. Earle
Ellis and Max Wilcox. Edinburgh: T. & T. Clark, 1969. Pp. 95–113.

Mussner, Franz. "Die bösen Winzer nach Matthäus 21, 33–46." Willehad Paul Eckert et al., Antijudaismus im Neuen Testament? Munich:
Chr. Kaiser Verlag, 1967. Pp. 129–134. (Abhandlungen zum christlich-jüdischen Dialog, 2)

———. "Gleichnisauslegung und Heilsgeschichte. Dargetan am Gleichnis von der selbstwachsenden Saat (Mk 4, 26–29)." TThZ 64 (1955),
257–266.

———. "I Q Hodajoth und das Gleichnis vom Senfkorn (Mk 4, 30–32
par)." BibZeit n.F. 4 (1960), 128–130.

Nagel, W. "Neuer Wein in alten Schläuchen (Mt 9,17)." VigChr 14
(1960), 1–8.

Nauck, Wolfgang. "Salt as a Metaphor in Instructions for Discipleship." StudTh 6 (1952), 165–178.

Neirynck, F. "Le discours anti-apocalyptique de Mc., xiii." ETL 45
(1969), 154–164.

Neuhäusler, Engelbert. "Mit welchem Massstab misst Gott die
Menschen? Deutung zweier Jesussprüche." Bibel und Leben 11
(1970), 104–113.

Newell, J. E. and R. R. "The Parable of the Wicked Tenants." *NovTest* 14 (1972), 226–237.

O'Hara, J. "Christian Fasting. Mk. 2:18–22." *Scripture* 19 (1967), 82–95.

Oliver, H. H. "The Lucan Birth Stories and the Purpose of Luke-Acts." *NTS* 10 (1963/64), 202–226.

Ott, Wilhelm. *Gebet und Heil. Die Bedeutung der Gebetsparänese in der lukanischen Theologie.* Munich: Kösel Verlag, 1965. (Studien zum Alten und Neuen Testament, 12)

Pallis, Alex. *Notes on St. Luke and the Acts.* London: Oxford University Press, 1928.

————. *Notes on St. Mark and St. Matthew.* New ed. London: Oxford University Press, 1932.

Pedersen, Sigfred. "Zum Problem der *vaticinia ex eventu.* (Eine Analyse von Mt. 21, 33–46 par; 22:1–10 par)." *Stud Th* 19 (1965), 167–188.

Pesch, Rudolf. *Naherwartungen. Tradition und Redaktion in Mk 13.* Düsseldorf: Patmos-Verlag, 1968. (Kommentare und Beiträge zum Alten und Neuen Testament)

————. "Das Zöllnergastmahl (Mk 2, 15–17)." *Mélanges Bibliques en hommage au R. P. Béda Rigaux.* Gembloux: J. Duculot, 1970, Pp. 63–87.

Quispel, Gilles. "The Gospel of Thomas and the NT." *VigChr* 11 (1957), 189–207.

Riddle, Donald W. "Mark 4:1–34: The Evolution of a Gospel Source." *JBL* 56 (1937), 77–90.

————. "Die Verfolgungslogien in formgeschichtlicher und soziologischer Beleuchtung." *ZNW* 33 (1934), 271–289.

Riesenfeld, Harald. "The Parable of the Sower and Its Interpretation." *NTS* 14 (1967/68), 165–193.

————. "Tradition und Redaktion im Markusevangelium." *Neutestamentliche Studien für Rudolf Bultmann zu seinem siebzigsten Geburtstag . . . 1954.* Berlin: Alfred Töpelmann, 1954. Pp. 157–164. (BZNW, 21)

Robinson, James M. *Das Geschichtsverständnis des Markus-Evangeliums.* (Aus dem englischen Manuskript ins Deutsche übertragen von Karlfried Fröhlich.) Zürich: Zwingli Verlag, 1956. (ATANT, 30)

————. *The Problem of History in Mark.* London: SCM Press, 1957. (SBT, 21)

Robinson, William C., Jr. "On Preaching the Word of God." In *Studies in Luke-Acts.* Edited by Leander E. Keck and J. Louis Martyn. Nashville: Abingdon Press, 1966. Pp. 131–138.

————. *Der Weg des Herrn: Studien zur Geschichte und Eschatologie im Lukas-Evangelium.* (Aus dem Ms. übers. von Gisela und Georg Strecker.) Hamburg-Bergsted: Herbert Reich, Evangelischer Verlag, 1964. (Theologische Forschung, 36)

Roloff, J. "Das Markusevangelium als Geschichtsdarstellung." *EvTheol* 29 (1969), 73–93.

Rüger, H. P. "Mit welchem Mass ihr messt, wird euch gemessen werden." *ZNW* 60 (1969), 174–182.

Sanday, William. *Studies in the Synoptic Problem.* Oxford: The Clarendon Press, 1911.

Schäfer, Karl Th. " '. . . und dann werden sie fasten, an jenem Tage' (Mk, 2,20 und Parallelen)." *Synoptische Studien. Alfred Wikenhauser zum siebzigsten Geburtstag . . . dargebracht.* Munich: Karl Zink Verlag, 1953. Pp. 124–147.

Schippers, R. "The Son of Man in Matt. xii.32 = Lk. xii.10, compared with Mk. iii.28." In *Studia Evangelica*, IV. Edited by F. L. Cross. Papers presented to the Third International Congress on New Testament Studies held at Christ Church, Oxford, 1965. Part I: *The New Testament Scriptures.* Berlin: Akadamie-Verlag, 1968. Pp. 231–235. (TU, 102)

Schmid, Josef. "Das textgeschichtliche Problem der Parabel von den zwei Söhnen." *Vom Wort des Lebens. Festschrift für M. Meinertz.* Münster: Aschendorff, 1951. Pp. 68–84. (Neutestamentliche Abhandlungen, Erg.-Bd., 1)

Schmid, Josef. See also Hoffmann, P.

Schmidt, Karl Ludwig. *Der Rahmen der Geschichte Jesu. Literarkritische Untersuchungen zur älteste Jesusüberlieferung.* Darmstadt: Wissenschaftliche Buchgesellschaft, 1969. (= repr. of 2d [1919] ed.)

Schnackenburg, Rudolf. " 'Ihr seid das Salz der Erde, das Licht der Welt.' " *Mélanges Kardinal Eugene Tisserant.* Vol. I: *Écriture Sainte —Ancien Orient.* Vatican City: Biblioteca Apostolica Vaticana, 1964. Pp. 365–387. (Studi e Testi, 231) (= *Schriften zum NT*, 177–200)

————. *Schriften zum Neuen Testament.* Munich: Kösel-Verlag, 1971.

Schneider, Gerhard. "Das Bildwort von der Lampe. Zur Traditionsgeschichte eines Jesus-Wortes." *ZNW* 61 (1970), 183–209.

Schrage, Wolfgang. "Evangelienzitate in Oxyrhynchus-Logien und im koptischen Thomas-Evangelium." *Apophoreta. Festschrift für Ernst Haenchen zu seinem siebzigsten Geburstag.* Berlin: Alfred Töpelmann, 1964. (BZNW, 29)

————. *Das Verhältnis des Thomas-evangeliums zur synoptischen Tradition und zu den koptischen Evangelien-übersetzungen. Zugleich ein Beitrag zur gnostischen Synoptikerdeutung.* Berlin: Alfred Töpelmann, 1964. (BZNW, 29)

Schramm, Tim. *Der Markus-Stoff bei Lukas. Eine literarkritische und redaktionsgeschichtliche Untersuchung.* Cambridge: At the University Press, 1971. (SNTS Monograph series, 14)

Schreiber, Johannes. "Die Christologie des Markusevangeliums." *ZThK* 58 (1961), 154–183.

————. *Theologie des Vertrauens. Eine redaktionsgeschichtliche Untersuchung des Markusevangeliums.* Hamburg: Furche-Verlag, 1967.

Schürer, Emil. *Geschichte des jüdischen Volkes im Zeitalter Jesu Christi.* 3 vols. 4. Aufl. Leipzig: J. C. Hinrichs, 1901–09.

Schürmann, Heinz. "Das Thomasevangelium und das lukanische Sondergut." *BibZeit* 7 (1963), 236–260.

Schulz, Siegfried. "Die Bedeutung des Markus für die Theologiegeschichte des Urchristentums." In *Studia Evangelica,* II. Edited by F. L. Cross. Berlin: Akademie-Verlag, 1964. Pp. 135–145.

————. "Gottes Vorsehung bei Lukas." *ZNW* 54 (1963), 104–116.

————. "Markus und das AT." *ZThK* 58 (1961), 184–197.

————. "Die neue Frage nach dem historischen Jesus." *Neues Testament und Geschichte. Historisches Geschehen und Deutung im Neuen Testament. Oscar Cullmann zum 70. Geburtstag.* Hrsg. von Heinrich Baltensweiler und Bo Reicke. Zürich/Tübingen: Theologischer Verlag/J. C. B. Mohr (Paul Siebeck), 1972. Pp. 33–42.

————. *Die Stunde der Botschaft. Einführung in die Theologie der vier Evangelisten.* Hamburg/Zürich: Furche-Verlag/Zwingli Verlag, 1967. 2. durchges. Aufl., 1970.

Schweizer, Eduard. "Anmerkungen zur Theologie des Markus." *Neotestamentica et patristica (Cullmann Festschrift).* Leiden: E. J. Brill, 1962. Pp. 35–46. (= *Neotestamentica. Deutsche und Englische Aufsätze, 1951–1963.* Zürich/Stuttgart: Zwingli Verlag, 1963. Pp. 93–104.)

————. *Beiträge zur Theologie des Neuen Testaments. Neutestamentliche Aufsätze (1955–1970).* Zürich: Zwingli Verlag, 1970.

————. "Zur Frage des Messiasgeheimnisses bei Markus." *ZNW* 56 (1965), 1–8. (= *Beiträge,* 11–20.)

————. "Mark's Contribution to the Quest of the Historical Jesus." *NTS* 10 (1963/64), 421–432.

————. "Die theologische Leistung des Markus." *EvTheol* 24 (1964), 337–355. (= *Beiträge,* 21–42. Cf. Engl. in *NTS* 10 [1963/64], 421–432.)

Siegmann, E. F. "Teaching in parables (Mk iv, 10–12; Lk viii, 9–10; Mt xiii, 10–15)." *CBQ* 23 (1961), 161–181.

Simon, Marcel. *Verus Israel. Étude sur les relations entre chrétiens et juifs dans l'empire romain (135–425)*. Paris: E. de Boccard, 1948. (Bibl. des Écoles Françaises d'Athènes et de Rome, fasc. 166)

Smith, B. T. D. *The Parables of the Synoptic Gospels. A Critical Study*. Cambridge: The University Press, 1937.

Smith, Charles W. F. *The Jesus of the Parables*. Philadelphia: Westminster Press, 1948.

————. "The Mixed State of the Church in Matthew's Gospel." *JBL* 82 (1963), 149–168.

Souček, Josef B. "Salz der Erde und Licht der Welt. Zur Exegese von Matth. 5, 13–16." *ThZeit* 19 (1963), 169–179.

Spicq, C. "La vertu de simplicité dans l'Ancient et le Nouveau Testament." *RSPT* 22 (1933), 5–26.

Sprenger, G. "Jesu Säe- und Erntegleichnisse, aus den palästinischen Ackerbauverhältnissen dargestellt." *Palästinajahrbuch des Deutschen evangelischen Instituts für Altertumswissenschaft des heiligen Landes zu Jerusalem* 9 (1913), 79–97.

Stendahl, Krister. *The School of St. Matthew and Its Use of the OT*. Philadelphia: Fortress Press, 1968. (ASNU, 20)

Strecker, Georg. "Das Geschichtsverständnis des Matthäus." *EvTheol* 26 (1966), 57–74.

————. "Die Leidens- und Auferstehungsvoraussagungen im Markusevangelium." *ZThK* 64 (1967), 16–39.

————. *Der Weg der Gerechtigkeit. Untersuchung zur Theologie des Matthäus*. 2. durchges., um einen Nachtrag erw. Aufl. Göttingen: Vandenhoeck & Ruprecht, 1966. (FRLANT, 82)

Streeter, Burnett Hillman. *The Four Gospels: A Study of Origins*. London/New York: Macmillan & Co. Ltd./St. Martin's Press, 1924 (repr., 1956).

Suhl, Alfred. *Die Funktion der alttestamentlichen Zitate und Anspielungen im Markusevangelium*. Gütersloh: Gütersloher Verlagshaus (Gerd Mohn), 1965.

Swaeles, R. "L'Arrière-fond scripturaire de Matt. xxi 43 et son lien avec Matt. xxi 44." *NTS* 6 (1959/60), 310–313.

Talbert, Charles H. "An Anti-Gnostic Tendency in Lucan Christology." *NTS* 14 (1967/68), 259–271.

Trilling, Wolfgang. *Christusverkündigung in den synoptischen Evangelien*. Munich: Kösel-Verlag, 1969. (Biblische Handbibliothek, IV)

————. *Das wahre Israel. Studien zur Theologie des Matthäusevangeliums*. 3. umgearb. Aufl. Munich: Kösel-Verlag, 1964. (Studien zum Alten und Neuen Testament, 10)

Turner, C. H. "*ho hyios mou agapētos*." *JTS* 27 (1926), 113–129.

————. "Markan Usage: Notes, Critical and Exegetical, on the Second Gospel. I: The Impersonal Plural." *JTS* 25 (1924), 378–386.

Tyson, Joseph B. "The Blindness of the Disciples in Mark." *JBL* 80 (1961), 261–268.

Van Iersel, Bastiaan M. F. *"Der Sohn" in den synoptischen Jesusworten. Christusbezeichnung der Gemeinde oder Selbstbezeichnung Jesu?* Leiden: E. J. Brill, 1961. (Suppl. to Novum Testamentum, 3)

————. "La vocation de Lévi (Mc, ii, 13–17; Mt., ix, 9–13; Lc., v, 27–32)." I. de la Potterie et al., *De Jésus aux Évangiles.* Gembloux/ Paris: J. Duculot/P. Letthielleux, 1967. Pp. 212–232. (BETL, 25/2)

Walker, Rolf. *Die Heilsgeschichte im ersten Evangelium.* Göttingen: Vandenhoeck & Ruprecht, 1967. (FRLANT, 91)

Weiser, Alfons. *Die Knechtsgleichisse der synoptischen Evangelien.* Munich: Kösel-Verlag, 1971. (Studien zum Alten und Neuen Testament, 29)

————. "Von der Predigt Jesu zur Erwartung der Parusie. Überlieferungsgeschichtliches zum Gleichnis vom Türhüter." *Bibel und Leben* 12 (1971), 25–31.

Weiss, Karl. "Mk 4,26 bis 29—dennoch die Parabel vom zuversichtlichen Sämann!" *BibZeit* 18 (1928/29), 45–67.

————. *Voll Zuversicht! Zur Parabel Jesu vom zuversichtlichen Sämann Mk 4, 26–29.* Munster: Aschendorff, 1922. (Neutestamentliche Abhandlungen, X, 1)

Wellhausen, Julius. *Einleitung in die drei ersten Evangelien.* Berlin: Georg Reimer, 1905. 2. Ausg., 1911.

White, K. D. "The Parable of the Sower." *JTS n.s.* 15 (1964), 300–307.

Wilckens, Ulrich. "Kerygma und Evangelium bei Lukas." *ZNW* 49 (1958), 223–237.

————. *Die Missionsreden der Apostelgeschichte.* Neukirchen: Neukirchener Verlag, 1961.

Wilkens, Wilhelm. "Die Redaktion des Gleichniskapitels Mk 4 durch Matt." *ThZeit* 20 (1964), 304–327.

Wilson, Robert McLachlan. " 'Thomas' and the Growth of the Gospels." *HTR* 53 (1960), 231–250.

Windisch, Hans. "Die Verstockungsidee in Mk 4,12 und das kausale *hina* der späteren Koine." *ZNW* 26 (1927), 203–209.

Wolff, Hans-Walter. "Das Thema 'Umkehr' in der atlichen Prophetie." *ZThK* 48 (1951), 129–138.

Wrede, William. *Das Messiasgeheimnis in den Evangelien. Zugleich ein Beitrag zum Verständnis des Markusevangeliums.* Göttingen: Vandenhoeck & Ruprecht, 1901. 3. unveränd. Aufl., 1963. (Engl. tr. by C. G. Greig. Edinburgh: J. T. Clarke, 1971)

Wrege, Hans-Theo. *Die Überlieferungsgeschichte der Bergpredigt.* Tübingen: J. C. B. Mohr (Paul Siebeck), 1968. (Wissenschaftliche Untersuchungen zum NT, 9)

Zerwick, Max. *Üntersuchungen zum Markus-Stil. Ein Beitrag zur stilistischen Durcharbeitung des Neuen Testaments.* Rome: Pontifical Biblical Institute, 1937.

INDEXES

Index of Passages

14:15 — 85
14:20 — 88
14:21 — 41
14:25–35 — 87–88
14:25 — 87, 89
14:26 — 130
14:27 — 88
14:28–32 — 87, 89
14:34 f. — 46 ff.,
   87 ff., 174–178
14:34 — 88
14:35 — 73, 88, 139
15:1 f. — 116
15:1 — 12, 93
15:2 — 59
15:3 — 62
15:7 — 60
15:17 ff. — 79
16:3 f. — 79
16:14 f. — 93
17:5 — 85
17:6 — 158
17:8 — 85
17:9 — 180
17:30 f. — 120
17:37 — 85
18:1 — 62
18:4 f. — 79
18:6 — 87
18:8 — 201
18:9 — 56, 62
18:11 — 56
18:12 — 118
18:22 — 68
18:43 — 55
19:1–10 — 61
19:3 — 87
19:7 — 116
19:11–27 — 85
19:11 — 83
19:12–27 — 200, 201
19:25 — 79
19:26 — 6
19:46 — 61
19:47–20:1 — 81
19:47 — 76
20:1 — 76
20:9–19 — 222
20:9–18 — 40, 41,
   76–81, 178–190

20:9–16 — 79
20:9 — 56, 62, 72, 76,
   78
20:10 ff. — 76
20:10 — 78
20:11 — 78
20:12 — 78
20:15 — 79
20:16 — 79
20:17 — 56, 79, 80
20:18 — 80
20:19 — 55, 62, 76
20:20 — 59, 80
20:37 — 61
20:39 — 58
20:45 — 55, 81, 87
21:5–36 — 219
21:5 — 81
21:8 — 83
21:19 — 75, 82
21:20–24 — 81
21:25–28 — 81
21:27 f. — 81
21:28 — 83, 196
21:29 ff. — 45–46,
   81–84, 190–197
21:30 — 196
21:31 — 82
21:32 — 82, 83
21:33 — 83
21:34 ff. — 85
21:34 — 120, 201
21:36 — 201
21:37 — 81
21:38 — 55, 87
21:39 — 62
22:2 — 58
22:14–38 — 61
22:22 — 80
22:27 ff. — 86
22:27 — 86
22:53 — 81
22:71 — 61
23:27 — 55
23:35 — 55
24:9 — 56
24:10 — 56

John
2:12 — 111

3:2 — 121
4:46–54 — 169
7:20 — 131
8:12 — 49
8:48 f. — 131
8:52 — 131
9:5 — 49
10:21 f. — 131
12:46 — 49
14:1–3 — 201
14:18–21 — 120
14:20 — 120
16:23 — 120
16:26 — 120
19:17 — 42

Acts
2:12 — 71
2:23 — 44
4:11 — 80, 181
4:31 — 72
4:35 — 68
5:13 — 56
6:2 — 72
6:7 — 72
7:52 — 42
8:12 — 83
8:14 — 72
10:12 — 73
10:38 — 24
11:1 — 72
11:3 — 116
11:6 — 73
12:4 — 84
12:24 — 72
13:5 — 72
13:2 f. — 129
13:10 — 24
14:23 — 129
17:9 — 56
17:19 ff. — 65
19:8 — 71, 83
19:13 — 132
20:25 — 83
26:20 — 60
27:9 — 118
27:44 — 56
28:9 — 56
28:23 — 71, 83
28:24 — 57

244

INDEX OF PASSAGES

Hermas, Sim. v.1 —
120

Hippolytus, Haer. v.8
— 138
viii.9 — 138

Ignatius, Eph. vii.1 —
170
Phil. viii.2 — 65

Justin, Apol. I.15 —
113
I.16 — 49
I.44 — 65
I.59 f. — 65
Dial. Tryph. 7 — 65
34:2 — 181
36:1 — 181
85 — 132

Oxyrhynchus Pap.
1224 — 10

Ps.-Clem. II Cor 2 —
113
Hom. II.xix — 169
IV.1 — 169

Venetian Diatessaron
— 117

GREEK AND
ROMAN WRITERS

Aristotle, Nic. Eth.
viii.4 1156^b —
177

Cicero, Letters to
Atticus V.21 —
184
VI.1 — 184

Epictetus, Discourses
I.xv.7 — 82
III.v.9 — 88

Heliodorus viii.12 —
150

Herodotus, Hist.
II.142 — 194

Lucian, On Salaried
Posts 21 — 103

Pliny, Nat. hist.
xxxi.88 — 47
.102 — 47
xlv.98 — 175

Plutarch, De Defectu
Oraculorum 415E
— 194
438b — 66
Moralia 230F — 110

Strabo, Geog.
XV.iii.11 — 143

Tacitus, Dialogus 18
— 65

Theophrastus,
De causis plant.
III.xx.5 — 145
Hist. plant. VIII.vii.4
— 143

Thucydides V.14.3 —
103

Index of Authors

Abrahams, I., 115, 176, 213
Albertz, M., 164, 213
Ambrozic, A. M., 213
Aune, D. E., 213

Bacon, B. W., 172, 213
Baird, J. A., 213
Baltensweiler, H., 137, 203, 208, 213
Bammel, E., 184, 213
Barth, G., 4, 12, 203, 214
Bartsch, H. W., 213
Beasley-Murray, G. R., 190, 191, 193, 196, 197, 198, 199, 200, 213–214
Behm, J., 103, 118
Belkin, S., 165, 214
Berger, K., 214
Black, M., 97, 146, 150, 154, 155, 163, 164, 165, 173, 177, 188, 209, 214, 225
Bleek, F., 178
Bonnard, P., 4, 5, 7, 12, 15, 21, 25, 27, 33, 37, 38, 39, 41, 43, 48, 49, 80, 102, 115, 116, 135, 140, 141, 144, 167, 171, 180, 183
Boobyer, G. H., 99, 214
Bornkamm, G., 4, 5, 11, 43, 44, 102, 106, 167, 203, 214
Bover, J. M., 154, 214
Branscomb, B. H., 13, 99, 102, 118, 121, 123, 134, 136, 140, 164, 165, 166, 171, 177, 182, 190, 214
Braumann, G., 214
Braun, H., 49, 122, 214
Brown, J. P., 128, 214
Brown, R. E., 214
Brownlee, W. H., 122, 215
Bultmann, R., 14, 17, 18, 27, 30, 36, 38, 63, 69, 89, 100, 110, 114, 119, 121, 124, 128, 130, 133, 140, 142, 153, 165, 167, 183, 187, 190, 194, 195, 198, 215, 227

Burkill, T. A., 101, 137, 166, 170, 173, 215
Burkitt, F. C., 182, 187, 215

Cadbury, H. J., 61, 181, 215
Cadoux, A. T., 65, 76, 121, 127, 141, 142, 172, 176, 182, 205, 207, 215
Calvin, J., 125, 173, 174
Carlston, C., 10, 162, 166, 215
Cave, C. H., 141, 205, 215
Cerfaux, L., 5, 75, 142, 215, 219
Chrysostom, 48, 60
Colpe, C., 136, 216
Conzelmann, H., 56, 59, 60, 69, 75, 76, 82, 83, 85, 102, 191, 201, 216
Coppens, J., 219
Couroyer, B., 156, 216
Cousar, C. B., 195, 198, 216
Coutts, J., 216
Cranfield, C. E. B., 102, 114, 119, 121, 126, 139, 171, 174, 177, 182, 184, 191, 194, 199, 200, 216
Creed, J. M., 62, 63, 64, 67, 68, 73, 80, 83, 87, 88, 90, 93, 110, 111, 134
Cremer, F. G., 116, 124, 126, 216
Cross, F. L., 216, 225, 227, 228
Crossan, J. D., 76, 78, 216
Cullmann, O., 47, 88, 89, 176, 213, 216–217, 228, 229

Dahl, N., 142, 161, 207, 208, 217
Dalman, G., 23
Davies, W. D., 5, 31, 110, 154, 176, 217
Deden, D., 102, 217
de la Potterie, I., 111, 115, 217, 223, 230
Delorme, J., 115, 217
Derrett, J. D. M., 150, 179, 181, 183, 184, 217

245

246